Russian Anti-Proverbs of the 21st Century

A Sociolinguistic Dictionary

Andrey Reznikov

"Proverbium"
In cooperation with the
Department of German and Russian

The University of Vermont
Burlington, Vermont
2012

Supplement Series

of

Proverbium
Yearbook of International Proverb Scholarship

Edited by Wolfgang Mieder

Volume 35

Cover design: Boris Burakov

ISBN 978-0-9846456-1-9

Manufactured in the United States of America
By Queen City Printers Inc.
Burlington, Vermont

For my wife Irina

Contents

Acknowledgments

My research was supported by a grant from the Faculty Research Committee, Black Hills State University, and I would like to thank the committee members for their support of my work.

I wish to express my deepest gratitude to my editor and mentor, Professor Wolfgang Mieder: without his support, his encouragement, his suggestions and criticisms this book would have never been published.

Andrey Reznikov

Petrozavodsk, Russia – Spearfish, South Dakota

2009-2011

Introductory Notes

Why One More Dictionary?

During the last 10-15 years, several collections of modern versions of traditional proverbs (so-called *anti-proverbs*) have been published in Russia.[1] Thus, the obvious question is, why would anyone need one more dictionary?

Here is why.

The major problem with these collections is that they – surprisingly – do not represent modern folk wisdom; all they do is publish lists and lists of new coinages created for the sake of wordplay. A true proverb is used in speech; the vast majority of those proverbs that fill the pages of the dictionaries in question were never (and could not possibly have been) used in real speech or writing, as they are taken from internet sites where users submit their versions of traditional proverbs trying to be funny and witty (some time they are, sometimes they are not, but they never meet the criteria of proverbs). In other words, in no way do these collections illustrate the real state of proverbial wisdom in modern-day Russian language and culture, even though they do demonstrate the possibilities of Russian creativity and humor.

My dictionary is the first ever dictionary of modern Russian anti-proverbs that contains (and analyzes – see below) those modern versions of traditional Russian proverbs that have been actually used in speech or writing. All of my examples are taken from newspapers and magazines, and have concrete authors and URL addresses for anyone to check them. None of the examples is taken from those collections of language jokes that my predecessors have used.

This argument, in itself, is, in my opinion, more than enough to justify my collection. But there are more.

My other criticism of the dictionaries published earlier is based on the limited lexicographic analysis provided there. Many of them, especially the shorter ones, are nothing more than long lists of language jokes and puns, without any commentaries.

In order to correct that, several years ago I published my attempt to offer a linguistic analysis of the modern Russian anti-proverbs phenomenon. In that book, I suggested my own classification of the types of anti-proverbs, as well as gave a detailed description of the language mechanisms used in their creating.[2] Thus, it was the logical next step for me to apply the results of my analysis to the corpus of real-life anti-proverbs collected from modern newspapers and magazines.

Finally, there is one more and pretty obvious reason for another dictionary: all of the dictionaries of modern Russian anti-proverbs were published, as I have already mentioned, in Russia and, of course, in Russian – which makes them virtually non-existent for the western audience. The language of my dictionary is English, so it is accessible by all of my colleagues using this modern *lingua franca* as the means of international communication, no matter where they live.

***

Besides the dictionary itself, the book has introductory notes with the description of the structure of the entry, as well as the criteria for selecting traditional proverbs and the order of the entries. In the Appendix, there is a brief explanation of language mechanisms used in creating anti-proverbs, and an alphabetical index of all traditional proverbs analyzed in the dictionary.

Notes

[1] They are: Mokienko V., Nikitina N. *Tolkovy slovar yazyka sovdepii* (Dictionary of the Soviet Language). Saint-Petersburg: Saint-Petersburg University press, 1998; Walter, H., Mokienko V. *Anti-poslovitsy russkogo naroda* (Anti-Proverbs of the Russian People). Saint-Petersburg: Neva publishers, 2005; Mokienko V., Walter, H. *Pricolny slovar* (Dictionary of Jokes: Anti-Proverbs and Anti-Aphorisms). Saint-Petersburg: Neva Publishers, 2006; Adamchik, M.V. *Antiposlovisty, antipogovorki novogo russkogo naroda* (Anti-Proverbs and Anti-Sayings of New Russian People). Minsk: Sovremenniy literator, 2007.

[2] Andrey Reznikov. *Old Wine in New Bottles: Modern Russian Anti-Proverbs*. Supplement Series of *Proverbium*, vol.27. 2009.

For linguistic studies of anti-proverbs from various languages see: Wolfgang Mieder. *International Bibliography of Paremiology and Phraseology*, 2 vols. Berlin: Walter de Gruyter, 2009.

How traditional proverbs were selected

For any dictionary – be it a dictionary of words, sentences, or anything in between – the key question is the question of selecting the material. The lexicon of modern languages is virtually boundless, and even if lexicographers had unlimited space in their books, one still would have to decide, when and how to stop.

In my case, the answer was rather easy to find. As my starting point, I used a modern Russian publication, *Slovar russkih poslovits* (Moscow, 2007) – a Dictionary of Russian Proverbs, edited by one of the leading authorities in Russian paremiology, Professor V.M. Mokienko. What sets this dictionary apart from many other modern collections is shown in the subtitle: *About 1,000 actively used proverbs, with etymological commentary and stylistic characteristics.*

Thus, my analysis was from the very beginning limited by 1,000 proverbs – and not just any proverbs, but those that are actively used today! I need not explain why this is crucially important: if a proverb is actively used, it means it is alive in the language memory of modern Russian speakers, hence – it has many more chances to produce modern versions than some other traditional proverbs that exist only in dictionaries, but which no one uses anymore. As we will see, this assumption turned out to be correct: in many cases, the proverbs listed in the dictionary gave birth to anti-proverbs (sometimes, going into several dozens). My goal was not so much the quantity of new coinages but their quality; thus, there are about 200 traditional proverbs in my dictionary that did serve as a starting point for modern variations. Since the original list was about 1,000 proverbs, it means that roughly every fifth proverb produced at least one modern variation.

In this connection, a question could be asked: why have so many of the popular proverbs produced no variants? A possible answer may be in the question: it is exactly because they are so popular that they need no adjustment to modern times; and as long as Russian speakers keep using them in their original form, they may not need any new versions.

Structure of an Entry

Traditional proverb

- English translation
- Meaning, literal and/or figurative
- English equivalent, if there is one

Anti-proverb #1

- English translation
- Brief description of the context that will explain to readers its usage
- Language mechanism(s) used in creating this particular anti-proverb
- URL address of the publication from where the quote is taken

Anti-proverb #2, etc.

Comments on the entry.

<u>For example:</u>

Дыма без огня не бывает (There is no smoke without fire). Everything happens for a reason; thus, if people are talking about something, there must be some truth behind those talks and rumors.
English equivalent: There is no smoke without fire.

AP-1: *Дым без огня прописал москвичам респираторные маски* (Smoke without fire prescribed face masks to Muscovites).
Burning peat lands in Moscow region.
Syntactic extension.
http://www.gzt.ru/topnews/health/-dym-bez-ognya-propisal-moskvicham-respiratornye-/316521.html

AP-2: Электронные сигареты. Есть дым без огня (Electronic cigarettes. There is smoke without fire).

Electronic cigarettes.
Antonym.
http://bravedefender.ru/post123365136/

AP-3: *Дым не без огня* (Smokc is not without fire).
Same topic as in #1, criticizing inactivity of government to solve the problem once and for all.
Syntactic restructuring.
http://www.mospravda.ru/issue/2010/07/27/article23173/

AP-4: *Дым без огня – идеал коптильщика* (Smoke without fire – the dream of a meat smoker).
Smoking sausage at home.
Syntactic extension.
http://www.krestianin.ru/articles/16854.php

AP-5: *Дым не без огня* (Smoke is not without fire).
Moscow police wants to use more severe punishments for soccer fans using fireworks during games.
Syntactic restructuring.
http://www.newizv.ru/news/2008-08-11/95697/

AP-6: *Бывает ли дым без огня?* (Is there smoke without fire?)
Law suit of Jennifer Lopez against Marion Night, as Night allegedly wants to post a video of J Lo on the web.
Syntactic restructuring.
http://kino.km.ru/magazin/view.asp?id=9F8BB845998E4F4FA0764998A8B38012

AP-7: *Огонь без дыма, или биокамин* (Fire without smoke, or bio fireplace).
Ecological fireplaces.
Chiasmus.
http://stylehome.org/news/biokamin.html

AP-8: *Кабаева-Путин: дыма без огня не бывает?* (Kabaeva-Putin: there is no smoke without fire?)
An alleged love affair between Vladimir Putin and Alina Kabaeva, a Russian athlete.

Syntactic extension.
http://ua-reporter.com/novosti/28029

AP-9: *Нет клуба без огня* (There is no club without fire).
A fire in a Moscow night club.
New lexical content.
http://www.newizv.ru/news/2010-03-10/122999/

AP-10: *Дымовца без огня не бывает* (There is no Dymovets without fire).
The arrest of Grigory Dymovets, a former investigator.
Paronymy.
http://www.mk.ru/politics/article/2010/05/28/499453-dyimovtsa-bez-ognya-ne-byivaet.html

AP-11: *Нет калыма без огня* (There is no pay-off without fire).
Corruption among firefighters in Russia.
Metonymy.
http://www.runewsweek.ru/country/31629/

AP-12: *Дымовского без огня не бывает* (There is no Dymovsky without fire).
Police officer major Aleksey Dymovsky posted a video on the web addressed to the Russian president; the video describes corruption in the police.
Paronymy.
http://news.babr.ru/?IDE=82036

Comments: This is a very diverse group of anti-proverbs. Some of them use the traditional proverbs to state the same idea: there must be some facts behind the rumors about Putin's love affair, or Jennifer Lopez, or corruption in the police. At the same time, many of the new coinages use the proverb literally, and do talk about smoke without fire (electronic cigarettes, or smoking sausage); one anti-proverb reversing the proposition and stating that there is fire without smoke (bio fire-places). AP #1 and #3 both describe extensive fires in Moscow region, because of which Moscow was covered in smoke (though there was no fire in the city itself). Two anti-proverbs use wordplay based on the fact that the names mentioned in #10 and 12 have the same root as the Russian word *дым* (smoke): *Дымовиц* and *Дымовский*. In #11 there is an interesting example of metonymy (it talks about fire, but means firefighters who profit from fires). Finally, #9 simply and literally states the grim fact that there have been too many fires in night-clubs in Russia, which have resulted in many deaths.

Order of Entries

Ttraditional proverbs used as the starting point of every entry are listed in the order of the Russian alphabet, by the first notional word.

Thus, for example, the traditional proverb *Первый блин комом* (*The first pancake is a flop*) is listed under the Russian letter *Б*, because the first noun, *блин* (pancake), starts with this letter.

***

Russian alphabet

А, Б, В, Г, Д, Е, Ё, Ж, З, И, Й, К, Л, М, Н, О, П, Р, С, Т, У, Ф, Х, Ц, Ч, Ш, Щ, Ъ, Ы, Ь, Э, Ю, Я.

A

Аппетит приходит во время еды (Appetite comes with eating).
One really understands and starts to enjoy some vocation only when one is actually doing something.
The proverb is a calque from French: *L'appetit vient en mangeant.*
English equivalent: Appetite comes while eating.

AP-1: *Аппетит приходит... в момент кражи* (Appetite comes at the moment of stealing).
Thieves stole things both from a tailor shop and a grocery store during one night.
New lexical content.
http://www.gazetaeao.ru/component/k2/item/1780-appetit-prihodit-v-moment-kraji

AP-2: *Питание детей: Аппетит всегда приходит* (Feeding kids: Appetite always comes).
An article about feeding babies and small children.
Syntactic extension. New lexical content.
http://www.womenmagazine.ru/s.php/2332.htm.

AP-3: *Аппетит приходит и не во время еды* (Appetite comes not only with eating).
An international exhibition of food and equipment for the food industry in Moscow.
New lexical content.
http://www.newizv.ru/expo/news/2006-12-19/60385/

AP-4: *Аппетит приходит во время побед* (Appetite comes with victories).
Analysis of the results of the 2007 soccer season in Russia.
New lexical content.
http://www.rg.ru/2007/11/27/gadzhiev.html

AP-5: *Аппетит пришёл во время езды* (Appetite came with driving).

A person stole a car and decided to take a ride, then a little more, and more until he hit a lamp post.
Paronymy; hidden rhyme.
http://ozersk.chel.sudrf.ru/modules.php?name=press_dep&op=1&did=65

AP-6: *Страсть приходит во время еды. Куропаток* (Desire comes while eating. Partridges).
Correlation between food and sexual desire.
Syntactic extension. New lexical content. Parcelling.
http://www.km.ru/magazin/view.asp?id=FDFA52B0DBEA48B6BCF7FBF0B8AF45F4

AP-7: *Робот приходит во время еды* (Robot comes with eating).
New generation of robots looks more and more like human beings, including using food to generate energy.
New lexical content.
http://www.rbcdaily.ru/2010/07/21/cnews/496285

AP-8: *Диоксид приходит во время еды* (Dioxide comes with eating).
Artificial flavoring in different types of food.
Hidden rhyme.
http://www.compromat.ru/page_10599.htm

AP-9: *Гепатит приходит во время еды* (Hepatitis comes with eating).
Situation with hepatitis A in Moscow.
Hidden rhyme.
http://www.mk.ru/social/article/2010/04/12/466764-gepatit-prihodit-vo-vremya-edyi.html

AP-10: *Идеи приходят во время еды* (Ideas come with eating).
Contest for the design of napkins for a restaurant chain in Kiev.
New lexical content.
http://www.sostav.ua/news/2010/05/27/78/31790/

AP-11: *Числа приходят во время еды* (Numbers come with

eating).
An ad for a new restaurant chain in Moscow where one can play Russian lottery during a meal.
New lexical content.
http://www.gosloto.ru/press/news/26858163

AP-12: *Профицит приходит во время еды* (Surplus comes with eating).
Discussion of federal budget-2003 in the Russian parliament.
Hidden rhyme.
http://dlib.eastview.com/browse/doc/4406034

AP-13: *«Апатит» приходит во время еды* ("Apatit" comes with eating).
Privatizing of "Apatit" plant in Russia.
Paronymy.
http://www.novayagazeta.ru/data/2005/30/30.html

AP-14: *Знакомство приходит во время еды* (Knowing comes with eating).
Advice for women: how to define the type of their male friends by analyzing how men eat.
New lexical content.
http://www.chas.lv/win/2007/10/31/g_023.html?r=32&

Comments: From the point of view of meaning, we have two groups here: some new coinages while changing part of the original proverb, preserve its message, be it literal or figurative (# 1, 4, 5, 6, 12) while others (the majority) use the association with the traditional proverb simply as a catch phrase, but the original meaning is pretty much lost (#3, 4, 7, 8, 9, 10, 11, 13, 14): they either claim that some other event literally takes place while one is eating (# 8, 9, 10, 11, 14) or completely depart even from that superficial semantic association with the original proverb (# 7 and 13). Thus, #7 tells about robots that can, like human beings, use food to generate energy, and #13 discusses competition between several persons to own a well-known ore-processing plant in Russia.

The vast majority of new phrases use new lexical content. Linguistically, the most interesting cases are those when this new lexical content is supplemented by another mechanism: paronymy (## 5 and 13) or hidden rhyme (## 5, 8, 9,12, 13). In #6 there is a stylistic device of parceling in order to create a special emphasis on the word *partridges*.

Как аукнется, так и откликнется (*As you shout so you will hear the echo*).
As you treat other people so other people will treat you. In other words, whatever happens to you is the result of your own actions.
Note: traditionally, when a group of people go to the forest to pick up mushrooms or berries, they periodically shout to each other to make sure the group is all together and no one gets lost.
English equivalent: What goes around comes around. As you sow you shall reap.

AP-1: *В Бразилии аукнется – в России откликнется* (As they shout in Brazil so they will hear an echo in Russia).
The global economic crisis of 2009.
New lexical content.
http://old.polit.ru/documents/497898.html

AP-2: *Как на LSE аукнется, так у нас на KASE откликнется* (As they shout at LSE so we will hear at KASE).
Note: LSE is London stock exchange; KASE is Kazakhstan stock exchange.
Whatever happens with the British economy has direct influence on the economy of Kazakhstan.
New lexical content.
http://www.kase.kz/files/publications/2008/08_01_25_Respublica.pdf

AP-3: *Как в Югре аукнется с добычей нефти, так в России откликнется* (As they shout about oil production in Yugra [one of the main deposits of oil in Siberia] so they will hear the echo in Russia).
Dependence of the Russian economy on oil.

New lexical content.
http://hmcity.ru/news/13895/

AP-4: *Коапп аукнется, так и откликнется* (As KOAPP [Code of Administrative Offences] shout so they will hear the echo).
Discussion of the new version of the Code.
Paronymy.
http://gai-net.kzpa.ru/g98/KoAP-p08.html#0

Comments: Most of the new coinages have two things in common: they preserve the original meaning of the traditional proverb (though apply it to modern day and different situations) and they use new lexical content, with the exception of #4 which uses paronymy. Linguistically, the most interesting case is #4 where the wordplay is based on the fact that the first word (the abbreviated title of the Code on Administrative Offences of the Russian Federation) sounds very similar to the first word of the traditional proverb – the conjunction *как* (as). Thus, it is a very witty way to both refer to the traditional proverb and insert the name of the Code in question into the old proverb.

Б

Баба с возу – кобыле легче (It is easier for the horse when a woman is off the cart).
The proverb is usually used when someone refuses an offer of help (money, food, etc.).

AP-1: *Баба с возу, но кобыле не легче* (The woman is off the cart, but it is not easier for the horse).
Agricultural reform in Russia.
New lexical content.
http://elibrary.ru/item.asp?id=9234430

AP-2: *Чиновник с возу – народу легче* (It is easier for the people when bureaucrats are off the cart).
The government of Russia's decision about lowering the number of federal government officials.

New lexical content.
www.kp.ru/daily/24526/672784

AP-3: *Наташа Ростова с возу – выпускнику легче*? (Natasha Rostova [main character in Leo Tolstoy's *War and Peace*] is off the cart – is it easier for high school graduates?) Final exam in literature is not a required exam in Russian secondary schools any more.
New lexical content; metonymy.
http://www.izvestia.ru/education1/article3124722/

AP-4: *Хлам с возу — автопрому легче* (It is easier for car manufacturers when clunkers are off the cart).
How cash for clunkers program is being implemented in Russia.
Metaphor, new lexical content.
http://www.mk.ru/regions/novosib/article/2010/04/08/462551-hlam-s-vozu-avtopromu-legche.html

AP-5: *Дети с возу – таксисту легче* (It is easier for taxi-drivers when kids are off the cart).
Ban introduced in Russia in 2007 on having kids in the car without special child seats; most taxis do not have them.
New lexical content.
http://chelyabinsk.ru/news/14205.html

AP-6: *Россия зовёт! или народ с возу – государству легче* (Russia is calling! or it is easier for the government when people are off the cart).
Modern political and economic situation in Russia.
Note: "Россия зовёт!" (Russia is calling!) is the name of a forum that took place in Russia on September 29, 2009.
New lexical content.
http://www.proza.ru/2010/06/05/388

AP-7: *Премьер с возу — режиму легче* (It is easier for the regime when the prime-minster is off the cart).
Political future of Vladimir Putin.
New lexical content.
http://www.kasparov.ru/material.php?id=49AB926274FBD

AP-8: *Милевский – с воза, «Динамо» – легче* (It is easier for Dynamo [soccer club] when Milevsky is off the cart).
Soccer club Dinamo shows better results without its forward Milevsky.
New lexical content.
http://sport.mycityua.com/articles/2010/04/16/064943.html

AP-9: *Машина – с «возу», автовладельцу – легче* (When the car is off the cart, it is easier for the owner).
Cash for clunkers program in Russia.
New lexical content.
http://www.nepsite.com/node/7895

AP-10: *«Опель» с воза – Сбербанку легче* (When Opel is off the cart, it is easier for Sberbank.
Analysis of the failed contract between Opel and Sberbank, the biggest Russian bank.
New lexical content.
http://www.baltinfo.ru/stories/Opel-s-voza--Sberbanku-legche-113643/print

AP-11: *Аудит с возу – малому бизнесу легче* (When the audit is off the cart, it is easier for small businesses).
Bill in the Russian parliament about exempting small businesses from obligatory audit.
New lexical content.
http://www.mirnov.ru/arhiv/mn840/mn/03-2.php

AP-12: *Льготников с воза – правительству легче* (It is easier for the government when recipients of social benefits are off the cart).
A suggestion of the government of Russia to replace social benefits for pensioners and disabled persons by monetary compensation.
New lexical content.
http://www.politjournal.ru/index.php?action=Articles&issue=35&tek=1314&dirid=47

AP-13: *Сара с возу – Клуни легче!* (It is easier for Clooney

when Sara is off the cart!)
George Clooney's separation from his girlfriend Sara Larson.
New lexical content.
http://www.internovosti.ru/text/?id=4712

AP-14: *Страховка с возу — ипотека легче* (When insurance is off the cart it is easier for mortgages).
Constitutional Court of RF decision that the requirement to insure life and employability when one takes a home loan contradicts the law.
New lexical content.
http://www.teleport2001.ru/news/2008/02/06/1290/

AP-15: *Учебники с возу – родителям легче* (It is easier for parents when textbooks are off the cart).
A school in Blagoveshchensk decided to spend federal money on buying textbooks for the students, so parents do not have to spend their money on textbooks.
New lexical content.
http://tvgorod.ru/news/2642-Uchebniki_s_vozu_%E2%80%93_roditelyam_legche.html

AP-16: *CEO с воза – компании легче* (It is easier for the company when the CEO is off the cart).
About firing the CEO of Finnish-Swedish cell phone provider TeliaSonera.
New lexical content.
http://www.ko.ru/document_for_print.php?id=16554

AP-17: *Шестеро с воза – Пхеньяну легче* (It is easier for North Korea when the six are off the cart).
Refusal of North Korea to take part in six-party talks on the nuclear problem of the Korean peninsula.
New lexical content.
http://i-news.kz/news/153997

Comments: Two things are pretty obvious in these examples: (a) they all use the same syntax and the key words of the original proverb – which is enough for readers to recognize it – while filling it with a new lexical content reflecting some concrete situation; at the same time, the basic moral of the traditional proverb remain intact: when some person (problem, etc.) disappears it is easier for another person (team, company, etc.); and (b) the number of examples is a reliable proof of the high popularity of the traditional proverb in modern Russian culture. Besides, #3 and 4 also use metonymy and metaphor, respectively. The only exception to thus rule is #1 when the allusion to the traditional proverb is used mostly to catch readers' attention and has hardly any direct connection to the content of the article.

Бабушка надвое сказала (Grandmother said ambiguously; *literally*: grandmother said in two ways).
The proverb means that it is still unknown, hard to say with any certainty whether something will actually happen in the future.

AP-1: *Бабушка Сандры надвое сказала* (Sandra's grandmother said ambiguously).
A report about the adoption conflict between the Russian mother of the girl Sandra and her Portuguese foster family where the girl lived because the mother could not provide for her daughter. Now the mother and daughter are back in Russia, and the future of the girl is uncertain. The grandmother allegedly was supposed to visit Portugal.
Syntactical extension.
http://www.svobodanews.ru/content/article/1814875.html

AP-2: *Бельгия надвое сказала* (Belgium said ambiguously).
Parliament elections in Belgium where the Flamand party got the majority of votes; the party stands for dividing the country into two parts.
Polysemy; new lexical content.
http://www.kommersant.ru/doc.aspx?DocsID=1386082&NodesID=5

AP-3: *Ивановская гордума надвое сказала* (Ivanovo city hall said ambiguously).
Proposal to unite all drug stores in Ivanovo into two large associ-

ations.
Polysemy; new lexical content.
http://www.pharmvestnik.ru/text/14663.html

AP-4: *Политика надвое сказала* (Politics said ambiguously).
Discussion of the future of the Russian political elite.
New lexical content.
http://www.rg.ru/2007/07/04/politika.html

AP-5: *Власть надвое сказала* (Those in power said ambiguously).
The first year of presidency of Dmitry Medvedev; he did not manage to divide spheres of influence with Vladimir Putin.
New lexical content; polysemy.
http://www.vedomosti.ru/newspaper/article/2009/05/07/194608

AP-6: *Гельман надвое сказал* (Gelman said ambiguously).
Art exhibition "Russia-2" in Moscow, about the coexistence of two Russias: official and cultural.
New lexical content; polysemy.
http://www.gif.ru/themes/culture/russia-2/vn/view_print/

AP-7: *Комиссия надвое сказала* (Committee said ambiguously).
Special European (Venetian) committee on the reform of the Constitution of Moldova and the governing party could not find common ground.
New lexical content.
http://www.aif.md/component/content/article/2048

AP-8: *Дедушка надвое сказал* (Grandfather said ambiguously).
On 16 May, 1996 Boris Yeltsin signed a decree about eliminating the military draft after 2000; but during all these years the real development was in the opposite direction, strengthening the draft.
New lexical content.
http://dlib.eastview.com/browse/doc/3201323

Comments: These examples fall into two clear-cut groups: in one, the basic meaning of the traditional proverb remains intact; only the wording is different to reflect a concrete situation (#1, 4, 5, 7, and 8). The other is comprised of new coinages where the moral is based on the play on the two meanings of the word *надвое*: its usual meaning – "ambiguously," and its literal meaning – "in two ways." Thus, the play on these two meanings allows the authors of #2, 3, and 6 to express the idea of dividing something into two parts – be it a country, drug-store chain, or political power.

Кто про что, а вшивый все про баню (No matter what other people are talking about, a person who has lice will talk only about the bath-house [that is, about washing himself]).
The moral of the proverb is that whatever the conversation or the discussion is going about (among several people), you can always find someone among them who will only be talking about his or her own, very vital (for that person) problem(s).

AP-1: *Кто про что, а я снова про кодекс* (No matter what other people are talking about, I am talking again about the Code of conduct).
Problems with the conduct of migrants who come to live in Saint-Petersburg; the suggested Code of conduct will not solve the problem.
New lexical content.
http://www.baltinfo.ru/column/Kto-pro-chto-a-ya-snova-pro-kodeks-150395

AP-2: *Кто про что, а Тимошенко про свою победу на выборах* (No matter what other people are talking about, Timoshenko will talk only about her winning the [presidential[elections).
Presidential elections in Ukraine.
New lexical content.
http://inforotor.ru/news/5047167

AP-3: *Кто про что, а Ильвес – про оккупацию* (No matter what other people are talking about, Ilves will talk only about occupation).

Estonian president Hendrik Ilves interprets the liberation of Estonia by the Soviet army in 1944 as occupation.
New lexical context.
http://www.chas-daily.com/win/2007/02/22/v_005.html?r=3&

AP-4: *Кто про что, а мы про кулеры* (No matter what other people are talking about, we will talk about coolers).
Advertisement for coolers.
New lexical content.
http://www.glacialtech.ru/articles.aspx?anum=502

Comments: The new coinages are pretty uniform: they all leave enough of the original proverb intact (most importantly, the introductory phrase) and substitute the wording of the traditional proverb with a new content; this also means that the general moral or meaning of the modern versions of the proverb remains the same as that of the traditional one.

Не лезь поперек батьки в пекло (Do not get into fire ahead of your father).
One should not undertake a dangerous or difficult action ahead of a more experienced, or more advanced in age (or superior in position) person.

AP-1: *Добкин полез в пекло поперек батьки* (Drobkin got into the fire ahead of the father).
Mayor of the city of Kharkov and his political views.
New syntax; new lexical content.
http://h.ua/story/128908/

AP-2: *Казахстан: поперек России в нефтяное пекло* (Kazakhstan: ahead of Russia into the oil fire).
Kazakhstan signed a contract with China about the export of Kazakh oil.
New syntax; new lexical content.
http://news.mail.ru/economics/arc506904/

AP-3: *Не лезь поперек G8 в пекло* (Do not get ahead of G8 into the fire).

Chair of the board of a Kazakh bank stated that Kazakh banks should not use those regulatory measures that are still only discussed by G8.
New lexical content.
http://comment-resp.com/comment/showtopic/3939/

AP-4: *Не лезь поперек «Howo» в пекло* (Do not get ahead of "Howo" into fire).
A traffic accident with a huge truck and a small car: the truck driver simply could not see the car from the height of his seat.
New lexical content.
http://www.zabinfo.ru/modules.php?op=modload&name=News&file=article&sid=57291&mode=thread&order=0&thold=0

AP-5: *Поперек Белого дома в пекло Тбилиси явно не пойдет* (Tbilisi will clearly not get into fire ahead of the White House).
Position of Georgia to Armenia and Turkey relationships, and establishing diplomatic relations between them; taking into account that Washington welcomed this change.
New syntax; new lexical content.
http://www.georgiatimes.info/interview/20350-1.html

AP-6: *Кадыров лезет в пекло поперек премьера?* (Kadyrov gets into the fire ahead of the prime-minister?)
Businessman Telman Isamilov returned to Chechnya and promised investments to Ramazan Kadyrov, while prime-minister Putin publicly accused this businessman of economic crimes, and several criminal cases were started against him in Russia.
New syntax; new lexical content.
http://www.compromat.ru/page_28845.htm

AP-7: С Северной Кореей конфронтации у России тоже никогда не возникало, и трудно вообразить себе, что *Москва вдруг полезет поперек американского батьки в северо-корейское пекло* (Russia has never had any confrontations with North Korea, and it is difficult to imagine that Moscow will get into the North Korea fire ahead of the American father).

New military doctrine in Russia allows preventive nuclear attack on possible aggressors.
New syntax; new lexical content.
http://www.pochtaonline.info/node/345

AP-8: *Поперек батьки в пекло? Лезть!* (Ahead of the father into the fire? Get!)
The union of scientists of Kazakhstan filed a law suit against the executive body of the Federation of trade-unions of the Republic of Kazakhstan asking the court to find unlawful its decision to exclude the union of scientists from the Federation.
Syntactic restructuring.
http://www.respublika-kz.info/news/society/6668/

Comments: These examples demonstrate one new feature that we have not seen yet: not only do they substitute – as is done usually – a word from the original proverb by a new word or phrase, but they also change the syntactical structure of the traditional proverb: the original phrase is structured as an imperative (command, addressed to a younger or a less experienced person), while the majority of anti-proverbs are structured as a declarative (## 1, 2, 5, 7) or interrogative (#6) sentence. The only exceptions are # 3 and 4 that repeat the syntax of the original proverb, while # 8 defies it: it starts with a question and continues as an imperative, but it gives directly opposite advice.

Семь бед – один ответ (Seven troubles – one/the same responsibility).
The proverb is used when one has decided to do something prohibited or risky again, fully understanding his or her responsibility for such actions.
English equivalent: As well be hanged for a sheep as for a lamb. In for a penny, in for a pound.

AP-1: *Семь бед один диабет* (Seven problems one diabetes).
The title of an article about diabetes.
Internal rhyme; new lexical content; hidden rhyme.
(http://www.russia-today.ru/2008/no_12/12_SF_05.htm)

AP-2: *Семь бед – один Club Med* (Seven problems one Club Med).
An advertisement for the French travel agency *Club Med.*
Internal rhyme; new lexical content; hidden rhyme.
http://www.kommersant.ru/doc.aspx?DocsID=347693)

AP-3: *Семь бед – один градсовет* (Seven problems – one city council).
The problems of the developing the city of Odessa.
Internal rhyme; new lexical content; hidden rhyme.
HTTP://ATV.ODESSA.UA/NEWS/2009/04/22/GRADSOVET_3781.HTML

AP-4: *Семь бед – один иммунитет* (Seven problems – one immune system).
An advertisement of food supplements strengthening the immune system of the human body.
Internal rhyme; new lexical content; hidden rhyme.
HTTP://WWW.VISIONBUY.COM/ARTICLES/52.HTML

Comments: This is a pretty uniform group of anti-proverbs: they all use the syntax and the rhyme of the traditional proverb, but substitute lexical content by one new word in such a way as to preserve the internal rhyme (and thus creating hidden rhyme). The only (and peculiar) difference is in AP #2, where the Russian word is rhymed with an English one: *бед – Med.* From the point of view of meaning, all new proverbs preserve a part of the traditional message: there is one solution for many problems, be it diabetes, developing a city, or choosing a good travel agency.

Лиха беда начало (Beginning is a difficult problem).
It is difficult to start doing something, but once you start, it is easier to continue; often said in order to encourage someone before starting some difficult task.
Cf. *an English proverb*: A good beginning makes a good ending.

AP-1: *Лиха беда. Начало* (Difficult problem. Beginning).
The title of an article from *Russian Newsweek* (11/09/2009)

about the swine flu epidemic in Russia.
Syntactic restructuring.
http://www.runewsweek.ru/society/31064/

AP-2: *Лиха беда начало сезона* (Difficult start of a new [TV] season).
About the new TV season on Russian TV.
New lexical content; syntactic extension.
http://www.novayagazeta.ru/data/2002/79/21.html

AP-3: *Лихо – беды начало* (Carelessness is the beginning of a problem).
Ministry of the Interior of Belarus about traffic accidents.
Syntactic restructuring; polysemy; paronymy.
http://mvd.gov.by/modules.php?name=News&file=print&sid=1420

Comments: Though few in number, these anti-proverbs show a variety of linguistic mechanisms that we have not met before: two of them use syntactic restructuring – that is, though using the same words, they use different syntactic relations, and hence create a different phrase. Thus, #1 divides the original proverb into two short sentences, while #3 makes the original nominal phrase a complete clause where the noun *лихо* (which looks very much like the adjective *лиха*) becomes the subject of the sentence, while *начало* is now a subject complement. Moreover, this new proverb also uses polysemy, as it utilizes the word *лихо* in a different meaning: if in the traditional proverb it is used in its dated meaning "difficult," in #3 it is used in one of its modern meanings – "careless" – often used about drivers who violate traffic rules. Hence the new moral of the new proverb: careless drivers are the reason for traffic accidents.

Бедность не порок (Poverty is not a flaw).
The proverb is used to say that material problems should not be looked upon as somebody's defect; often said as a consolation to those who are ashamed of their being poor.

AP-1: *Бедность не порок, а шанс на новоселье* (Poverty is not

a flaw but a chance to get hew housing).
Low-income people in Russia have a chance to get free municipal housing.
Syntactic extension.
http://www.rg.ru/2005/03/11/zhiliyo.html

AP-2: *Бедность не порок, но футболу мешает* (Poverty is not a flaw, but it hinders soccer).
Soccer clubs in the south of Russia cannot compete financially with clubs from such cities as Moscow or oil regions.
Syntactic extension.
http://www.sport-express.ru/newspaper/2005-07-21/4_3/

AP-3: *Бедность — не порок. Это хуже...* (Poverty is not flaw. It is worse…)
An article about the world summit in New York.
Defeated expectancy.
http://pda.sb.by/post/46980/

AP-4: *Бедность — не порок, а...* (Poverty is not a flaw, but…)
Analysis of ways businesses reduce taxable amounts.
Syntactic extension.
http://yurpractika.com/article.php?id=10007398

AP-5: *Бедность — не порок, а несчастье* (Poverty is not a flaw, but a disaster).
Difficult life of common working people in Ukraine.
Syntactic extension.
http://rg.kiev.ua/page5/article14457/

AP-6: *Бедность не порок, а причина болезней психики* (Poverty is not a flaw, but the cause of many mental diseases).
WHO claims that poverty is the origin of many mental diseases.
Syntactic extension.
http://www.zabolel.net/403-bednost-ne-porok-a-prichina-boleznej-psixiki.html

AP-7: *Бедность не порок, а достопримечательность* (Poverty is not a flaw, but a point of interest).

Visiting Philippines.
Syntactic extension.
http://world.lib.ru/s/smerdow_igorx_walentinowich/philipines.shtml

AP-8: *Бедность – не порок, порочна система, её порождающая* (Poverty is not a flaw; the flaw is in the system that produces poverty).
Economic analysis of changes in the social sphere in Russia.
Syntactic extension.
http://www.yabloko.ru/Publ/Articles/yaryg-15.html

AP-9: *Бедность – не порок, но бороться с ней надо всем миром* (Poverty is not a flaw, but we should fight it altogether).
Fighting poverty in the USA.
Syntactic extension.
http://www.izvestia.ru/nyizvestia/article3094582/?print

AP-10: *Бедность – не порок, но она может стать поводом для лишения родительских прав* (Poverty is not a flaw but it can be the reason to deprive parent their custody of the children).
A mother was deprived of her parenting rights because she had too little money to take care of her daughter.
Syntactic extension.
http://cerkov.by/page/bednost-ne-porok-no-ona-mozhet-stat-povodom-dlja-lishenija-roditelskih-prav

AP-11: *Бедность не порок. Нищета – порок* (Poverty is not a flaw. Pauperism is a flaw).
The cost of living in Uzbekistan.
Syntactic extension.
http://www.uzmetronom.com/2007/08/30/bednost_ne_porok_nishheta__porok.html

AP-12: *Бедность – не порок, но вещь очень неприятная. И распространенная* (Poverty is not a flaw, but it is very unpleasant. And also very widely spread).
Poverty in the world today.
Syntactic extension.

http://www.intv.ua/ru/article/201232/

AP-13: *Бедность не порок, но...* С какой суммы для россиян начинается богатство (Poverty is not a flaw, but… Starting with what sum of money Russians consider someone to be rich).
Survey of Russian citizens who were asked how much money people need to be considered rich.
Syntactic extension.
http://www.point.ru/news/stories/11607/

AP-14: *Бедность не порок, а особенность нашего инвестиционного климата.* (Poverty is not a flaw, but the peculiarity of our investment climate).
Investments in Belorussia.
Syntactic extension.
http://www.belgazeta.by/20041004.39/040130242/

AP-15: *Бедность не порок, но недуг!* (Poverty is not a flaw, it is a disease!)
Poor people live 8.2 years fewer.
Syntactic extension.
http://www.gorod.lv/novosti/100915-bednost_ne_porok_no_nedug

Comments: This group, though big, is quite uniform. All of the modern variants use syntactic extension, in order to make their point. What is also interesting about these coinages is that none of them is an attempt to make it a joke; they all discuss serious problems, even though in vastly different areas (from soccer clubs to fighting poverty to correlation between poverty and health). Most of them start with reinforcing the moral of the original proverb, and make their point on that basis: yes, being poor is not your fault, but… Only one anti-proverb is different in this aspect – #3, as it in fact states that poverty is not just a flaw – it is much worse, utilizing a well-known stylistic device – defeated expectancy: instead of saying (as one expects) that it is ok to be poor, it goes on to claim – surprisingly – that it is not ok at all.

На безрыбье и рак рыба (In the absence of fish, even a lobster is fish).
One should be satisfied with having what one has, to be content with what is available.
English equivalent: *In the country of the blind one-eyed man is a king. Better a small fish than an empty dish.*

AP-1: *На безрыбье и американские трежерис – рыба* (In the absence of fish, even American treasures are fish).
Economic situation in the world, and American securities: because the economic situation is so bad, US securities are the most attractive ones.
New lexical content.
http://finmarket.net/ru/found_brouse/detail/37652/14/22/

AP-2: *На безрыбье и рак — олигарх* (In the absence of fish, even a lobster is an oligarch).
An article about Vladimir Kogan, one of the oligarchs in modern Russia who is active in politics.
New lexical content.
http://2000.novayagazeta.ru/nomer/2000/50n/n50n-s16.shtml

AP-3: *А на безрыбье и Соловьев аналитик. Точнее – шоу-мен. Но тоже на безрыбье.* (In the absence of fish, Soloviev is an analyst. To be more exact – a show-man. But also in the absence of fish).
Critical review of a Sunday analytical show on Russian TV hosted by Vladimir Soloviev.
Syntactic extension; new lexical content.
http://www.forum-tvs.ru/index.php?showtopic=10516&mode=linear

AP-4: *На безрыбье и Кличко – чемпион* (In the absence of fish, even Klichko is a champion).
About a boxing match between Vitaly Klichko (Ukraine) and Deny Williams (UK).
New lexical content.
http://www.pravda.ru/sport/individual/boxing/14-12-2004/48987-boxing-0/

Comments: All new proverbs use new lexical content, but preserve the old message: in the absence of something we would like to have, we have to be content with what we have – be it a poor TV show or bad politicians, or not the best way to invest money.

За одного битого двух небитых дают (In exchange for a beaten one they give two unbeaten).
An experienced ("beaten by life") person is much more valuable than those who lack life experience. The proverb is often used to encourage people that some negative experience will still benefit them.

AP-1: *За одного битого латгальца двух небитых латышей дают* (For one beaten person from Latgalia they give two unbeaten Latvians).
Situation in Latgalia – the poorest part of Latvia.
New lexical content.
http://nordeurope.kp.ru/daily/24334/525864/

AP-2: *За одного Битова трех не битых дают* (For one Bitov they do not give three unbeaten).
A criminal investigation in Uzbekistan against a citizen of Russia Bitov, who is charged with multiple crimes.
Homonymy.
http://www.newizv.ru/news/2009-02-05/105268/

AP-3: *За одного старого двух новых дают* (For one old one they give two new ones).
About new appointments in the Russian government: one deputy minister of regional development was fired and two new persons were appointed deputy ministers.
New lexical content.
http://www.rg.ru/2009/03/27/minregion.html

AP-4: *За одного врача двух медсестер дают* (They give two nurses for one doctor).
Problems of and importance of nurses in Ukraine – a report about the Ukrainian congress of nurses.

New lexical content.
http://www.zn.ua/3000/3450/61051/

AP-5: *За одного Павлюченко дают двух испанских футболистов* (For one Pavluchenko they give two Spanish soccer players).
British soccer club Tottenham wants to exchange Russian player Roman Pavluchenko for two players from a Spanish club.
New lexical content.
http://www.molgvardia.ru/groupchanges/2009/06/30/7876

AP-6: *Одного Ефимова за двух Березуцких дают* (They give two Bezrutskih for one Efimov).
Two brothers, well-known soccer players, will not play for the Russian national team because of injuries; instead, Sergey Efimov will play.
New lexical content.
http://www.gudok.ru/newspaper/detail.php?ID=254211&year=2007&month=03&SECTION_ID=13180

AP-7: *За одного крановщика двух экономистов дают* (They give two economists for one crane operator).
Belorussian plant Gomselmach does not need engineers or other persons with college degrees anymore; they have more than enough and even may have to fire some.
New lexical content.
http://sb.by/post/24556/

AP-8: *За одного ангела двух людей дают* (They give two people for one angel).
A review of a new play staged in one of the Moscow theaters "Two angels, four men."
New lexical content.
http://www.smotr.ru/2001/2001_tab_2ang.htm

Comments: With the exception of the first two anti-proverbs, the new variants depart from the original wording substantially, while leaving the syntactic structure intact, together with key words: *for one... two*. Surprisingly, though, it does not change the message: all of them (except #8) talk about preferring one more experienced person as opposed to two or more inexperienced ones. Anti-proverb #2 is interesting for another reason: it uses homonymy: the last name of the person – *Битова* – sounds very similar to the Russian word *битого* (beaten) from the original proverb, which is the basis of the play on words in this title of the article about a famous criminal case.

Первый блин комом (The first pancake is a flop).
The first attempt at something is usually unsuccessful.
English equivalent: *If at first you don't succeed, try and try again!*

AP-1: *Первый блин не комом* (The first pancake is not a flop).
Ice hockey world cup; victory of the Russian team in the first game.
New lexical content.
http://www.gazeta.ru/sport/2010/04/a_3351010.shtml

AP-2: *Первый артефакт – комом* (The first artifact is a flop).
Review of the movie "Artifact."
New lexical content.
http://www.proficinema.ru/distribution/reviews/detail.php?ID=51298

AP-3: *Первый гимн комом* (The first anthem is a flop).
Soccer federation of Russia did not approve the first version of its anthem.
New lexical content.
http://football.sport.ua/news/87178

AP-4: *Первый эскалатор — комом* (The first escalator is a flop).
Escalators installed in one of the new metro stations in Saint-Petersburg need repairs after only one year of work.
New lexical content.
http://www.kommersant.ru/doc.aspx?DocsID=1347182

AP-5: *Первый гриб комом* (The first mushroom is a flop).

Very few mushrooms in the forests in the Russian Far East in summer 2010.
New lexical content.
http://www.ampravda.ru/2010/07/20/026617.html

AP-6: *Первый гриб комом* (The first mushroom is a flop).
The first case of mushroom poisoning in the city of Riga.
New lexical content.
http://www.chas-daily.com/win/2010/07/08/g_042.html?r=32&

AP-7: *Google Nexus One: первый "гуглоблин" комом?* (The first "google-pancake" is a flop?)
Review of Google Nexus One phone.
Neologism.
http://www.cifrovik.ru/publish/open_article/16387/

AP-8: *Первый «ракетный блин» – комом* (The first rocket pancake is a flop).
Failed rocket launch during a military exercise in Leningrad oblast.
New lexical content.
http://www.tv100.ru/news/Pervyj-raketnyj-blin--komom-15664/

AP-9: *Первый Falcon вышел комом* (The first Falcon is a flop).
Failed first launch of the new Falcon rocket; March 28, 2006.
New lexical content.
http://news.cosmoport.com/2006/03/28/8.htm

AP-10: *Первый экшн комом* (The first action is a flop).
Problems in the organization of the first festival of action movies in Astana.
New lexical content.
http://www.focus.kz/ru_culture/5668/

AP-11: *"Казсат-1" – Первый спутник комом* (*Kazsat-1*: The first satellite is a flop).
Problems in the work of the first Kazakh communication satellite.
New lexical content.

http://tv.goldmir.net/index.php?newsid=406

AP-12: *Первый ЕГЭ комом* (The first Unified State Examination is a flop).
First experience of using the Unified State Examination in Russia, instead of traditional entrance exams in universities.
New lexical content.
http://www.hse.ru/news/1163609/2875239.html

AP-13: *Первый месяц комом* (The first month is a flop).
All types of bank deposits turned out to be without profit in January 2007, due to high inflation in Russia.
New lexical content.
http://www.banki.ru/news/daytheme/?id=258420

Comments: There are several interesting things about this group. One the one hand, they are all uniform in a sense that they all use the old pattern and fill it with new realities: thus, instead of a failed pancakes, they talk about failed sputniks, earnings, film festivals, entrance examinations, and everything in between. This proves, one more time, that the traditional proverb is alive and well in modern Russian society and culture. Also, #1 defies traditional wisdom claiming that the first attempt can in fact be successful. Anti-proverb #7 uses an interesting neologism – *гуглоблин* (literally, "google pancake"), which is a combination of the words *Google* and *pancake* in Russian. Even though the word does not exist, it is easily understood because it is part of the familiar syntactic structure of the traditional proverb.

Бог дал, бог и взял (God gave, God took back).
We should not be sorry or grieve about something lost because it does not depend on us; often used as a consolation for somebody.
English equivalent: *The Lord giveth and the Lord taketh away.*

AP-1: *Бог дал. Поп взял.* (God gave. Priest took back).
The cost of religious ceremonies in various religions in Russia.
New lexical content.
http://uisrussia.msu.ru/docs/nov/2000/23/nov_2000_23_33.htm

AP-2: *МЭРТ дал, бог взял* (Ministry of economic development gave, God took away).
A draft bill on church restitution in Russia.
New lexical content.
http://www.zagolovki.ru/article/12Mar2007/restituciya

Comments: Both examples have very little to do with the original moral; the first one criticizes ministers of various denominations for the high cost of religious ceremonies; the second one talks about returning to the church its property that was confiscated during the soviet time. Still, the association with the original proverb is strong enough for both new versions to make a catchy title.

Бог любит Троицу (God loves Trinity).
The proverb is used as a justification of proof that it is necessary to do something three times or with three people.
Cf. *English phrase*: Third time is the charm.

AP-1: *Хоккейный бог любит троицу* (Hockey god loves trinity).
Russian national ice hockey team plans to win the World Cup for the third time in a row in 2010.
New lexical content.
http://www.kp.ru/daily/24484/640601/

AP-2: *Чешский Бог троицу не любит* (Czech God does not love trinity).
Russian national ice hockey team lost the final game to the Czech team in the 2010 championship; it also happened on the day when the Russian Orthodox church celebrates Trinity holiday.
Polysemy.
http://www.mk.ru/sport/article/2010/05/24/494862-cheshskiy-bog-troitsu-ne-lyubit-foto.html

AP-3: *Кризис, как и бог, троицу любит* (Crisis, as well as God, loves trinity).
The third stage of the financial crisis in Kazakhstan.

New lexical content; syntactic extension.
http://www.respublika-kaz.info/news/finance/9217/

AP-4: Не только бог троицу любит (Not only God loves trinity).
Three German female athletes were photographed for the German version of Playboy magazine on the eve of the Olympics in Athens. 2004).
New lexical content.
http://www.pravda.ru/sport/cupper/hockey/18-08-2004/48146-nude-0/

AP-5: *Бог троицу любит... в Петербурге* (God loves trinity… in Saint-Petersburg).
The third forum of the law firms of CIS took place in Saint-Petersburg, August 2010.
New lexical content; syntactic extension.
http://yurpractika.com/article.php?id=100094964

AP-6: *"Куриный бог" троицу любит* ("Chicken god" loves trinity).
The festival of arts in Crimea, which lasted for three days in 2008; the name is taken from the stone amulet popular among many Slav peoples.
New lexical content.
http://www.kommersant.ua/doc.html?docId=1007856&IssueId=46980

AP-7: *Бог и закон троицу любят* (God and law love trinity).
The administration of Novosibirsk oblast is going to make a third attempt to buy apartments from the contractors to house people living in housing unfit for living.
Syntactic extension.
http://newsib.net/index.php?newsid=6376

AP-8: *Любит ли Бог троицу?* (Does God love trinity?)
Italian soccer club "Inter" twice lost the game in the final match in the championship of Italy; will it loose a third time?
New syntax.

http://m.football.ua/italy/news/98132.html

AP-9: *Мальцев не бог, но троицу любит* (Maltsev is not God, but he loves trinity).
Coach Alexander Maltsev (women's ice hockey national team, Kazakhstan) hopes to win the championship of Asia for the third time.
Syntactic extension.
http://i-news.kz/news/173985

Comments: Once again, the sheer number of new variants shows the popularity of the traditional proverb. Most of the new coinages narrow the meaning to some particular field (ice-hockey; soccer, economic crisis), while retaining the basic idea that something must be done three times in a row (or questioning if it is possible). Linguistically, the most interesting case is #2, as it utilizes a play on words: the Russian word *троица*, though literally meaning "Trinity," is understood in this context as a synonym of the number three. Thus, the article about the Czech victory not only says that the Russian team did not win three times in a row, but it also lost the game on the day when the Russian Orthodox church celebrates the holiday of Trinity. Also, in terms of the meaning, anti-proverb #4 is the farthest from the traditional prototype, and mostly uses the allusion to the traditional proverb as a catchy phrase to get readers' attention.

Бог терпел и нам велел (God suffered and told us to suffer, too).
We have no choice but get through the hard times. Often said as a consolation, mostly ironically, to oneself or others who are in a difficult situation.

AP-1: *Русский язык терпел и нам велел* (The Russian language suffered and told us to suffer).
History of spelling reforms in the Russian language.
New lexical content.
http://www.kp.ru/daily/24374.3/555587/

AP-2: *Сам терпел и нам велел* (Himself suffered and told us to

suffer).
Alexander Voloshin, head of the administration of the president of Russia, believes that only time and patience are needed to improve the situation in Russia.
New lexical content.
http://dlib.eastview.com/browse/doc/9523285

AP-3: *Запад терпел, а нам не велел* (The West suffered, but told us not to).
Criticism of the value and necessity of tolerance in liberal education, stripped of any ideology.
New lexical content.
http://www.wpfdc.org/ru//news/1-news//1-/news/1-news//76--q----q

AP-4: *ТС терпел и нам велел* (Customs Union suffered and told us to suffer).
Problems with the customs union of Russia, Belorussia, and Kazakhstan.
New lexical content.
http://www.expert.ru/printissues/kazakhstan/2010/04/tamozhnya/

AP-5: *Атлет терпел и нам велел* (The athlete suffered and told us to suffer).
An interview with Dmitry Kolokov, silver medalist at Olympic Games in China-2008, who believes that patience is the key virtue of an athlete.
New lexical content.
http://ufa1.ru/news/63796.html

Comments: This group is very uniform in its tendency to adjust the traditional proverb to a concrete situation while preserving its message: one has to be patient, whether we talk about an economic situation, spelling reform, or customs union: it takes time and, yes, some suffering before things get better.

До Бога высоко, до царя далеко (God is up high, the Tsar is far away).
It is useless to expect any help from those in power.

AP-1: *До Бога высоко, до чиновника далеко* (God is up high, bureaucrats are far away).
Problems with repairing municipal housing in Kiev.
New lexical content.
http://timeua.info/200310/16913.html

AP-2: *До Бога высоко, до Шойгу далеко* (God is up high; Shoigu [Minister of Emergency Situations] is far away).
Corruption in the personnel policy of the Ministry of Emergency Situations.
New lexical content.
http://www.sknews.ru/main/20687-do-boga-vy...jgu-daleko.html

AP-3: *До Бога высоко, до ЮНЕСКО – далеко* (God is up high; UNESCO is far away).
Parliamentary assembly of CIS will deal with the preservation of historic and cultural monuments.
New lexical content.
http://odessa-daily.com.ua/video-gal/10615-oxrana-pamyatnikov.html

AP-4: *До Бога высоко, до Царя... не так уж и далеко* (God is up high, the tsar is not that far away).
A retired person fought successfully against corrupt city hall officials, after he wrote a letter to President of Russia.
New lexical content.
http://news.mail.ru/inregions/south/26/2875348/

AP-5: *До Бога высоко, до Страсбурга далеко...* (God is up high; Strasburg is far away…)
How to file a complaint in the European Court on human rights.
New lexical content.
http://ru.trend.az/life/sitylife/940523.html

AP-6: *До трибун высоко, до ораторов далеко* (The podium is up high; the speakers are far away).
Violation of human rights in Russia, though many senior government officials deny it.
New lexical content.

http://www.npar.ru/op/anna-1005.htm

Comments: These new proverbs fall into two groups: one confirms the original message of the traditional proverb that it makes no sense to expect any help from those in power (#1, 2, 3, 6) while the second group states the opposite: it is possible to get help from those in power (#4 and 5): though it is far from easy, it is not hopeless.

На бога надейся, а сам не плошай (Trust in God but rely on yourself).
Only people themselves are responsible for the outcome of their actions; often said as advice not to rely on somebody's help but to act.
English equivalent: Heaven helps those who help themselves.

AP-1: *На Бооса надейся, а сам не плошай* (Trust in Boos [governor of Kaliningrad oblast] but rely on yourself).
Situation in Kaliningrad oblast.
Paronymy.
http://kaliningrad.ru/news/analytics/item/5091

AP-2: *На заграницу надейся, а сам не плошай!* (Trust in overseas but rely on yourself!)
Comparing cost of imported and Russian prescription drugs.
New lexical content.
http://www.apteka.ua/article/21962

AP-3: *На банк надейся, а сам не плошай* (Trust in the bank but rely on yourself).
Responsibility of taxpayers to check whether the bank transferred the money to the budget.
New lexical content.
http://yurpractika.com/article.php?id=100097232

AP-4: *На МВФ надейся, а сам не плошай* (Trust in the International Monetary Fund, but rely on yourself).
Citizens of Belorussia look for help from the International Monetary Fond, and not its own government.

New lexical content.
http://www.ej.by/economy/2010-06-27/na_mvf_nadeysya
a_sam_ne_ploshay.html

AP-5: *На Минздрав надейся, а сам не плошай!* (Trust in the Ministry of health, but rely on yourself!)
You are responsible for your own health.
New lexical content.
http://demoscope.ru/weekly/2010/0417/tema06.php

AP-6: *На пенсию надейся, а сам не плошай* (Trust in retirement money, but rely on yourself).
Social security system in the Netherlands.
New lexical content.
http://www.gollandia.com/Pensioen.htm

AP-7: *На импорт надейся, а сам не плошай...* (Trust in imported goods, but rely on yourself).
Italy's dependence on imported electricity explains the major blackout on 28 September 2003.
New lexical content.
http://www.e-m.ru/er/2004-02/22464/

AP-8: *На антивирус надейся, а сам не плошай!* (Trust in antivirus, but rely on yourself)
Importance of using common sense to protect your computer from viruses and spam.
New lexical content.
http://dialognauka.ru/main.phtml?/press-center/press-
release&newser=0000001234295476.txt&arh=1&start=91

AP-9: *На ментов надейся, а сам не плошай!* (Trust in cops, but rely on yourself!)
Means of self-defense available for Russian citizens.
New lexical content.
http://diesel.elcat.kg/lofiversion/index.php?t82374.html

AP-10: *На дождь надейся, а сам не плошай!* (Trust in rain, but rely on yourself!)

How to effectively water garden plants when there is no rain.
New lexical content.
http://www.e1.ru/articles/comfort/page_1/006/876/article_6876.html

AP-11: *На чудо надейся, но сам не плошай* (Trust in miracles but rely on yourself).
Advice on job hunting in Russia today.
New lexical content.
http://www.vacansia.ru/index.php?act=info&story=3784

AP-12: *На фонды надейся, да сам не плошай* (Trust in funds, but rely on yourself).
How retired persons live in other countries and where their retirement money comes from.
New lexical content.
http://www.mk.ru/economics/article/2009/12/21/403364-na-fondyi-nadeysya-da-sam-ne-ploshay.html

AP-13: *На БАД не надейся. И сам не плошай!* (Do not trust food supplements. And rely on yourself!)
Prosecutor's office in Krasnoyarsk investigating a firm selling food supplements allegedly guaranteeing immediate results.
New lexical content.
http://www.newslab.ru/blog/170651

AP-14: *На «БОИНГ» надейся, а сам не плошай* (Trust in Boeing, but rely on yourself).
Problems of the aircraft industry in Russia today.
New lexical content.
http://www.bujet.ru/article/18214.php

AP-15: *"Зеленая карта" или на страховку надейся, да сам не плошай* ("Green card" [European international car insurance] or trust in insurance, but rely on yourself)
Car insurance for Russian citizens travelling abroad by car.
New lexical content.
http://www.zr.ru/a/4831/

AP-16: *На Запад надейся, а сам не плошай* (Trust in the West, but rely on yourself).
Health care reform in Russia should be based on national health care traditions and models.
New lexical content.
http://medgazeta.rusmedserv.com/2005/63/article_1383.html

Comments: One more time, the number of modern versions shows the popularity of the traditional proverb with the Russian speakers. Nearly all of the anti-proverbs confirm the traditional wisdom: yes, one should trust in some authority (be it an anti-virus program, or police protection, or international community), but at the same time, one should rely first of all on oneself. Linguistically, #1 is the most interesting case, as it uses the similarity between the last name of the governor of Kaliningrad region (*Боос*) and the Russian word for God (*Бог*) to create a play on words, based on paronymy. Also, #13 defies the original moral, encouraging the readers not to rely on food supplements (in the particular situation which was under investigation).

B

Кому война, а кому мать родна (What is war to some people is mother to others).
The proverb is used to describe people who even during difficult times for everyone seek their own interests or profit, ignoring other people's problems.

AP-1: *Кому жара, а кому мать родная* (What is heat for some is mother to others).
Drought leads to price growth on grain – which is good for Ukraine.
Hidden rhyme.
http://www.aif.ua/money/article/20415

AP-2: *Кому казна, кому мать родна* (What is treasury for some is mother for others).
Budget problems in Ukraine and corruption in spending.
Hidden rhyme, internal rhyme.

http://www.zn.ua/2000/2600/67650/

AP-3: *Кому девальвация, а кому мать родна?* (What is currency devaluation to some is mother to others?)
Devaluation of Kazakh national currency was a disaster for common people, but some businesses actually made huge profits during a couple of days.
New lexical content.
http://www.respublika-kz.info/news/finance/9797/

AP-4: *Кому волна, а кому мать родна* (What is a wave to some is mother to others).
A second wave of the financial crisis in Russia is actually good for some players, for example, banks who will again ask for more money from the government.
Hidden rhyme; internal rhyme.
http://www.ippnou.ru/article.php?idarticle=006401

AP-5: *Кому – «Ега», а томским школьникам – «мать родна»!* (What is USE to some is "mother" to Tomsk school graduates!)
New Unified State Exams give high school graduates in every Russian region better chances to enter not only a regional university, but also any prestigious Moscow or Saint-Petersburg university.
Neologism; internal rhyme.
http://www.hse.ru/news/1113255.html

AP-6: *Кому безработица беда, кому – мать родна* (What is unemployment to some is mother to others).
Personnel agencies promise unemployed persons to find a job for a fee; after getting money they do not fulfill their promises.
Internal rhyme.
http://www.grani21.ru/node/18202

AP-7: *Кому – Вона, а кому – мать родна* (What is she to some is mother to others).
A meeting in Kiev on choosing Yulia Timoshenko as a candidate for president of Ukraine.

Paronymy, hidden rhyme, internal rhyme; polysemy.
http://www.diary.ru/~politics-ua/p83926085.htm

AP-8: *Кому газовая война, а кому...* (What is gas war to some, to others is…).
A conflict between Minsk and Moscow about prices for gas is good for those who are interested in new gas pipelines, not via the territory of Ukraine or Belorussia.
Ellipsis.
http://www.chaspik.info/bodynews/6757.htm

Comments: This old Russian proverb produced a very interesting group of modern variants. First of all, most of them repeat the internal rhyme of the original proverb. Secondly, most of them have a hidden rhyme (rhyming substitution) by means of which a new lexical content rhymes with the original wording of the proverb: thus, most new versions include words that rhyme with the Russian word *война* (war): *жара, казна, Волна, ега, беда, вона.* At the same time, two anti-proverbs stand out in this group: #5 and #7. In the first one, we have a neologism *ега* which is based on the abbreviation *ЕГЭ* (Unified State Examination), but made into a word resembling a character from Russian Fairy tales – the evil witch Baba Yaga; the implication being that for some students these new exams are scary and terrifying, but for children from far away regions of Russia they give an equal chance of entering prestigious colleges and universities. In #7, the Ukrainian form of the personal pronoun *she* (*вона*) not only perfectly rhymes with the original proverb, but it is also a clear allusion to Timoshenko's advertisements where she used this pronoun to talk about Ukraine under her leadership if she is elected.

Волка ноги кормят (Legs feed the wolf).
In order to earn a living, one must be active, do something, and not just sit and wait.
English equivalent: A hound's food is in its legs.

AP-1: *Виктор Никулин: «Дрессировщика, как и волка, ноги кормят...»* (Victor Nikulin: "Legs feed not only the wolf, but

the animal trainer, too…")
The work of the animal trainer of wolves in a circus in Ukraine.
Syntactic extension.
http://www.time4news.org/content/viktor-nikulin-%C2%AB dressirovshchika-kak-i-volka-nogi-kormyat%E2%80%A6% C2%BB

AP-2: *Не только волка ноги кормят* (Legs feed not only the wolf).
Prevention of diseases of legs and feet.
Syntactic extension.
http://svital.com/klub-zozh-urok-33-ne-tolko-volka-nogi-kormyat/

AP-3: *Ноги волка кормят, а зайца спасают* (Legs feed the wolf and save the rabbit).
Different types of legs in various animals.
Syntactic extension.
http://zoosite.ru/v2/909

AP-4: *Молодых ноги кормят* (Legs feed the young).
Problems with finding jobs among high school and college students.
New lexical content.
http://www.expert.ru/printissues/kazakhstan/2010/21/trud/

AP-5: *Почтальона ноги кормят* (Legs feed mail-carriers).
The work of mail carriers.
New lexical content.
http://dv.aif.ru/issues/546/16_01

AP-6: *Депутата ноги кормят* (Legs feed deputies).
Video of voting in the Russian parliament: only 88 members of the parliament were in the room, and they were voting for those absent. As a result, they managed to get 450 votes; May 28, 2010.
New lexical content.
http://inotv.rt.com/2010-05-28/Deputata-nogi-kormyat

AP-7: *Волкову ноги кормят* (Legs feed Volkova).
Russian бегунья Katya Volkova got the gold medal in the World Cup 2007 in 2,000 meters race.
Paronymy.
http://www.kp.ru/daily/23957/72215/

AP-8: *Кого ноги кормят?* (Whom do legs feed?)
Selling of obligatory boot covers in medical facilities is a profitable business.
Polysemy.
http://www.zakon.kz/170294-kogo-nogi-kormjat-torgovlja-bakhilami.html

AP-9: *Месси ноги кормят* (Legs feed Messi).
Argentinean soccer player Lionel Messi was awarded "Golden Football-2009."
New lexical content.
http://news.21.by/sport/2009/12/02/414371.html

AP-10: *Си-волкера ноги кормят* (Legs feed C-walkers).
Modern dance C-walk.
Paronymy; neologism; English word with a Russian morphological ending.
http://www.molodoi-gazeta.ru/article-8027.html

Comments: These anti-proverbs fall into two groups: one (#1, 2, 3) is using syntactic extension to add something to the meaning of the original proverb; in other words, they confirm the original meaning but also add something to it; in the second group the original noun *волк* (wolf) is substituted by something new: young people, mail-carriers, athletes, members of the parliament. Anti-proverb #8, making the proverb a question, talks about people who make profits by selling boot covers, and thus using the words *legs* in its direct meaning, while in the original proverb (Legs feed the wolf) it is used metonymically. Finally, we have two examples of paronymy: in #7, the last name of the female athlete happens to be *Volkova*, which nearly perfectly coincides with the form of the Russian word *volk* (wolf) in the original proverb; in #10 we have a rare case of an English word (*C-*

walker) written in Russian but acquiring the morphological ending of the Russian genitive case; it is also paronymical with the Russian word *волк* (wolf).

И волки сыты, и овцы целы (Both the wolves have eaten and the sheep are unhurt).
Said about a situation when both opposing sides are satisfied with a decision.
English equivalent: To have one's cake and eat it, too.

AP-1: *Генералы сыты, преступники целы* (The generals have eaten, and the criminal are unhurt).
Misuse of money allocated for investigative criminal work of Russian police.
New lexical content.
http://mk-piter.ru/2006/11/22/014/

AP-2: *И люди целы, и собаки сыты* (Both the people are unhurt, and the dogs have eaten).
A shelter for homeless animals in Ulyanovsk.
http://saveanimals.ru/node/3

AP-3: *И дороги целы, и люди сыты* (Both the roads are intact, and the people have eaten).
A new asphalt plant in Ukraine will bring both more taxes and work for people.
New lexical content.
http://www.tehnichka.com/index.php?option=com_content&view=article&id=1542:2009-07-08-08-42-41&catid=132:-25-16062009&Itemid=99

AP-4: *И инвесторы сыты, и собственники целы, и все довольны...* (Both investors have eaten, and the owners are un-hurt, and everyone is satisfied…)
Reconstructing and preserving historic buildings in the old center of Irkutsk.
New lexical content; syntactic extension.
http://news.babr.ru/?IDE=28381

AP-5: *И деньги целы, и сотрудники сыты* (Both the money is intact, and the employees have eaten).
Many companies organize cafeterias for their employees, which is not only good for the people but allows companies to reduce taxes.
New lexical content.
http://www.penza-job.ru/view/1709.html

AP-6: *Волки сыты, овцы не целы* (The wolves have eaten; the sheep are not unhurt).
Economic situation in Armenia; government does nothing to make the lives of common people better, looking only to improve macroeconomic data.
New lexical content.
http://www.armtown.com/news/ru/lra/20100505/13657/

AP-7: *И елки целы, и гости сыты* (Both the spruces are unhurt, and the guests have eaten).
Sales of spruce trees in Moscow in December 2004 fell 20%.
Hidden rhyme.
http://www.prazdnikinfo.ru/5/11/i21_15654p0.htm

AP-8: *И кошки сыты, и мышки целы* (Both the cats have eaten, and the mice are unhurt).
A review of a new performance of the play *Cats and Mice* in the Moscow theater named after Chekhov.
New lexical content.
http://www.izvestia.ru/culture/article969312/?print

AP-9: *Наследники сыты, и депутаты целы* (Both heirs have eaten, and the deputies are unhurt).
Russian parliament passed the bill on taxes on inheritance and gifts; June 2005.
New lexical content.
http://www.mk.ru/editions/daily/article/2005/06/11/195091-nasledniki-syityi-i-deputatyi-tselyi.html?action=comments

Comments: This is a pretty uniform group; most new coinages use new lexical content to fill the same syntactic structure (Both _______have eaten and ______ are unhurt) in order to apply it to various situations; however, the basic message of the new proverbs is exactly the same as it is in the traditional one: a situation when opposing parties are satisfied with a decision. The only exception is anti-proverb #6, which states the opposite: only one side (the government) is satisfied, while the people are hurting.

Волков бояться – в лес не ходить (If you are afraid of wolves, do not go to the forest).
If you are afraid of taking risks, do not do risky things; in other words, risks are part of achieving something in life.

AP-1: *Борис Немцов: «Путина бояться – в сортир не ходить»* (Boris Nemtsov: "If you are afraid of Putin, do not go to the outhouse.")
About the report by Boris Nemtsov about the results of 10 years of governing by Putin.
New lexical content.
http://svpressa.ru/politic/article/26417/

AP-2: *Взрыва бояться – в метро не ходить* (If you are afraid of bombs, do not go to the metro).
Explosions in Moscow metro; March 29, 2010.
New lexical content.
http://www.interfax.ru/society/txt.asp?id=131501

AP-3: *ЕГЭ бояться – в ВУЗ не ходить* (If you are afraid of Unified State Examinations, do not go to college).
Results of the new type of final school exams in Russia.
New lexical content.
http://www.ogirk.ru/news/2010-07-02/ege.html

AP-4: *Второй волны кризиса бояться – в инвесторы не ходить* (If you are afraid of the second wave of the crisis, do not become an investor).
Analysis of the economic situation in Russia and the possibility of the second stage of economic crisis.
New lexical content.

http://www.bigness.ru/articles/2010-04-30/krizis/108544

AP-5: *Начальников бояться – работать не ходить* (If you are afraid of your bosses, do not go to work).
Relationships with your boss.
New lexical content.
http://wwwomen.ru/s.php/2514.htm

AP-6: *Волкера бояться – в банки не ходить* (If you are afraid of Volcker, do not go to the bank).
Paul Volcker and his role in American economy.
Paronymy.
http://www.spekulant.ru/magazine/Volkera_boyatsya_v_banki_ne_hodit.html

AP-7: *Путина бояться – в Кремль не ходить* (If you are afraid of Putin, do not go to the Kremlin).
The government of Moscow denied its participation in the publication in a Moscow newspaper criticizing Vladimir Putin.
New lexical content.
http://www.kasparov.ru/material.php?id=48764BABD51A3

AP-8: *Путина бояться – на марши не ходить…* (If you are afraid of Putin, do not go to the march…)
Participation in the so-called "March of Those who Disagree"
New lexical content.
http://news.babr.ru/?IDE=41308

Comments: All these anti-proverbs use the same device: they take the familiar structure (*If you are afraid of____, do not____*) and fill it with new content, be it the Moscow underground, economic crisis, or your boss. From the point of view of its etymology, the very first coinage is the most interesting. It is an allusion to the famous Putin's promise "to whack terrorists everywhere, including outhouses." In September 1999 Putin (he was prime-minister of Russia then) said: "Russian airplanes are striking and will continue striking the bases of terrorists in Chechnya, and this will continue no matter where terrorists might be. We will follow the terrorists everywhere, if in the airport, then it will be in the airport. So, we will, if you excuse me, catch them in the outhouse, we will whack them there, eventually. That is all, the question is closed." The statement immediately acquired proverbial status, and is known to literally any person in Russia. Another interesting example is anti-proverb #7, where the name Волкер (Volcker) sounds very similar to the Russian word *волков* (wolves) in the genitive case; thus, we have paronymy here.

Г

С глаз долой – из сердца вон (Out of sight, out of heart).
People tend to forget those – relatives, friends, loved ones – whom they do not see around.
English equivalent: Out of sight, out of mind.

AP-1: *С глаз – долой, из «С Украиною в сердце» – вон* (Out of sight – out of "With Ukraine in the Heart").
"With Ukraine in Heart" is Yulia Timoshenko's organization supporting her during presidential elections in Ukraine in January 2010.
New lexical content.
http://news.yottos.com/ShowNews/11-12-2009

AP-2: *С глаз — долой, из чарта — вон!* (Out of sight, out of [music] chart!)
Russian translation of the title of the movie "Music and Lyrics" (2007) starring Hugh Grant and Drew Barrymore.
New lexical content.
http://www.kinopoisk.ru/level/1/film/251918/

Comments: Those only two in number, both anti-proverbs are quite interesting in its meaning and structure. The first one is the title of the article describing how Yulia Timoshenko fired a number of her representatives and replaced them by new ones. The title uses the similarity between the well-known proverb and the name of her organization. The second one is the Russian version of the title of a movie; instead of literally translating the original title it tries to interpret its message, and does it quite well. Again, the wording is based on the fact that everyone will recognize the traditional proverb and will see at once the main idea: once a singer does not appear in public his or her songs are immediately forgotten.

Не говори гоп, пока не перепрыгнешь (Do not say "gop" until you have jumped over).
The proverb is used as a warning to those who start boasting about something before that something is complete or done.
English equivalent: Don't count your chickens before they're hatched; There's many a slip between the cup and the lip.

AP-1: *Не говори гол, пока вратаря не обвёл* (Do not say goal until you have tricked the goal-keeper).
Soccer game photos.
Paronymy; internal rhyme.
http://volgograd.kp.ru/photo/496230/

AP-2: *Последний экзамен: не говори "ГАК", пока не перепрыгнул* (The last exam: do not say GAK [state examination committee] until you have jumped over).
A list of topics for a final exam in journalism.
Paronymy.
http://mediart.ru/blog/metodichki/661-1-poslednii-ekzamen-ne-govori-gak-poka-ne-pereprignul.html

AP-3: *Не говори ГОК, пока не перепрыгнешь* (Do not say GOK [ore-processing plant] until you have jumped over).
Changing ownership in one of the biggest ore-processing combines in Russia.
Paronymy.
http://www.kommersant.ru/doc.aspx?DocsID=139215

Comments: All three proverbs use paronymy to create an association with the original proverb (on top of preserving its syntactic structure and the second part of the phrase intact). Besides, #1 uses internal rhyme; this is especially interesting in this case: though internal rhyme is a very common feature of traditional Russian proverbs, it is absent in this one; still, the new coinage uses it, which makes it easier for readers not only to remember it, but to associate it with other proverbs.

Дурная голова ногам покою не дает (Silly head does not allow the legs to have some rest).
The proverb is used to describe some action that was not thought over well or done in haste, and as a result led to new problems or troubles. Often used humorously about oneself.

AP-1: *Дурная «Булава» покоя не дает* (Silly "Bulava" does not give any rest).
A failed launch of the new Russian missile Bulava.
Hidden rhyme.
http://www.gazeta.ru/politics/2010/01/12_a_3310785.shtml

AP-2: *Дурная голова врачам покоя не дает* (Silly head does not give any rest to doctors).
New methods of treating drug addiction.
Hidden rhyme.
http://www.adic.org.ua/teenager/m-ain-alp/stereotox.htm

AP-3: *Как на Украине дурная голова языкам покою не даёт* (How silly head does not give any rest to tongues in Ukraine).
Ukrainian opposition against better relationships with Russia.
Syntactic extension; hidden rhyme.
http://dkvartal.ru/news/64147295

AP-4: *Дурная погода голове покоя не дает* (Silly [here: bad] weather does not give any rest to the head).
Advice to weather-dependent people: how to treat headaches connected with changes in the weather.
Polysemy.
http://www.sobesednik.ru/publications/healthy/2008/07/14/golova_pogoda/

AP-5: *Дурная голова Луке покоя не дает* (Silly head does not give any rest to Luka).
Belorussian president Alexander Lukashenko did not let the journalists of two Russian newspapers to the summit of CIS (The

Commonwealth of Independent States), which took place in Minsk in 2006.
New lexical content.
http://charter97.org/rus/news/2006/11/29/luka

Comments: Though relatively few, all of the new coinages are interesting in their own way. Thus, #1, 2 and 3 have hidden rhymes (rhyming substitution) with various parts of the original proverb: the Russian word *голова* (head) rhymes with the name of the new Russian missile – *Булава* in the first case, while the Russian word *врачам* (doctors) rhymes with the word *ногам* (legs) in #2; in #3: *языкам* (tongues) once again rhymes with *ногам* (legs), but on top of that it uses syntactic extension. In #4, the tables are turned, and now it is the head that suffers because of bad weather; this anti-proverb uses a play on different meanings of the word *дурная*: in the original proverb (and in most new variants) it means "silly," while here it utilizes its other meaning – "bad" (weather).

Повинную голову и меч не сечет (The sword does not chop off the head admitting guilt).
Those who admit their fault or wrong-doing are not punished.
English equivalent: A fault confessed is half redressed.

AP-1: *Повинную голову меч не сечет, ее лишь штрафуют* (The head admitting guilt is not chopped off by the sword; it is only fined).
An advertising company was fined for violating the law on advertisements.
Syntactic extension.
http://www.rt-online.ru/articles/144_24441/56835/

Comments: This lone example is a good illustration of adjusting a traditional proverb to modern circumstances and narrowing its meaning by way of syntactic extension.

Голь на выдумки хитра (Poor people are creative).
Usually said in a situation when people using some cheap improvised means solve difficult problems as a rule requiring a lot

of material resources; in other words, people who cannot afford to spend a lot of money have to be creative; often said humorously.
English equivalent: Necessity is the mother of invention.

AP-1: *Не только голь на выдумки хитра* (Not only poor people are creative).
About toothpaste with the smell of alcohol.
Syntactic extension.
http://www.tv100.ru/news/Ne-tolko-gol-na-vydumki-hitra-27786/

AP-2: *Власть на выдумки хитра* (Government is creative).
Suggestions about new taxes in order to improve economic situation in different countries.
New lexical content.
http://krsk.sibnovosti.ru/business/95550-vlast-na-vydumki-hitra

AP-3: *Боль на выдумки хитра* (Pain is creative).
Methods of fighting pain suggested by various people in a popular show on Russian TV.
Hidden rhyme; metonymy.
http://malahov-plus.com/main/synopsises/1042-bol-na-vydumki-khitra.html

AP-4: *Алко-голь на выдумки хитра* (Alco-hol is creative).
A gang of thieves stole alcohol from little stores in Estonia.
Hidden rhyme; neologism.
http://www.chas-daily.com/win/2010/01/27/lk034.html?r=2&

AP-5: *Молодость на выдумки хитра* (Youth is creative).
Haute couture exhibition of young couturieres in Rostov.
New lexical content.
http://www.rostov-gorod.ru/?ID=7269

AP-6: *Любовь на выдумки хитра* (Love is creative).
A short story about two young people who fall in love with each other.
Metonymy.

http://www.sobinform.ru/info.php?id=174

Comments: All new coinages confirm the message of the original proverb: someone tends to be creative, be it young people, those in power, or thieves. They use both hidden rhymes (# 3 and 4) and new lexical content (#2, 5, 6), as well as syntactic extension (#1). Linguistically, the most interesting example is #4, where the Russian word *алкоголь* (alcohol) is jokingly interpreted as a combination of *алко-* and *-голь* (that is, alco- and -hol); the second part coinciding with the word *голь* (poor people). Thus, creating this non-existent new word, the title of the article attracts attention, as this nonce word condenses both meanings: alcohol and creative (thieves). Finally, we have two examples of metonymy: in # 6, "love" means "people who are in love," while in #3, "pain" means "people who are in pain."

Незваный гость хуже татарина (An uninvited guest is worse than a Tatar).
The proverb used to describe a person who came to somebody's house without an invitation or at a bad time. The origin of the proverb goes back to the period of Tatar Yoke (1237 - 1480), when Russia was occupied by Asian invaders.

AP-1: *Незваный гость хуже Саакашвили* (An uninvited guest is worse than Saakashvili).
An unexpected visit of Michael Saakashvili (president of Georgia) to Ukraine.
New lexical content.
http://www.segodnia.ru/index.php?pgid=2&partid=11&newsid=12097

AP-2: *Чудные клоуны или... незваный проповедник хуже татарина* (Miraculous clowns or… uninvited preacher is worse than a Tatar).
Street healers violate the Constitution of Ukraine.
Syntactic extension.
http://ajr.org.ua/?p=56

AP-3: *Турецкий гость хуже незваного* (A Turkish guest is

worse than uninvited).
Council of Muftis of Russia was reprimanded for inviting an extremist organization to the international conference "Russia-Islamic World."
New lexical content.
http://www.kommersant.ru/doc.aspx?DocsID=1310063

AP-4: *Пьяный милиционер хуже незваного гостя* (A drunken policeman is worse than an uninvited guest).
A drunken policemen stole things from a person's summer house.
New lexical content.
http://ufa.kp.ru/daily/24413/586859/

AP-5: *Незваный артист хуже «засрака»* (Uninvited artist is worse than "honored artist")
Devaluation of honorary awards given to singers and actors in Russia today, as compared with soviet times.
http://www.mk-piter.ru/2006/12/06/038/

AP-6: *Незваный инвестор хуже террориста?* (An uninvited investor is worse than a terrorist?)
The discussion in the Latvian parliament about allowing foreign investors from the third world countries to do business in Latvia.
http://www.chas-daily.com/win/2010/03/12/g_035.html?r=32&

AP-7: *Незваный Кучма хуже Лукашенко* (Uninvited Kuchma is worse than Lukashenko).
The visit of Ukrainian president Leonid Kuchma to the NATO summit, even though he was advised not to go because of the suspicion that he was selling weapons to Iraq.
New lexical content.
http://dlib.eastview.com/browse/doc/4524293

AP-8: *Незваный эмпиризм – хуже схоластики!* (Uninvited empiricism is worse than scholasticism).
This research paper criticizes Russian economic science for a gap between its theoretical research and the real problems of today's Russian economy.

New lexical content.
http://elibrary.ru/item.asp?id=9167320

AP-9: *Незваному гостю хуже татарина* (It is worse for an uninvited guest than it is for a Tatar).
Conditions in Moscow jail for foreign workers who violated the immigration law of Russia.
Syntactic restructuring.
http://2004.novayagazeta.ru/nomer/2004/27n/n27n-s50.shtml

Comments: The traditional proverb is doing very well today judging by these coinages: in most cases, the only content that is left is "Uninvited______ is worse than_______" (this is only two words in Russian), and it is still easily recognized by modern Russian speakers. Thus, even when the anti-proverb compares something vastly different (see # 8 – which is not about people at all) it is understood as a version of the traditional phrase. Linguistically, the most interesting example is the last one, where the syntax is changed: here, "uninvited guest" is not the subject of the sentence but an indirect object (of an impersonal construction); consequently, his situation is worse than that of a Tatar.

Пока гром не грянет, мужик не перекрестится (Until the thunder roars, a Russian will not cross himself).
Necessary measures are taken only when circumstances force someone to act immediately; often used to criticize lack of foresight on the part of someone.

AP-1: *Пока «Фосфор» не грянет, Шойгу не перекрестится...* (Until "Phosphor" roars, Shoigu [Minister of Emergency Situations] will not cross himself).
A dangerous situation at the Phosphor plant, while the Ministry of Emergency Situations does nothing about it.
New lexical content.
http://www.flb.ru/infoprint/18085.html

AP-2: *Пока кризис не грянет, Путин не перекрестится* (Until crisis roars, Putin will not cross himself).

Measures to help small businesses in Russia are long overdue.
New lexical content.
http://znamkaluga.ru/content/view/553/19/

AP-3: *Пока гром не грянет, кабмин не перекрестится* (Until thunder roars, the cabinet of ministers will not cross themselves). Measures taken by the Kazakhstan government to fight price increase on grain are correct, but the problem should have been discussed earlier.
New lexical content.
http://www.press-uz.info/index.php?title=analitik&nid=2598&my=102007&st=7&date=20071102

AP-4: *Пока гром не грянет, украинский банк не перекрестится* (Until thunder roars, the Ukrainian bank will not cross itself).
A criticism of the work of the bank of Ukraine.
New lexical content.
http://www.lel.com.ua/href&child_tbl_name=news&id=2325

AP-5: *Пока Громов не грянет, "Эхо" не перекрестится* (Until Gromov roars, "Echo" [a Moscow radio station] will not cross itself).
A line from the article – birthday greetings to Alexey Gromov, deputy head of the administration of the president of Russia, signed by the directors of three major Russian TV stations.
Paronymy.
http://www.kommersant.ru/doc.aspx?DocsID=1376237&print=true

AP-6: Россия будет идти своим привычным путем, и пока гром не грянет, Минфин не перекрестится. А и перекрестившись, ничего не сделает, пока не увидит примера «большого брата» (Russia will go its usual way, and until thunder roars, the Ministry of Finances will not cross itself. And having crossed itself, will do nothing, until it sees the example of the "Big Brother").
An article criticizing the monetary policy of the Russian Ministry of Finances.

Anadiplosis.
http://2000.novayagazeta.ru/nomer/2000/03n/n03n-s13.shtml

Comments: With one exception, all anti-proverbs, using new lexical content, repeat the message of the traditional proverb, adjusted to a concrete situation; they all mean that someone (or some entity) does nothing to prevent a problem, and waits till the very last moment, when sometimes it is too late to do anything. Linguistically, the most interesting cases are #5 and 6. The first one is a play on words, using paronymycal relations between the last name *Громов* and the Russian word *гром* (thunder); it is also the only one where the main idea is simply a world play, not criticizing someone or something; the second one uses anadiplosis – which is quite a rare mechanism used in creating anti-proverbs.

Не было ни гроша, да вдруг алтын (There was not a single penny, and all of a sudden there are several; literally: There was not a *grosh* [an old Russian coin equal to 1/2 of a kopeck] and all of a sudden there is an *altyn* [an old Russian coin equal to 3 kopecks].
After a period of bad luck, lack of money there comes success, luck, well-being.

AP-1: *Не было ни гроша, да вдруг Алтай* (There was not a single penny, and all of a sudden there is Altay [a region in Russia]).
An article about business leaders in the Republic of Altay and republic of Tyva in Russia.
Paronymy.
http://dlib.eastview.com/browse/doc/3663212

Comments: This single example uses paronymy, as the name of the region (*Altay*) sounds similar to the name of the old Russian coin *altyn.*

Назвался груздем, полезай в кузов (You say you are a mushroom, so get into the basket).
If you start doing something, you should finish it, without trying

to shift responsibility to others.
English equivalent: In for a penny, in for a pound.

AP-1: *Назвался водкой, полезай в рюмку* (You say you are vodka – so get into the glass).
A review of the alcohol market in Saint-Petersburg.
New lexical content.
http://www.4p.ru/main/research/3811/

AP-2: *Назвался мэром – полезай в СИЗО* (You say you are a mayor – so get into jail).
The arrest of the mayor of a small settlement in Irkutsk oblast of Russia.
New lexical content.
http://news.babr.ru/?IDE=44804

AP-3: *Назвался президентом – полезай в ковш* (You say you are president – so get into the bucket).
President Medvedev's visit to a mine in Siberia where he talked to miners and even got into the bucket of a front loader.
New lexical content.
http://www.chslovo.com/index.php?idst_p=7275

AP-4: *Назвался вузом – полезай в кузов* (You say you are a college – so get into the basket).
Negative public opinion about non-government higher educational institutions in Russia.
Hidden rhyme.
http://www.ug.ru/99.15/t5_3.htm

AP-5: *Назвался десантником – полезай в фонтан?* (You say you are a paratrooper – so get into the fountain?)
Celebration of the Day of Airborne Troops of Russia in Saint-Petersburg; there were no problems that are usually expected on that day, among them traditional bathing in city fountains.
New lexical content.
http://www.nvspb.ru/stories/nazvalsya-desantnikom-polezay-v-fontan-43039

AP-6: *Назвался ЧУПом – полезай в пекло* (You say you are a small business – so get into the fire).
Problems of registration of small businesses in Belorussia.
Hidden rhyme.
http://www.perspektyva.org/news/regions/1412.html

AP-7: *Назвался Груздевым – полезай в скафандр* (You say you are Gruzdev – so get into the space suit).
A member of the Russian parliament from the United Russia party, Mr. Gruzdev, wants to become a space tourist.
Paronymy.
http://magmetall.ru/contribution/962.htm

AP-8: *Назвался ядерной державой – полезай в блокадный кузовок* (You say you are a nuclear country – so get into the embargo basket).
Food crisis in North Korea, because of new nuclear tests, has gotten even worse.
New lexical content.
http://deyerler.org/ru/print:page,1,2870-nazvalsja-jadernojj-derzhavojj-polezajj-v.html

Comments: All anti-proverbs use new lexical content to fill the traditional structure; at the same time, not all of them repeat the traditional moral. Thus, #5 in fact defies the traditional wisdom that paratroopers have to get into the city fountains to celebrate their holiday, while #7, using paronymy between the last name of the member of parliament and the Russian word *груздь* (mushroom), simply coins the catchy phrase in order to tell readers about the wish of the deputy to become a space tourist; the idea of obligation or necessity to finish some business is completely absent here.

Гусь свинье не товарищ (A goose and a swine cannot be friends).
Persons who are different in their character, interests, way of life, occupation or social status cannot have anything in common.

AP-1: *Грипп свинье не товарищ* (Flu and a swine cannot be friends).
The swine flu threat.
Metonymy.
http://www.aif.ru/politic/article/26706

AP-2: *Русь свинье не товарищ* (Russia and a swine cannot be friends).
Russian Ministry of Healthcare denies there is the first case of swine flu in Russia; 22 September 2009.
Hidden rhyme; metonymy.
http://www.mk.ru/social/health/article/2009/09/21/354223-rus-svine-ne-tovarisch.html

AP-3: *Птица свинье не товарищ* (A bird and a swine cannot be friends).
Vaccine against regular flu can prevent avian flu.
Metonymy.
http://www.gudok.ru/newspaper/detail.php?ID=277472&year=2006&month=03

AP-4: *Фондовый рынок свинье не товарищ* (Stock market and a swine cannot be friends).
The swine flu epidemic negatively influences world markets, and prices for raw materials fall.
Metonymy.
http://www.kazakh-zerno.kz/index.php?option=com_content&view=article&id=6628&catid=17%3A2010-02-24-11-07-38&Itemid=1

AP-5: *Страус свинье не товарищ* (An ostrich and a swine cannot be friends).
Poultry breeding on the territory that suffered radioactive contamination is an effective way to produce “clean” meat in Belorussia.
New lexical content.
http://old.belniva.by/index.php?option=com_content&task=view&id=174&Itemid=43

AP-6: *Медведь свинье не товарищ* (A bear and a swine are not friends).
Wild bears in the Kamchatka region of Russia killed three pigs from a farmer's herd.
New lexical content.
http://kamchatka.aif.ru/issues/1514/3?print

AP-7: *Гусь свинье товарищ. Его ждали с воздуха, а он пришел с земли* (A goose and a swine are friends. We expected it from the air, and it came from land).
Swine flu is similar to avian flu because it mutated and can be transmitted from person to person.
Metonymy.
http://www.info-tses.kz/red/article.php?article=55951

Comments: These examples fall into two groups: in the first group, the word "swine" is used in its figurative meaning and is a metonymy for the "swine flu" (#1, 2, 3 , 4, 7). In the other group (#5 and 6), the word "swine" is used in its direct meaning – a domestic animal. At the same time, these groups are united by another feature: they all have little if anything to do with the message of the original proverb, and the association with it is used mostly to make a catchy title. Linguistically, the most interesting cases are #2 and 7: in the first one, we have hidden rhyme: the word *Русь* (Russia) rhymes with the word *гусь* (goose) in the original proverb; the second contradicts the traditional proverb, stating that a goose and a swine are friends, which in this case means that avian flu and swine flu have a similar feature: they can be transmitted from person to person, not only from birds and pigs respectively.

Д

Дают – бери, бьют – беги (If they offer you something, take it; if they start beating you, run).
Often used as advice to use an opportunity to do or get something, as such an opportunity may not be repeated in the future.

AP-1: *Дают бери, не дают – проси* (If they offer you some-

thing, take it; if they do not offer – ask for it).
The current state of the Ukrainian stock market.
New lexical content.
http://fundmarket.ua/blogs/4a5d6dedd6d25/

AP-2: *Дают? Не бери!* (They offer you something? Do not take it!)
Bribes were allegedly taken by government officials in one of the districts of the Russian city of Tver.
Syntactic restructuring.
http://www.tverinfo.ru/obshestvo/daut_ne_beri.html

Comments: While preserving the structure, rhythm, and most of the vocabulary of the original proverb (and thus, easy association with it), #1 changes the meaning substantially, and of course, by the combination of it being recognized and different at the same time, makes this one a good catchy title. The second anti-proverb, by means of restructuring the original phrase (making it a question-answer structure), changes its meaning to exactly the opposite of the moral of the original phrase.

Дело (работа) не волк, в лес не убежит (The work is not a wolf – it will not run away into the forest).
Usually said to suggest that one need not hurry to do some work; it can be postponed; it can also be said to someone who is in no hurry to do some job.

AP-1: *Студент не волк, в лес не убежит* (A student is not a wolf, he will not run away into the forest).
Full-time students who have a job while studying.
New lexical content.
http://www.energy.nstu.ru/archive/49/282

AP-2: *Аппетит не волк, в лес не убежит* (Appetite is not a wolf, it will not run away into the forest).
The importance of controlling your appetite, which is both possible and necessary.
http://www.ressina-privivka.ru/dieta/appetit.htm

AP-3: *Коррупция не волк, в лес не убежит* (Corruption is not a wolf, it will not run away into the forest).
New laws against corruption were passed by Victor Yanukovich, president of Ukraine; but the date they will take effect was postponed till 1 January, 2011.
New lexical content.
http://comments.com.ua/?art=1275580184

Comments: From the point of view of meaning, the first two anti-proverbs have very little to do with the original one, and use the association with it simply to catch readers' attention. The third one, on the contrary, confirms the original message, criticizing the Ukrainian president for postponing the enforcement of anti-corruption laws.

Делу – время, потехе – час (There is time for work, and there is a time [literally: hour] for play).
Note: The Russian word "hour" in this proverb has retained its old meaning – time in general, not just a unit of time equal to 60 minutes.
The proverb is usually used to encourage someone to work, not waste time.

AP-1: *Делу – время, потехе – деньги* (There is time for work, and there is money for play).
An article on documenting the hours of work correctly, so that the hourly pay should be correct.
New lexical content.
http://yurpractika.com/article.php?id=10002478

Comments: Though violating the rhythm of the original proverb (one-syllable word *час* is replaced by two-syllable *деньги*) this version preserves enough of the original structure to establish the association with it – and at the same time conveys a completely different message.

Летний день год кормит (A summer day feeds a year).
In summer, during the harvest, every day is very important in order to make enough food reserves for the whole year.

AP-1: *Летний день учебный год кормит* (A summer day feeds a school year).
Summer camps for school children.
New lexical content.
http://www.tverlife.ru/news/19342.html

AP-2: *День с металлоискателем год кормит* (A day with a metal detector feeds a year).
Searching for hidden treasures.
New lexical content.
http://poryvaev.ru/news_detail.php?id=121&PHPSESSID=c4e8c7ec71ff16eb071ab6062813a3d7

AP-3: *Летний день, что кормит год, порой уходит на ремонт* (A summer day that feeds the year is often spent on repairs).
The poor state of agricultural machinery and loss of precious summer days for its repairs.
New syntactical structure; internal rhyme.
http://www.kostroma.rfn.ru/rnews.html?id=10137&date=18-07-2006

Comments: While the first two proverbs continue the message of the traditional saying, the most interesting case is #3. This is in fact a brand new proverb, built according to all the traditional criteria: rhythm and internal rhyme: *год* – *ремонт* (year – repairs), which are not present in the traditional proverb.

Не в деньгах счастье (Happiness is not in money).
Money itself does not make people happy.

AP-1: *Счастье не в деньгах и не в их количестве* (Happiness is not in money and not in the amount of money).
Results of a survey conducted by US researchers who polled 136,000 respondents in 132 countries.
Syntactic extension.
http://infox.ru/03/soul/2010/07/02/Schastye_nye_v_dyeng.phtml

AP-2: *Не в деньгах счастье, а в их качестве* (Happiness is not

in money, but in its quality).
An economic forum in Astana, the capital of Kazakhstan.
Syntactic extension.
http://www.np.kz/?newsid=6092

AP-3: *Не в деньгах счастье, а в женах* (Happiness is not in money, but in wives).
Financial statements of top government officials of Russia (the prosecutor general and his deputies) show that they get relatively small salaries and have very little property, but that is compensated by the big earnings of their wives.
Syntactic extension. Defeated expectancy.
http://www.kp.ru/daily/24485/642262/

AP-4: *Не в деньгах счастье, а в знаниях. Они помогут заработать...* (Happiness is not in money but in knowledge. It will help you earn money…)
Importance of education in order to get a well-paying job in the future.
Syntactic extension.
http://www.hse.ru/news/bird/4568544.html

AP-5: *Аукцион по-московски: не в деньгах счастье, а в объективности* (Tender Moscow style: happiness is not in money, but in objectivity).
New rules of conducting tenders in Moscow.
Syntactic extension.
http://www.kdo.ru/author/daily/2009/01/28/daily_10896.html

AP-6: *Счастье не в деньгах, а в их количестве у соседей* (Happiness is not in money, but in the amount of money your neighbors have).
A research study by British psychologists shows that people are happy when they have more money than their friends and relatives.
Syntactic extension.
http://www.gzt.ru/topnews/world/-denjgi-prinosyat-schastje-toljko-togda-kogda-/297376.html

AP-7: *Не в деньгах счастье, а в «икспириенсе»* (Happiness is not in money, but in experience).
Lifestyle engineering.
Syntactic extension; neologism.
http://sundaybytes.com/2008/03/03/the-experience-point/

AP-8: *Не в деньгах счастье, счастье в регулярном сексе* (Happiness is not in money, happiness is in regular sex).
Results of the survey of 16,000 people which showed that increasing sex life from once a month to once a week brings as much happiness as an unmotivated salary increase of $50,000.
Syntactic extension.
http://www.rol.ru/news/med/news/06/07/11_001.htm

Comments: There are two groups of anti-proverbs here: the first continues the message of the traditional proverb that money itself cannot bring happiness, and that there are more important things that will make one happy, be it life experience or a regular sex life. At the same time, there is another group that not so much denies the traditional message but modifies it, sometimes in an unexpected way. Thus, #6 claims that people are happy when they make more money than their friends and relatives. The most interesting example of this second group is #3. At first, it looks like it should belong to our first group, as at its face value it claims that wives are more important for men than money. But when one reads the article itself, it becomes clear that we have a textbook example of defeated expectancy: the article is about tax returns of top Russian government officials (the prosecutor general and his deputies), who all declare modest salaries, but this is compensated by the amounts earned by their wives. Incidentally, the same is true for the spouses of ministers and other top bureaucrats: their wives all are successful business ladies.

Деньги дело наживное (Money is something that can be earned).
Said with the intention to encourage someone who has material problems.

AP-1: *Валюта – дело наживное* (Currency is something that can be earned).
Additional emission in Belorussia.
Synonyms.
http://pda.sb.by/blog/83320/

AP-2: *Опыт – дело наживное* (Experience is something that can be earned).
The work of a college graduate.
New lexical content.
http://www.zem-nn.ru/gaz/10_11/01.html

AP-3: *Страх – дело наживное* (Fear is something that can be earned).
New regulations of auto insurance in Russia.
Homonym.
http://legalru.ru/document.php?id=14379

AP-4: *Восток – дело наживное* (Orient is something that can be earned).
A review of the movie "Prince of Persia."
New lexical content.
http://www.e-vid.ru/index-m-192-p-63-article-33037.htm

AP-5: *Спорт – дело наживное* (Sports is something that can be earned).
The cost of the Olympic Games in Sochi in 2014.
New lexical content.
www.kommersant.ru/doc.aspx?DocsID=1402455

Comments: There are two groups of new proverbs here: the first one confirms the traditional message: if you lack something (currency, or experience) it can be earned (#1 and 2). Anti-proverb #3 has a clever play on words: the Russian word *страх* (fear) has the same origin as the Russian word *страхование* (insurance); thus, you pay for insurance to get rid of your fear of an accident, and that is how insurance companies make money. The remaining two proverbs belong to that type of modern variants that has nothing to do with the original message, and use the formal association with it simply to create a catchy title. One can suspect that the authors of such articles either do not know or do not care about the original meaning of the proverb.

Деньги не пахнут (Money has no smell).
This is a famous Latin expression, allegedly said by the Roman emperor Vespasian to his son, Tit. The son accused the father of introducing a tax on public lavatories, so the emperor made him smell the first money collected in this way, and asked him, whether it had any smell. The son had to admit that the money had no smell: "Non olet" (It does not smell). Now, of course, used in a much broader sense: the origin of money is of no importance, money is money.

AP-1: *Если деньги не пахнут, значит их нет* (If money has no smell, it means there is no money).
An embezzlement scandal in the Ministry of Emergency Situations of Russia.
Syntactic extension. Wellerism.
http://www.compromat.ru/page_9251.htm

AP-2: *Траур рекламе не помеха, или деньги не пахнут-2* (Mourning is not an obstacle for commercials, or money has no smell-2).
Some Russian TV stations refused to cut advertisements on the day of official mourning announced in Moscow on March 29th after explosions in Moscow metro stations.
Syntactic extension.
http://nnm.ru/blogs/girlfriendHudo/traur_reklame_ne_pomeha_ili_dengi_ne_pahnut-2/

AP-3: *Деньги не пахнут, деньги светятся* (Money has no smell; money glows).
Luminous paper money invented in Korea.
Syntactic extension.
http://www.novate.ru/blogs/040410/14469/

AP-4: *Деньги не пахнут снегом* (Money does not smell like snow).

Investors should take into account not the time of the year while buying stocks and shares but important economic criteria.
Syntactic extension.
http://www.luxurynet.ru/russian-market/3863.html

AP-5: *Деньги не пахнут. Даже если это вредит соседям* (Money has no smell. Even if it brings harm to neighbors).
Special "alcohol" tour buses between Estonia and Finland (offered by Estonia in order to fight economic crisis), where Finnish tourists can start drinking right on the bus; the bus will have 110 liters of beer and 90 liters of vodka on board.
Syntactic extension. Wellerism.
http://www.chaspik.info/bodynews/5998.htm

AP-6: *Дума: деньги не пахнут – ни табаком, ни водкой* (Russian Parliament: money has no smell of either tobacco or vodka).
The Russian parliament killed two bills that would limit alcohol and tobacco companies in financing political parties.
Syntactic extension.
http://www.km.ru/magazin/view.asp?id=%7BAA1B4428-185D-488B-B12A-5994C3C37F4B%7D

AP-7: *Деньги пахнут газом.* Создан коллективный портрет интеллигенции, борющейся за сохранение Петербурга (Money smells of gas. A collective portrait of intelligentsia fighting for preservation of Saint-Petersburg has been created).
About the fight of prominent public figures against the building of Gasprom skyscraper in Saint-Petersburg.
Syntactic extension.
http://www.spb.yabloko.ru/pbl/4739.php

Comments: All of the anti-proverbs, using the traditional phrase as their starting point, develop the idea further, but in different ways. Some of them in fact confirm the original message (and criticize it) in a concrete situation (#2, 5, 6, 7); some others use it to send a different message: money is always connected with corruption (#1), new type of paper money (#3), and good times for investments (#4). Consequently, all the new proverbs use syntactic extension, and one of them (#5) comes very close to a wellerism, as the added phrase completely changes the message of the traditional proverb.

Деньги счет любят (Money likes to be counted).
Said to encourage and justify thriftiness.

AP-1: *Чужие деньги счет любят* (Other people's money likes to be counted).
Depositing money in banks.
Defeated expectancy.
http://www.dtkt.com.ua/show/1cid1659.html

AP-2: *Деньги счет любят: программы учета финансов* (Money likes to be counted: accounting software).
New software for accounting.
Syntactic extension.
http://www.pcmag.ru/reviews/detail.php?ID=35724

AP-3: *Деньги любят счет, а эмиграция – расчет* (Money likes to be counted, and emigration – to be planned).
Teaching Russian readers how to correctly plan emigration to Czech republic.
Syntactic extension, rhythm, internal rhyme.
http://futurumtour.ru/index.php?c=92

AP-4: *У бердских следователей деньги не любят счет* (Investigators from the city of Berdsk do not like to count money).
First deputy-mayor of Berdsk was charged with tax evasion; the charge was dropped after the court found inadmissible evidence gained during house search.
Syntactic extension.
http://fedpress.ru/federal/polit/vlast/id_191799.html

AP-5: *Деньги любят счет, особенно бюджетные* (Money, especially money in the budget, likes to be counted).
The federal agency dealing with financial control and supervision.
Syntactic extension.
http://www.ampravda.ru/2009/10/22/023606.html

AP-6: *Деньги точный счет любят* (Money likes to be scrupulously counted).
Changes in accounting and financial reports for businesses.
New lexical content.
http://www.ippnou.ru/article.php?idarticle=001809

AP-7: *Деньги любят счет, или Зачем нужен финансовый отчет* (Money likes to be counted, or why we need financial reports).
How to achieve financial independence.
Syntactic extension, internal rhyme.
http://www.personal-trening.com/node/273

AP-8: *Деньги счёт любят. А государственные — требуют* (Money likes to be counted. And public money demands to be counted).
Misuse of budget allocations.
Syntactic extension.
http://novayagazeta-nn.ru/2008/33/dengi-schyot-ljubyat-a-gosudarstvennye-trebujut.html

AP-9: *Счет любит деньги* (Counting/score likes money).
Popularity of soccer games in Europe leads to better financial situation of the soccer clubs.
Syntactic restructuring; homonym.
http://www.novayagazeta.ru/data/2000/21/24.html

AP-10: *Деньги любят и счет, и проверку* (Money likes both to be counted and checked).
New equipment for banks.
Syntactic extension.
http://www.taxesplus.spb.ru/bank/bank1n22.html

AP-11: *Деньги счет любят, особенно партийные* (Money, especially party money, likes to be counted).
Changes in the law about political parties that are meant to make financing political campaigns more transparent.
Syntactic extension.
http://www.stolitsa.ee/news?5510

AP-12: *Деньги любят счет и не любят счетоводов* (Money likes to be counted and does not like those who count).
Mistakes in the government financial support for Russian auto industry.
Syntactic extension.
http://analyseman.blogspot.com/2010/05/blog-post_17.html

AP-13: *Зарплата счет любит* (Salary likes to be counted).
Pluses and minuses of the system when salary is deposited to debit cards as opposed to cash.
Synonyms.
http://moneynew.ru/viewpage.php?page_id=82

AP-14: *Деньги любят счет, а кредиторы – гарантии* (Money likes to be counted, and creditors like guarantees).
Insurance industry.
Syntactic extension.
http://www.kubnews.ru/newspaper/2/601/

AP-15: *Любят ли деньги счет или зачем нужно управление финансами* (Does money like to be counted, or why we need financial management).
Title of the article on the topic.
Syntactic extension.
http://konsultant.biz/?ContentID=752505

AP-16: *Деньги счет не любят* (Money does not like to be counted).
Results of the survey according to which 70% of respondents do not keep track of their family budget.
New lexical content.
http://www.tv100.ru/news/view/22318/

AP-17: *Деньги любят не только счет* (Money likes not only to be counted).
Investing in stock exchange.
New lexical content.
http://vyatka24.ru/news/23123.html

AP-18: *Деньги любят счет, а тепло – учет* (Money likes to be counted, and heating – to be measured).
The cost of heating and using meters to reduce the cost.
Syntactic extension.
http://novodar.ru/index.php?option=com_content&view=article&id=772:dlsatu-05-2010&catid=265:zkhps-cat&Itemid=179

AP-19: *Деньги любят комфорт* (Money likes comfort).
Importance of good customer service in the banking business.
New lexical content.
http://www.pmoney.ru/txt.asp?sec=199&id=353938

AP-20: *Деньги любят счет. Банковский* (Money likes to be counted/account. Bank account).
Encouraging people to keep their money in banks.
Polysemy. Defeated expectancy.
http://www.asb.by/ru/press/smi_about_bank/16615

AP-21: *Деньги любят честный счет* (Money likes to be counted honestly).
Additional fees imposed by banks on their customers.
New lexical content.
http://sb.by/post/97444/

Comments: Once more time, we see two different groups of new coinages. The first one (the largest) confirms the traditional message, just adjusting it to a concrete situation, by means of either a new lexical content or syntactic extension. The other group (smaller) uses the traditional proverb as a starting point for sending their own message; thus, #9 using the play on words (the Russian word *счет* (score) and *счет* (count) look and sound the same), establishes a connection between scoring more goals and getting more profit for soccer clubs; in a similar fashion, #20, using the play on different meanings of the word *счет* (count and account), encourages people to keep their money in banks. This anti-proverb also uses the defeated expectancy device, as the usual expectation after reading the first part will be to interpret the word *счет* in its usual meaning here – to count, while adding a one-word sentence (Bank [account]) destroys this expectation and shows that a different meaning is targeted. The same device – only more emphatic – is used in #1. At first reading, it looks like this phrase contradicts the universal maxim that it is not good manners to count other people's money. This, in itself, makes the reader stop and read further. However, the article encourages people to keep money in banks, arguing that banks look after "other people's money" very diligently, hence – a completely new meaning of the title: it is necessary to guard other people's money.

Маленькие детки – маленькие бедки *(*Little kids – little problems).
Said to parents of grown-up kids when they get into trouble or have problems.

AP-1: *Маленькие детки — большие бедки* (Little kids – big problems).
Lack of kindergarten and daycare centers, and how difficult it is for parents to get their kids into one.
Antonym.
http://kursk.aif.ru/issues/751/01_01

AP-2: *Маленькие детки – немаленькие бедки* (Little kids – not little problems).
The cost of raising children in today's Russia.
Antonym.
http://www.ural56.ru/news/46/2970/

AP-3: *Маленькие детки – нечаянные бедки* (Little kids – unexpected problems).
Teaching young parents first aid essentials.
New lexical content.
http://articles.gazeta.kz/art.asp?aid=113757

Comments: The first two anti-proverbs defy traditional wisdom and claim that there are big problems even with little kids, be it the cost of raising a child or lack of kindergartens and day-care centers; they both use antonymous substitution in the original wording to achieve that goal. The last proverb is completely different: without getting into the debate about how big or little the problems are, it teaches young parents first aid essentials.

Чем бы дитя ни тешилось, лишь бы не плакало (Whatever the child plays with, the most important thing is that it does not cry).
Anything is worth allowing the child to do as long as it does not cry. Figuratively (and often ironically) said about adults who do something unusual or strange for a grown-up person, but like it anyway.

AP-1: *Чем бы дитя ни тешилось, лишь бы... не было войны!* (Whatever the child plays with, the most important thing is... that there be no war!)
An interview with the ambassador of Armenia in Russia.
New lexical content.
http://www.regnum.ru/news/1136294.html

AP-2: *Чем бы мэр ни тешился, лишь бы не работал* (Whatever the mayor plays with, the most important thing is that he should not work).
An article criticizing the work of the mayor of Kishinev, the capital of Moldova.
New lexical content.
http://www.cnc.md/ru/snews/3716/

AP-3: *Чем бы дитя ни тешилось, лишь бы не свергало власть капитала* (Whatever the child plays with, the most important thing is that it should not overthrow the power of capital).
Student riots in France in 1968.
New lexical content.
http://scepsis.ru/tags/id_175.html

AP-4: *Чем бы звезда не тешилась, лишь бы не растолстела* (Whatever the star plays with, the most important thing is that she should not gain weight).
Types of sports that American movie stars use to stay fit.
New lexical content.

http://minus5.ru/articles/583

AP-5: *«Регионалы» будут действовать по принципу «чем бы дитя ни тешилось – лишь бы власть мирно отдало»* ("Party of the regions" will act according to the principle: "Whatever the child plays with, the most important thing is that it should give power back peacefully").
Results of presidential elections in Ukraine in 2010: Yushchenko lost to Yanukovich.
Syntactic extension, new lexical content.
http://www.rk.org.ua/rk/494/2.html

Comments: All the new variants preserve the original message to some extent – at least, the key part of it: no matter what someone does, as long as he or she does (does not) do something, it is ok. The variety of situations in which the proverb is used confirms it being alive and well in modern Russian culture.

От добра добра не ищут (One does not leave something good for another good thing).
Changes, even if they promise profit or convenience, may bring negative consequences.
English equivalent: Better is the enemy of good.

AP-1: *От зерна добра не ищут* (One does not expect something good from grain).
Lower than expected grain production in Russia in 2010.
Hidden rhyme.
http://www.kommersant.ru/doc.aspx?DocsID=1379055

AP-2: *От огра добра не ищут* (One does not expect something good from the ogre).
A review of the latest issue of the Shrek movie release in Russia.
Hidden rhyme; internal rhyme.
http://www.vremya.ru/2010/84/10/253925.html

AP-3: *От рубля добра не ищут* (One does not expect something good from the ruble).
Russian markets of securities.

New lexical content.
http://www.itinvest.ru/analytics/review/719/71164/

AP-4: *От доллара добра не ищут* (One does not expect something good from the dollar).
Weakening of US dollar as compared to the euro and other currencies.
New lexical content.
http://www.ng.by/ru/issues?art_id=20875

AP-5: *От ларька добра не ищут* (One does not expect something good from a kiosk).
The market of pirate videocassettes (sold in street kiosks, hence the title).
Metonymy.
http://www.zakon.kz/104069-ot-larka-dobra-ne-ishhut.-kompanija.html

Comments: With the exception of #4, all the new coinages keep the rhythm of the traditional proverb, replacing the first word *добро* (good) by something else; besides, in most cases the substitution rhymes with it, which creates an even stronger association with the original wording. Interestingly, in spite of all this material semblance, none of the new coinages repeats, even partially, the message of the traditional proverb, which is used simply to make an unusual title: they all talk about problems with something (harvest of crops, foreign currency, pirate video), with the exception of #2, which is mostly a joke more than anything else; this last one also uses internal rhyme: *огра – добра* (Ogre – good), which makes it look even more like a traditional Russian proverb.

Доверяй, но проверяй! (Trust but verify!)
Said as advice to check everything one more time so that it will be possible to act with confidence.
English equivalent: Better safe than sorry.

AP-1: *Доверяй, но ПРОверяй!* (Trust, but ABM-fy!)
New anti-missile treaty between US and Russia.

Homophone; neologism.
http://www.aif.ru/politic/article/30428

AP-2: *Женщине доверяй, но проверяй, особенно если она за рулем* (Trust but verify a woman, especially if she is driving).
Results of the survey among men: one-third of men are nervous when their wife or girlfriend is driving.
Syntactic extension; new lexical content.
http://news.infocar.com.ua/jenshchine_doveryay_no_proveryay_osobenno_esli_ona_za_rulem_44161.html

Comments: The first anti-proverb is a very interesting example: on the surface, it simply repeats the original proverb, but the first three letters of the Russian word *проверяй* (verify) are capitalized. At the same time, this coincides with the Russian abbreviation for the ABM treaty; thus, this new word condenses two meanings: verify everything in this treaty. Linguistically, this is a very well-done play on words. The second anti-proverb is an example of narrowing the traditional message to a concrete situation.

Долг платежом красен (The debt is made red by the payment).
The literal meaning is that one should promptly return the money one owes to somebody. Figuratively, it can also mean that anything that you owe someone (not necessarily money) should be promptly returned.
Note: The Russian word *красен* (red) in this context is used in its old meaning – beautiful, good, pleasant.

AP-1: *Налоговый долг платежом красен* (Tax debt is made red by the payment).
A new law would allow tax agencies to deduct money from the bank accounts of the debtors without their consent.
New lexical content.
http://34banka.ru/news/213089.html

AP-2: *Долг Пушкина литературным платежом красен* (the debt of Pushkin is made red by literary payment).

The prototype of one of the characters in Pushkin's poem *Queen of Spades*.
New lexical content.
http://exlibris.ng.ru/kafedra/2009-08-13/4_pushkin.html

AP-3: *Гражданский долг платежом красен* (Civil debt/duty is made red by the payment).
The proposal to draft people avoiding child support payment into the army on a contract basis, and to use their salaries to pay what they owe in child support.
New lexical content.
http://www.vz.ru/society/2009/3/12/264478.html

AP-4: *Священный долг платежом красен* (Sacred debt/duty is made red by the payment).
The problems of the military draft in Russia [to defend their country is a "sacred duty" of Russian citizens].
New lexical content.
http://www.hse.ru/news/1091312.html

AP-5: *Когда долг платежом не красен* (When debt is not made red by the payment).
Businesses' debts to the federal budget.
New lexical content.
http://www.ligazakon.ua/news_old/ga012694.html

AP-6: *Уругвай-Германия: долг платежом красен* (Uruguay – Germany: debt is made red by the payment).
The match for the third place in the World Soccer Cup 2010.
New lexical content.
http://www.sports.ru/tribuna/blogs/muyzhnek/97057.html

AP-7: *GM платежом красен* (GM is made red by the payment).
GM corporation returned money loaned by the US government.
New lexical content.
http://www.gazeta.ru/auto/2010/04/21_a_3355404.shtml

Comments: This group, though very diverse in context and narrow meaning of the new coinages (created mostly by adding some new lexical content), is united by one feature: all seven anti-proverbs confirm the traditional message: it is good to pay back what you owe – be it money, a return soccer game, or duty to serve your country. Consequently, when someone does not do what is good, such actions are criticized (#5).

Мой дом – моя крепость (My home is my castle).
One is master in one's own house, and is free to establish the rules.
English equivalent: My home is my castle.

AP-1: *Мой дом – моя крепость, мой друг и мой доктор* (My home is my castle, my friend, and my doctor).
Title of a book.
Syntactic extension.
http://www.koob.ru/fedorovich/my_home_castle

AP-2: *Мой умный дом – моя крепость* (My clever home is my castle).
Software used to automate managing home appliances.
New lexical content.
http://www.xakep.ru/post/50167/

AP-3: *Мой дом – моя крепость, а кухня сердце крепости* (My home is my castle, and my kitchen is the heart of the castle).
Kitchen design.
Syntactic extension.
http://domosedka.com/publ/moj_dom_moja_krjepost_a_kukhnja_sjerdcje_krjeposti/19-1-0-487

AP-4: *Мой дом — моя крепость, мое лицо — мой пропуск* (My home is my castle, my face – my ID).
Biometric control.
Syntactic extension.
http://www.compress.ru/article.aspx?id=11165&iid=444

AP-5: *Мой дом – не моя крепость* (My home is not my castle).

Illegal reconstructions of apartments in apartment buildings that are dangerous for the building.
New lexical content.
http://union.makeevka.com/2009/09/07/moj-dom--ne-moja-krepost/

Comments: All five anti-proverbs, using the traditional proverb as their starting point, have their own message to the reader, be it kitchen design or the danger of unlawful reconstructions, or a new software for home appliances. These messages (with the exception of #1) have very little to do with the original meaning. At the same time, the traditional proverb is clearly very popular and easily recognized, otherwise these variants would not be possible.

В доме повешенного не говорят о веревке (In the house of a person who was hanged one does not talk about a rope).
One should not talk in the presence of somebody about a topic that may be unpleasant to that person.

The proverb is a calque from French: Il ne faut parler de corde dans la maison d'un pendu. Its *English equivalent*: Name not a rope in the house of him that hanged himself. The proverb exists in other languages, as well.

AP-1: *В доме повешенного говорят о веревке* (In the house of the person that was hanged one does talk about a rope).
Antonym.
The execution of Iraq vice-president Yaha Yasin Ramadan.
http://www.kommersant.ru/doc.aspx?DocsID=751647&print=true

Comments: This single example of an anti-proverb based on the traditional international proverb is interesting in its meaning: it ignores the usual (figurative) meaning of the proverb and goes back to the original literal meaning, based on the superstitious belief that the tools of murder should not be mentioned in the place where the murder took place, lest the ghost of the deceased return from the other world. Thus, it is about hanging – the method of execution that was used in this case.

Все дороги ведут в Рим (All roads lead to Rome).
What is predestined to be, will inevitably happen. Said when something that is happening seems to be logical and unavoidable.
This is an international proverb; its *English* version is: All roads lead to Rome.

AP-1: *Не все дороги ведут в Рим* (Not all roads lead to Rome).
The title of a song.
New lexical content.
http://mp3lemon.org/album/41848/

AP-2: *Не все дороги ведут в Рим* (Not all roads lead to Rome).
A popular article about other inhabited worlds in the Universe.
New lexical content.
http://class-fizika.narod.ru/g4.htm

AP-3: *2438 км или все дороги ведут в Рим* (2,438 kilometers, or all roads lead to Rome).
The title of a movie.
Syntactic extension.
http://www.vedomosti.md/news/2438_Km_Ili_Vse_Dorogi_Vedut_V_Rim#

AP-4: *Все дороги ведут в Рим. Поиски любви ведут туда же...* (All roads lead to Rome. Search for love leads there, too).
A review of the movie “Once in Rome.”
Syntactic extension.
http://review-kino.net/reviews/893-vse-dorogi-vedut-v-rim-poiski-lyubvi-vedut-tuda-zhe.html

AP-5: *Все дороги опять ведут в Рим* (All roads again lead to Rome).
Real estate markets in Europe.
New lexical content.
http://www.burocrats.ru/realty/050805105526.html

AP-6: *Все любовные дороги ведут в Рим* (All love roads lead to Rome).
Another review of the movie "Once in Rome."
New lexical content.
http://kino.itop.net/Node/do/625309

AP-7: *Тур Италия: Этим летом все дороги ведут в Рим!* (Tour of Italy: This summer, all roads lead to Rome).
An ad for a travel agency's tours to Rome.
Syntactic extension.
http://aditec.ru/tur/tur-details_38739.htm

AP-8: *Все дороги ведут… в Тибет!* (All roads lead to…Tibet!)
Tibet as spiritual center of the world.
New lexical content.
http://www.chernetskaya.ru/blog/643

AP-9: *Дороги ведут в Рим и в Москву* (Roads lead to Rome and Moscow).
The visit of the delegation of the Russian railroad company to Italy.
Syntactic extension.
http://www.vmdaily.ru/article/30973.html

AP-10: *Все дороги ведут к тебе, Как стремились когда-то в Рим* (All roads lead to you, as they lead to Rome once).
A line from a poem by Evgeniya Renar.
Syntactic extension.
http://poem.com.ua/renar-zhenya/vse-dorogi-vedut-k-tebe.html

AP-11: *Все дороги ведут в Рим, а российские военные железные дороги – в Бабушкино* (All roads lead to Rome, and Russian military railroads – to Babushkino).
Research institute of Russian military railway troops.
Syntactic extension.
http://dlib.eastview.com/browse/doc/2570160

AP-12: *Леди вне конкуренции, или Все дороги ведут к успеху* (Ladies are winners, or all roads lead to success).

The title of a book for businesswomen.
Syntactic extension; new lexical content.
http://book.tr200.net/v.php?id=187697

AP-13: *Все дороги ведут в Рим, а бездорожье – к нам!* (All roads lead to Rome, and lack of roads – to us!)
The poor condition of roads in Ukraine.
Syntactic extension.
http://worldnews.org.ua/news154877.html

AP-14: *Все дороги ведут не в Рим, все дороги ведут в Иерусалим.* Кто владеет святыней человечества – владеет миром (All roads lead not to Rome, but to Jerusalem. He who owns the holy place of humanity owns the world.)
Foreign policy of the US, Russia, Israel and the UK in the Middle East.
Syntactic extension.
http://www.kavkazmonitor.com/blogs/yusuf/2007/04/05/32.shtml

Comments: These numerous examples, none of which uses the figurative meaning of this international proverb, make one wonder whether this meaning is still recognized by modern Russian speakers. There is no doubt that the construction itself is easily recognized, but it seems equally obvious that the traditional meaning is lost. All these examples interpret the traditional proverb in its literal meaning, and, using mostly syntactic extension, modify it according to their context.

После драки кулаками не машут (One does not wave fists after the fight).
Said when it is too late to change something or to try to do something to correct the situation.
English equivalent: It is no use crying over spilt milk. An ounce of prevention is worth a pound of cure.

AP-1: *После драки кулаками не машут. И молотками тоже!* (One does not wave fists after the fight. And hammers, too!)
An art project in the form of a hammer.

Syntactic extension.
http://www.novate.ru/blogs/030709/12412/

AP-2: *Финал ЧМ-2010: голландцы машут кулаками после драки* (The final match in the world soccer cup-2010: the Dutch team wave their fists after the fight).
The Dutch soccer team criticized the referee in their game against the Spaniards.
New lexical content.
http://www.vokrug.tv/article/show/Final_CHM-2010_gollandtsy_ne_umeyut_proigryvat_dostoino_6081/

AP-3: *Тренер «Вердера» обещает после драки кулаками не махать* (The coach of "Verder" promises not to wave fists after the fight).
The soccer match of the German club against "Shakhter" from Donetsk.
New lexical content.
http://ura.dn.ua/21.05.2009/78207.html

AP-4: *После драки кулаками не машут. Но не на Украине* (One does not wave fists after the fight. But not in Ukraine).
Professional boxing association in Ukraine.
Syntactic extension.
http://fightnews.ru/forum/showthread.php?t=30

AP-5: *Возле драки кулаками не машут* (One does not wave fists near the fight).
Russian foreign policy, especially concerning presidential elections in Iran.
New lexical content.

AP-6: *Девушки после драки кулаками не машут* (Girls do not wave fists after the fight).
Female boxing tournament between Russia and Kazakhstan.
New lexical content.
http://diapazon.kz/aktobe/aktobe-city/1608-devushki-posle-draki-kulakami-ne-mashut.html

AP-7: *После капоэйры кулаками не машут* (One does not wave fists after capoeira).
An exotic type of wrestling, incorporating dancing, singing and playing musical instruments.
New lexical content.
http://newspaper.moe-online.ru/view/218282.html

AP-8: *После драки кулаками машут* (One does wave fists after the fight).
The government of Armenia banned changes to the state coat of arms after it had changed it.
New lexical content.
http://armtoday.info/default.asp

AP-9: *После драки кулаками не машут (только крыльями)* (One does not wave fists after the fight (only wings).
Cartoon caption about Yulia Timoshenko, who lost the presidential elections in Ukraine.
Syntactic extension.
http://durdom.in.ua/ru/main/photo/photo_id/12498/user_id/4267/filter/interesting/order/asc.phtml

AP-10: *И до драки кулаками машут* (One does wave fists before the fight, too).
Mutual insults in the mass media of two professional boxers: Vitaly Klichko (Ukraine) and Nikolay Valuev (Russia).
New lexical content.
http://www.sobesednik.ru/scandals/sobes_9_10_boks/

AP-11: *После матча кулаками не машут... а вот во время...* (One does not wave fists after the fight… but as to during the fight…)
Fights between fans of two Israel soccer teams.
Syntactic extension.
http://www.isra.com/news/33733

Comments: Once again, the anti-proverbs fall into two major groups: one is comprised of new coinages that treat the meaning of the traditional proverb literally, and hence, use it in their context, talking about fights between soccer players, their fans, or someone else. The other group uses the original proverb in its typical – figurative – meaning, and talks about situations when someone (or some entity) was late to change the situation or do something, be it lost elections in Ukraine, or the foreign policy of Russia. Finally, in #1, the original proverb has nothing to do with the content of the article, and is used (as it happens quite often) simply as a catchy phrase.

Скажи мне кто твой друг, и я скажу тебе кто ты (Tell me who your friend is, and I will tell you who you are).
One's choice of friends tells a lot about the person.
English equivalent: A man is known by his friends.

AP-1: *Скажи мне, кто твой друг, и я скажу, кто твой враг. И наоборот* (Tell me who your friend is, and I will tell you who your enemy is. And vice versa).
Andrey Illarionov, former economic advisor to the president of Russia, writes about countries which the Russian government considers friendly or unfriendly.
New lexical content.
http://aillarionov.livejournal.com/112953.html

AP-2: *Скажи мне свою группу крови, и я скажу, кто ты* (Tell me your blood type, and I will tell you who you are).
The correlation between temperament and blood type.
New lexical content.
http://smi.marketgid.com/news/686

AP-3: *Скажи мне, кто твой друг, и я скажу тебе твой вес* (Tell me who your friend is, and I will tell you how much you weigh).
An alleged correlation between types of friends and the weight of a person: if your friends are obese, you will start to gain weight, etc.
New lexical content.
http://www.mycharm.ru/articles/text/?id=2566

AP-4: *Скажи, кто твой «четырехколесный» друг – и я ска-*

жу, кто ты... (Tell me what “four-wheeled friend” you drive, and I will tell you who you are…)
The type of car as a means of self-expression for men.
New lexical content.
http://www.autocentre.ua/news/SIA/21870.html

AP-5: *Скажи, какие анекдоты тебе нравятся, и я скажу, кто ты* (Tell me what types of jokes you like, and I will tell you who you are).
Different types of jokes.
New lexical content.
http://1001.ru/books/people/issue2/

AP-6: *Скажи мне, кто твой пес, и я скажу, кто ты* (Tell me who your dog is, and I will tell you who you are).
Correlation between aggressiveness in people and in their pets.
New lexical content.
http://www.newsland.ru/News/Detail/id/536753/

AP-7: *Юлия Высоцкая: Скажи мне, кто твой муж, и я скажу, кто ты* (Yulia Vysotskaya: tell me who your husband is, and I will tell you who you are).
An interview with the wife of Andrey Konchalovsky, a famous Russian producer.
New lexical content.
http://www.vmdaily.ru/article/47584.html

AP-8: *Скажи мне, кто твой кумир, и я скажу, кто ты* (Tell me who your idol is, and I will tell you who you are).
Idols in the lives of common people.
New lexical content.
http://pedsovet.org/forum/index.php?autocom=blog&blogid=74&showentry=6970

AP-9: *Расскажи мне, кто твоя подруга, и я скажу, кто ты* (Tell me who your ladyfriend is, and I will tell you who you are).
Friendship among women.
New lexical content.
http://www.myjane.ru/articles/text/?id=6095

AP-10: *Скажи мне твой любимый фрукт, и я скажу кто ты* (Tell me what your favorite fruit is, and I will tell you who you are).
An alleged correlation between a favorite fruit and personality type.
New lexical content.
http://dnevnik.bigmir.net/article/480625

AP-11: *Скажи мне, что ты слушаешь, и я скажу каков твой IQ* (Tell me what music you listen to, and I will tell you your IQ).
The type of music and IQ.
New lexical content.
http://daolubvi.ws/index.php?newsid=2446

AP-12: *Скажи, каков твой запах, и я скажу, кто ты* (Tell me what your smell is, and I will tell you who you are).
The unique smell of every person.
New lexical content.
http://www.computerra.ru/xterra/biomed/31262/

Comments: The most interesting feature about this group of anti-proverbs is their similarity: all of them reconfirm the message of the original proverb: a person is known by …., differing only in details: books, music, pets, idols, cars, blood type, etc. Indeed, all of these characterize a person, to an extent, and in that sense, the new coinages develop and expand the meaning of the traditional proverb.

Старый друг лучше новых двух (An old friend is better than two new friends).
Said by people who have old friends or who regret that they do not have them.
English equivalent: Old friends and old wine are the best.

AP-1: *Старый друг лучше новых труб* (An old friend is better than new pipes).
The price Ukraine will have to pay for Russian gas.
Internal rhyme; rhyming substitution.

http://www.kommersant.ru/doc.aspx?DocsID=1343148

AP-2: *Когда старый друг не лучше новых двух* (When an old friend is not better than two new ones).
A review of the movie "Forbidden Love."
New lexical content.
http://102vechera.ru/iview/231468.html

AP-3: *Старый супруг лучше новых двух* (An old spouse is better than two new ones).
Relationships between former spouses.
Internal rhyme; rhyming substitution.
http://vesti70.ru/stats/full/?id=15948

AP-4: *Старый друг лучше новых двух, или верность Windows XP SP2* (An old friend is better than two new ones, or loyalty to Windows XP SP2).
Syntactic extension.
http://adminoff.square7.ch/seo

Comments: The most interesting example is #1: even though the direct translation sounds strange, the message is clear: an old friend (that is, old price for gas) is better than new pipelines (with their new prices). It is also interesting linguistically: the Russian word *труб* (pipes) rhymes with the word *двух* (two); thus, the AP has a hidden rhyme on top of preserving the internal rhyme present in the traditional proverb. The same is true for #3, though this time the hidden rhyme is with another key word from the original proverb: *друг – супруг* (friend – spouse).

Друзья познаются в беде (Friends are tested during bad times).
Said when someone was helped in difficult times, or, on the contrary, was left alone.
English equivalent: A friend in need is a friend indeed.

AP-1: *Друзья познаются в беде, а управляющие – во время кризиса!* (Friends are tested during bad times, and managers – during crisis!)

An interview with the CEO of a company managing pension funds.
Syntactic extension.
http://www.nlu.ru/news_all.htm?id=113218

AP-2: *Друзья познаются не в беде, а в успехе* (Friends are tested not during bad times, but during success).
An interview with Natalia Podolskaya, a popular singer.
Syntactic extension.
http://www.kleo.ru/items/planetarium/nataljia_podolskaya_druzjia_po.shtml

AP-3: *Друзья познаются в беде, а модемы – на плохих линиях* (Friends are tested during bad times, and modems – by bad lines).
Modems for phone lines with poor quality.
Syntactic extension.
http://softsearch.ru/articles/2-303-read.shtml

AP-4: *Страны, как друзья, познаются в беде* (Countries, as friends, are tested during bad times).
Flood in Germany.
Syntactic extension.
http://www.novayagazeta.ru/data/2002/62/17.html

Comments: All new coinages develop the message of the traditional proverb, adjusted to other situations by means of syntactic extension: relationships between countries, or the testing of modems, or managers. The only exception is #2, which in fact, refutes the original idea, by stressing that a successful period in one's life is the right time to test your friends.

Дружба дружбой, а табачок врозь (We are friends, but we will not share tobacco). Friendship should not hinder one's personal interests or the performing of one's duties.

AP-1: *Дружба – дружбой, а имущество – врозь!* (We are friends, but we will not share property!)
Local elections in Ukraine.

New lexical content.
http://www.reporter.com.ua/articles/345/

AP-2: *Эстония и Литва: дружба дружбой, а «табачок» – врозь* (Estonia and Latvia: we are friends, but we will not share "tobacco").
Estonia is not going to follow Latvia's example in creating a professsional army.
Contextual synonym.
http://www.kp.kg/online/news/141581/

AP-3: *Дружба дружбой, а собственность, как говорится...* (We are friends, but as the saying goes, property…)
A speech of the Tatarstan president M. Shaimiev at Kazan technical university.
Ellipsis; new lexical content.
http://shaimiev.tatar.ru/pub/view/830

AP-4: *Дружба – дружбой, а мужичок врозь!* (We are friends, but we will not share men!)
Female friendship.
Hidden rhyme.
http://www.wild-mistress.ru/wm/wm.nsf/publicall/2010-07-02-452702.html

AP-5: *Дружба дружбой, а экспортный табачок врозь* (We are friends, but we will not share the export of tobacco).
Export of tobacco to Moldova, and conflicts between former partners in business for the profit.
Polysemy.
http://www.compromat.ru/page_13529.htm

AP-6: *Дружба дружбой, а желтая майка врозь* (We are friends, but we will not share the yellow jersey).
Tour de France cycling competition.
Metonymy.
http://www.newizv.ru/news/2010-07-22/130177/

AP-7: *Украина и Россия: Дружба дружбой, а газ – врозь*

(Ukraine and Russia: we are friends, but we will not share gas).
Gas supply conflict between Russia and Ukraine.
New lexical content.
http://news.finance.ua/ru/~/2/0/all/2010/05/27/198339

AP-8: *Дружба дружбой, а ресурсы – врозь* (We are friends, but we will not share resources).
Russian cabinet meeting and relationships with economic partners of Russia.
New lexical content.
http://www.izvestia.ru/economic/article3122671/

AP-9: *«Дружба» дружбой, а преференции врозь* (We are "Friends," but we will not share preferences).
Russian-Belorussia conflict about the price of oil.
Polysemy.
http://www.expert.ru/printissues/expert/2010/03/preferbcii_vroz/

AP-10: *Дружба дружбой, а интересы врозь?* (We are friends, but we will not share interests?)
Problems with creating the customs union of Russia, Belorussia and Kazakhstan.
New lexical content.
http://www.ng.by/ru/issues?art_id=46767

AP-11: *Дружба дружбой, а бомба – врозь* (We are friends, but we will not share the bomb).
Relationships between Russia and Iran.
New lexical content.
http://www.vestikavkaza.ru/analytics/politika/2398.html

AP-12: *Дружба дружбой, а киловатт врозь* (We are friends, but we will not share kilowatts).
The governor of Kirov oblast asks Vladimir Putin to stop the reform of the electrical energy sector.
New lexical content.
http://www.kommersant.ru/doc.aspx?DocsID=1215987

AP-13: *Дружба дружбой, а пряники – врозь* (We are friends,

but we will not share gingerbread).
Conflicts between political parties in Ukraine.
New lexical content.
http://www.vd.net.ua/rubrics-3/1100/

AP-14: *"Дружба" "Дружбой", а асфальт врозь* (We are "Friends," but we will not share asphalt).
Roads problem in a new district of Alma-Ata *Druzhba* [Friendship].
Metonymy.
http://www.vecher.kz/?S=7-200908010720

AP-15: *Киргизия: дружба дружбой, а сухофрукт врозь* (Kirgizia: We are friends, but we will not share dry fruit).
Kirgizstan and its relationships with Russia.
New lexical content.
http://www.vmdaily.ru/article/16864.html

AP-16: *Дружба дружбой, а никель врозь* (We are friends, but we will not share nickel).
Dividing the nickel market between Russian oligarchs.
New lexical content.
http://www.finiz.ru/economic/article1148006

AP-17: *Дружба дружбой, а храмы врозь* (We are friends, but we will not share churches).
Church property in Ukraine.
New lexical content.
http://www.portal-credo.ru/site/?act=news&id=10783

AP-18: *Дружба дружбой, а ужин врозь* (We are friends, but we will not share supper).
European tour of Barack Obama and why he refused to have supper with Nicolas Sarcozy.
New lexical content.
http://www.zagolovki.ru/article/08Jun2009/obam4enko

AP-19: *Дружба дружбой, а спутники врозь* (We are friends, but we will not share satellites).

Europe intends to create its own global navigation system.
New lexical content.
http://www.izvestia.ru/internet/article16207/

AP-20: *Дружба дружбой, а Крым врозь* (We are friends, but we will not share Crimea).
The status of Crimea.
New lexical content.
http://www.aif.ua/society/article/16192

AP-21: *Дружба – дружбой, а Табаков – врозь!* (We are friends, but we will not share Tabakov [famous Russian actor]!)
Kazakh students about master class of Oleg Tabakov.
Paronymy.
http://www.express-k.kz/show_article.php?art_id=26162

AP-22: *Дружба дружбой, а гражданство врозь...* (We are friends, but we will not share citizenship…)
Estonian government refused to grant citizenship to several prominent persons.
New lexical content.
http://www.meeting.lv/print/news_print?id=BCR9IK387

Comments: The sheer number of new versions confirms the popularity of the traditional proverb. In fact, once again, all anti-proverbs build on the original message, only narrowing it to a specific context, which is pretty obvious in the examples above. Linguistically, the most interesting cases are #4, 14, and 9; in the first one, the new word *мужичок* (man, with a diminutive suffix) not only rhymes with the original word *табачок* (tobacco, with a diminutive suffix), but also preserves the rhythm of the original proverb: both are three-syllable words, and both have the stress on the last syllable. In #14, there is a play on words between the name of the association of home owners (Дружба – Friendship) and the same word in the original proverb; thus, the message is, though we are members of the same HOA, we are not going to pay for the roads. A similar situation is in #9, where there is a play on two meanings of the word *дружба* (friendship): one is the name of the oil and gas pipeline from the territory of Russia through the territory of former soviet republics – Ukraine and Belorussia; the other is, of course, the literal meaning of this word. Thus, the proverb says something like this: though we do have this common pipeline, you (Belorussia) will still have to pay for oil. Finally, #18 stands a little apart from the rest, as it talks not so much about not sharing something (resources, tobacco, etc.), but rather about not participating in something (in this case – supper). In spite of that, the old proverb with a new word serves as a perfect title for the article about the European tour of President Obama.

Заставь дурака богу молиться – он и лоб расшибет (If you force a fool to pray to God, he will hurt his forehead [while bowing to the floor as required by formal Orthodox prayer]).
Too assiduous a person can bring harm even without realizing it. Said when someone is annoyed by such actions creating additional problems.

AP-1: *Заставь кабмин богу молиться, он себе лоб расшибет* (If you force the cabinet of ministers to pray to God, they will hurt their foreheads).
Efforts of Kazakh government to provide better conditions for small businesses.
New lexical content.
http://www.respublika-kz.info/news/politics/6023/

AP-2: *Заставь депутата богу молиться, он всем лоб расшибет* (If you force members of Parliament to pray to God, they will heart everybody's foreheads).
Bills submitted to Russian parliament banning financial transactions with certain countries and regions.
New lexical content.
http://www.businesspress.ru/newspaper/article_mId_40_aId_395347.html

AP-3: *Заставь дурака богу молиться — он ТЕБЕ лоб расшибет* (If you force a fool to pray to God, he will hurt YOUR forehead).
Presidential elections in Russia 2004.

New lexical content.
http://www.vestnik.com/issues/2004/0107/win/baymukhametov.htm

AP-4: *Заставь чиновника богу молиться, он и лоб расшибёт. Добро бы себе...* (If you force a bureaucrat to pray to God, he will hurt the forehead. Unfortunately, not his forehead…)
Dismantling the last monument to Stalin on the territory of the former USSR – in the city of Gori (Georgia), where he was born. The article criticizes how it was done: in haste, without asking the citizens, during night time.
New lexical content; syntactic extension.
http://forum-msk.org/material/society/3546889.html

Comments: All modern variants confirm traditional wisdom, though, again, adjust it to various contexts. An interesting common feature of the new coinages is that they all criticize government officials (of various branches of government) for making hasty actions that lead to creating more problems (#2, 4) or for not solving existing problems (#1, 3).

Дуракам закон не писан (A fool observes no rules).
Usually said as a negative reaction to someone's strange or improper behavior.
English equivalent: Fools rush in where angels fear to tread.

AP-1: *Рунету закон не писан* (Runet observes no rules).
Regulating the Internet in Russia.
New lexical content.
http://www.rbcdaily.ru/2010/04/19/media/472488

AP-2: *"Мигалкам" закон не писан* ("Flashing lights" observe no rules).
Problems with government official cars in Moscow [these cars have flashing lights on top and they have the right to use oncoming traffic lanes].
New lexical content.
http://www.dw-world.de/dw/article/0,,5602018,00.html

AP-3: *Ветеранам закон не писан* (War veterans observe no rules/have no rules written for them).
War veterans in Moscow, 200 families, who complain that they did not receive municipal apartments promised to them by the Moscow government.
Polysemy; defeated expectancy.
http://www.gazeta.ru/realty/2010/05/25_a_3372916.shtml

AP-4: *Лагерям закон не писан* (Summer camps observe no rules).
Summer camps for children and their problems.
New lexical content.
http://www.mk.ru/incident/article/2010/07/12/515877-lageryam-zakon-ne-pisan.html

AP-5: *Вершителям правосудия закон не писан* (Those who exercise justice observe no rules).
Violations of law in building a new courthouse for the Arbitrazh Court in Saint-Petersburg.
New lexical content.
http://www.zaks.ru/new/archive/view/71110

AP-6: *Аптекам закон не писан* (Drug-stores observe no rules).
Cost of medicine in Russia.
New lexical content.
http://www.izvestia.ru/zdorov/article3140561/

AP-7: *Для такси закон не писан* (Taxis observe no rules).
Problems with taxis in Russia: technical inspection, medical exams are often a formality, etc.
New lexical content.
http://info.sibnet.ru/?id=281954

AP-8: *Господам закон не писан и мордобой разрешен* (Masters observe no rules and are allowed to throw punches).
The driver of the advisor for the president of Russia defended the right of his boss to use the oncoming traffic lane by fist fight.
New lexical content; syntactic extension.
http://www.ekonbez.ru/news/cat/4693

AP-9: *ФСБ закон не писан* (FSB observes no rules).
A drunken FSB officer hit a girl with his car and continues working without any punishment.
New lexical content.
http://corrupcia.net/news/crime/fact-1769.html

AP-10: *Коллекторам закон не писан!* (Collectors observe no rules!)
Absence of a law about collecting money of debtors allows collectors to use any methods they like to force the debtors to pay.
New lexical content.
http://buildbeauty.ru/news/1142-kollektoram-zakon-ne-pisan.html

AP-10: *ХАМАС – остальному миру: «Для нас закон не писан»* (Hamas to the rest of the world: "We observe no rules").
Hamas confirming that they did have their headquarters in a hospital during war in Gaza strip.
Syntactic extension.
http://samsonblinded.org/newsru/8770

AP-11: *Для Газпрома закон не писан* (Gasprom [biggest state-owned company in Russia] observes no rules).
Plans to build Gazprom skyscraper in Saint-Petersburg in violation of law.
New lexical content.
http://www.apn-spb.ru/publications/print5789.htm

AP-12: *Электронным деньгам закон не писан. Но пишется* (Electronic money observes/has no rules. But there will be rules).
Necessity to have a law on electronic transactions in Russia.
Polysemy. Syntactic extension. Defeated expectancy.
http://webdress.ru/articles/web_money.html

AP-13: *Кому, помимо дураков, в России закон не писан* (Who, besides, fools, observe no rules in Russia).
Immunity of deputies of the parliament, judges, prosecutors, and other government officials in Russia.

New lexical content.
http://blog.aif.ru/users/844254/post131185760/

AP-14: *Ментам закон писан* (Cops observe/have laws written for them).
President Medvedev signed five new laws on the Ministry of the Interior of Russia.
Polysemy. New lexical content.
http://russianews.ru/second/33257/

Comments: There are two types of anti-proverbs based on this traditional proverb: the first – most numerous – type uses the message of the original proverb and adjusts it to a new situation or group of people; thus, instead of fools we have members of parliament, judges of the Supreme Arbitrazh Court, an FSB officer, Hamas, collectors, etc. The other – and more interesting – group uses a play on a different meaning of the expression *закон не писан*: it usually means, as was mentioned, "to observe no rules", but literally, it says "rules are not written," and this is how the mechanism of wordplay – and defeated expectancy – works here: in #3, it talks about veterans who were promised municipal housing but did not get it, but at first reading it seems that the phrase says, as usual, veterans observe no rules. In a similar way, in #12, it says about the necessity of having a law regulating electronic transactions, not that electronic transactions observe no rules; finally, #14 is about new laws on police passed by the Russian parliament and signed by president Medvedev – not that the police observe any rules.

Чужая душа – потемки (Another man's soul is dark).
One cannot know the inside of someone else's mind.
English equivalent: Still waters run deep.

AP-1: *Чужая душа — потемки, а страна тем более* (Another man's soul is dark, and the country – the more so).
Economic reform in Ukraine.
Syntactic extension.
http://smi2.ru/Wellda/c364280/?comm_id=717131

AP-2: *Если чужая душа – потемки, то предсказать собственное поведение и вовсе невозможно* (If another man's soul is dark, then it is impossible to foresee one's own behavior).
The first line of an article about hiking in the Caucasus Mountains.
Syntactic extension.
http://poxod.ru/literature/hair/p_hair_gissar_a.html

Comments: Both examples use the traditional proverb as a springboard in order to make their own conclusions, which in both cases have very little to do, if anything, with the original message. Thus, once again, it is simply a catch phrase to draw readers' attention, with no real reference to the traditional proverb.

Дыма без огня не бывает (There is no smoke without fire).
Everything happens for a reason; thus, if people are talking about something, there must be some truth behind those talks and rumors.
English equivalent: There is no smoke without fire.

AP-1: *Дым без огня прописал москвичам респираторные маски* (Smoke without fire prescribed face masks to Moscovites).
Burning peat lands in Moscow region.
Syntactic extension.
http://www.gzt.ru/topnews/health/-dym-bez-ognya-propisal-moskvicham-respiratornye-/316521.html

AP-2: *Электронные сигареты. Есть дым без огня* (Electronic cigarettes. There is smoke without fire).
Electronic cigarettes.
Antonym.
http://bravedefender.ru/post123365136/

AP-3: *Дым не без огня* (Smoke is not without fire).
Same topic as in #1, criticizing the inactivity of government to solve the problem once and for all.
Syntactic restructuring.

http://www.mospravda.ru/issue/2010/07/27/article23173/

AP-4: *Дым без огня – идеал коптильщика* (Smoke without fire – the dream of a meat smoker).
Smoking sausage at home.
Syntactic extension.
http://www.krestianin.ru/articles/16854.php

AP-5: *Дым не без огня* (Smoke is not without fire).
Moscow police wants to use more severe punishments for soccer fans using fireworks during games.
Syntactic restructuring.
http://www.newizv.ru/news/2008-08-11/95697/

AP-6: *Бывает ли дым без огня?* (Is there smoke without fire?)
Law suit of Jennifer Lopez against Marion Night, as Night allegedly wants to post a video of J Lo on the web.
Syntactic restructuring.
http://kino.km.ru/magazin/view.asp?id=9F8BB845998E4F4FA0764998A8B38012

AP-7: *Огонь без дыма, или биокамин* (Fire without smoke, or bio fireplace).
Ecological fireplaces.
Chiasmus.
http://stylehome.org/news/biokamin.html

AP-8: *Кабаева-Путин: дыма без огня не бывает?* (Kabaeva-Putin: there is no smoke without fire?)
An alleged love affair between Vladimir Putin and Alina Kabaeva, a Russian athlete.
Syntactic extension.
http://ua-reporter.com/novosti/28029

AP-9: *Нет клуба без огня* (There is no club without fire).
A fire in a Moscow night club.
New lexical content.
http://www.newizv.ru/news/2010-03-10/122999/

AP-10: *Дымовца без огня не бывает* (There is no Dymovets without fire).
The arrest of Grigory Dymovets, a former investigator, who allegedly got half a million dollars bribe from two suspects.
Paronymy.
http://www.mk.ru/politics/article/2010/05/28/499453-dyimovtsa-bez-ognya-ne-byivaet.html

AP-11: *Нет калыма без огня* (There is no pay-off without fire).
Corruption among firefighters in Russia.
Metonymy.
http://www.runewsweek.ru/country/31629/

AP-12: *Дымовского без огня не бывает* (There is no Dymovsky without fire).
Police officer major Aleksey Dymovsky posted a video on the web addressed to the Russian president and talking about corruption in the police.
Paronymy.
http://news.babr.ru/?IDE=82036

Comments: This is a very diverse group of anti-proverbs. Some of them use traditional proverbs to state the same idea: there must be some facts behind the rumors about Putin's love affair, or Jennifer Lopez, or corruption in the police. At the same time, many of the new coinages use the proverb literally, and do talk about smoke without fire (electronic cigarettes, or smoking sausage); one anti-proverb reversing the proposition and stating that there is fire without smoke (bio fire-places). #1 and 3 both describe extensive fires in Moscow region, because of which Moscow was covered in smoke (though there was no fire in the city itself). Two anti-proverbs use wordplay based on the fact that the names mentioned in #10 and 12 have the same root as the Russian word *дым* (smoke): *Дымовиц* and *Дымовский.* In #11 there is an interesting example of metonymy (it talks about fire, but means firefighters who profit from fires). Finally, #9 simply and literally states the grim fact that there have been too many fires in night-clubs in Russia, which have resulted in many deaths.

E

Тише едешь – дальше будешь (The slower you go, the farther you get).
If people take time thinking their actions over, they will achieve their results quicker than doing something in haste.
English equivalent: Haste makes waste.

AP-1: *Тише музыка — дальше выселение* (The quieter music is – the farther is eviction).
Tenants will be evicted from their apartments for loud music and other violations.
New lexical content; polysemy.
http://www.rbcdaily.ru/2009/07/09/focus/422315

AP-2: *Тише едим – дальше будем* (The slower we eat, the farther we get).
The webpage of a plastic surgery clinic Westmed.
Paronymy.
http://www.westmed.ru/about/press/detail.php?ID=2228

AP- 3: *Тише скажешь — дальше будешь* (The quieter you talk, the farther you get).
Suggestion to increase speed limit in Latvia made by the Minister of regional development.
New lexical content; polysemy.
http://www.gorod.lv/novosti/1175-tishe_skazhesh_dalshe_budesh

AP-4: *Едем тише. Дальше будем?* (We go slowly. Will we get farther?)
Analysis of the slow growth of the transport industry in Russia in 2005-2006
Syntactic restructuring.
http://www.companion.ua/Articles/Content/Forprint/?Id=7606&Callback=0

Comments: All new proverbs use the formal association with the traditional proverb to make their own point. Thus, #1, preserving the structure and the key words *тише – дальше* (slower – farther) has nothing to do with it. Besides, using the key word *тише* in a different meaning (with verbs of motion it means "slowly," but with the noun "music" it means "quietly") it creates a completely different message that has nothing to do with not being in a haste when making some decisions. In #2, there is a paronym *едим* (eat), which looks very much like the original word *едем* (go) but again has nothing to do with the original meaning, and the whole structure is used simply to catch readers' attention. The same is true for #3, where the key word *тише* is used in the meaning "quietly." Anti-proverb #4 is the only one that has at least some connection with the original message, but interprets it literally, and hence, asks the rhetorical question whether the Russian transportation industry is indeed growing.

Ж

Семеро одного не ждут (Seven [persons] don't wait for one). When one person out of several is late, the others will not wait for him. Usually said when the majority starts doing something without waiting for those who are late.

AP-1: *Двое одного не ждут* (Two don't wait for one).
Will Belorussia remain in the customs union with Russia and Kazakhstan.
New lexical content.
http://bk-brest.by/ru/23/politics/665/

AP-2: *Одного не ждут?* (Don't wait for one?)
Nine renters want to buy out the rented building, but one of them refused. They are seeking legal advice in the situation.
Ellipsis.
http://www.gazeta-yurist.ru/consult.php?i=386

AP-3: *Семь чудес одного не ждут* (Seven wonders do not wait for one).
Citizens of Kharkov chose seven wonders of the city; their models were to be displayed in one of the city squares.

New lexical content.
http://www.segodnya.ua/blogs/faktorovskyblog/13046859.html

AP-4: *Семеро Россию не ждут* (Seven don't wait for Russia). G7 countries doubt if Russia should be part of it and thus become G8; December 2005
New lexical content.
http://www.kommersant.ru/doc.aspx?DocsID=632418

AP-5: *История крымских аквапарков. Шестеро четверых не ждут* (The history of aqua parks in Crimea. Six don't wait for four).
About aqua parks in Crimea. The first six were built successfully and gain profit, while four more have been designed but not built due to various political, legal, economic, and national problems.
New lexical content.
http://www.aq-media.info/node/2647

AP-6: *Один наследник семерых не ждет* (One heir doesn't wait for seven).
A legal advice column: each of the heirs has the right to have his or her share of the inheritance without waiting for the others.
Syntactic restructuring.
http://www.law.edu.ru/doc/document.asp?docID=1231897

AP-7: *Восемь овощей одного не ждут* (Eight vegetables don't wait for one).
Campbell Soup company tries to get into the Russian juice market with its vegetable juices – V8 and V-Fusion.
New lexical content.
http://www.kommersant.ru/doc.aspx?DocsID=1014168

AP-9: *Один семерых ждет* (One waits for seven).
Only one stadium in Donetsk, of all Ukrainian cities, is ready for the Euro-2012 soccer cup.
Chiasmus; antonomy.
http://www.sports.ru/football/6184735.html

Comments: There are several groups of anti-proverbs here: one develops the message of the original proverb simply adjusting it to a different situation (#1, 2, 4, 6); another group sends an opposite message (one does not wait for many, # 6 and 7); a third one, represented by #9, reverses and refutes the original proverb, stating (at least, on the surface of it) that one waits for seven (though the message is completely different from the original meaning). Linguistically, the most interesting example is #2, where there is an elliptical construction (no subject and no object in the Russian sentence), which shows that the verbal part of the traditional proverb is enough for it to be recognized and the nouns (numbers) are not that important; this is also proven by the variety of numbers used in anti-proverbs, in spite of which they are all easily associated with the original phrase.

Куй железо, пока горячо (Strike while the iron is hot).
Something planned should be done without delay, while the circumstances are favorable.
English equivalent: Make hay while the sun shines.

AP-1: *Куй железо, пока оно есть* (Strike the iron while there is iron).
Kuznetsk metallurgical combine in Kemerovo oblast of Russia.
New lexical content.
http://www.compromat.ru/page_25563.htm

AP-2: *Куй «железного человека», пока горячо* (Strike the “Iron Man” while it is hot).
Review of the sequel to the movie “Iron Man.”
Cognate words.
http://www.kp.ru/daily/24482.4/638631/

AP-3: *Куй атом пока горячо* (Strike the atom while it is hot).
Cooperation between Russia and Ukraine in nuclear energy and creating a joint company.
New lexical content.
http://www.trust.ua/news/26174.html

AP-4: *Куй, пока горячо!* (Strike while it is hot!)
Review of the movie “The Adventures of Tintin” by Steven

Spielberg.
Ellipsis.
http://www.mirf.ru/News/Kui_poka_goryacho_10799.htm

AP-5: *Куй топа, пока горячо* (Strike top [managers] while it is hot).
Training top-managers for corporations in special educational institutions – so-called corporate universities.
New lexical content.
http://www.expert.ru/printissues/expert/2008/24/kuy_topa_poka_goryacho/

AP-6: *Куй карьеру, пока горячо: Жить хорошо, а в кресле босса лучше* (Strike your career while it is hot. Life is good, but in the boss's chair it is even better).
The title of a book.
http://shop.top-kniga.ru/books/item/in/273034/

AP-7: *Куй "Железничар" пока горячо* (Strike "Zheleznichar" while it is hot).
Israeli national soccer team beat the Bosnian team in the European Champions League tournament.
Paronymy.
http://www.all-news.net/?id=1004034

AP-8: *«Куй ТВ» пока горячо* ("Strike/Kuy TV" while it is hot).
A new TV station in Ukraine , "Kuy TV."
Homonyms.
http://lopata.in.ua/novosti-dnepropetrovsk/glavnie/%C2%ABkui-tv%C2%BB-poka-goryacho-1-sentyabrya-nachnet-veshchanie-novyi-ukrainskii-telekanal

AP-9: *Куй счастье, пока горячо!* (Strike happiness while it is hot!)
Modern blacksmiths and the traditional belief that blacksmiths bring happiness to people.
New lexical content.
http://www.nasha.lv/article.php?id=5600557&

AP-10: *Куй розу, пока горячо* (Strike the rose while it is hot).
A blacksmith from Khabarovsk manually creates iron lace which one can see on many buildings in the city.
New lexical content.
http://www.toz.khv.ru/page.php?page=440536&date_id_num=2010-07-31&year=2001&month=04&day=30

Comments: The majority of the new proverbs repeat the original message: it is a good time to do something. Linguistically, the most interesting cases are #7 and #8: the former uses paronymy between the word *железо* (iron) in the traditional proverb and the name of the Serbian soccer team in the anti-proverb, *Железничар* (Zheleznichar); in the latter, the name of the new TV station, *Куй* (Kuy), coincides (but has nothing to do) with the imperative mood of the verb *ковать* – *куй* (strike) in the traditional proverb. Another unusual example is #4 where there is no object of the transitive verb *куй* (strike).

Жизнь прожить – не поле перейти (Living a life is not like crossing a meadow). Usually said when one faces problems, troubles, and life turns out to be more difficult than it seemed earlier.
English equivalent: Life is not a bed of roses.

AP-1: *Ахмадинеджада убить – не поле перейти* (Killing Ahmedinedzad is not like crossing a meadow).
An attempt to assassinate the president of Iran.
New lexical content.
http://www.rus-obr.ru/days/7487

AP-2: *Постичь брэндреализм – не поле перейти* (Understanding brand realism is not like crossing a meadow).
A new art exposition in Moscow.
New lexical content.
http://www.kp.ru/daily/24490/645623/

AP-2: *Счет открыть – не поле перейти* (Opening an account is not like crossing a meadow).

Advice to business owners: how to correctly open a bank account.
New lexical content.
http://www.buhgalteria.ru/article/n42954

AP-3: *Сдать ЦТ – не поле перейти* (Passing the final exam [in high school] is not like crossing a meadow).
Reporters from the Belorussian newspaper "Vecherniy Brest" tried to take the final test that high school students take when they graduate from school.
New lexical content.
http://vb.by/article.php?topic=5&article=10400

AP-4: *Мастера найти – не поле перейти* (Finding a specialist is not like crossing a meadow).
Firms specializing in recruiting specialists for companies.
New lexical content.
http://www.zakon.kz/62760-mastera-najjti-ne-pole-perejjti..html

AP-5: *Вырастить сад – не поле перейти* (Growing a garden is not like crossing a meadow).
How to grow a garden.
New lexical content.
http://biznessmens174.ru/main/188-vyrastit-sad-ne-pole-perejti.html

AP-6: *Крышу покрыть – не поле перейти* (Building a roof is not like crossing a meadow).
Roofing.
New lexical content.
http://www.sz138.net/kry.html

AP-7: *Смету составить – не поле перейти* (Developing a budget is not like crossing a meadow).
Accounting.
New lexical content.
http://www.akdi.ru/nalog/pr_news/298.htm

AP-8: *Жизнь издать – не поле перейти* (Publishing a life is

not like crossing a meadow).
A new edition of the works of Boris Pasternak in 11 volumes.
New lexical content.
http://exlibris.ng.ru/fakty/2005-09-15/2_pasternak.html

AP-9: *Кафе открыть – не поле перейти* (Opening a café is not like crossing a meadow).
Problems with café businesses in Vitebsk.
New lexical content.
http://vitbichi.vitebsk.biz/post/129/

AP-10: *В поход сходить – не поле перейти* (Going camping is not like crossing a meadow).
A reporter describes her experience of camping in Crimea.
New lexical content.
http://mivina.biz/ua/presscenter/publications_in_mass/165.html?pg=11

AP-11: *Сыр сварить – не поле перейти* (Making cheese is not like crossing a meadow).
Making competitive cheese in Belorussia today.
New lexical content.
http://www.director.by/index.php/section-blog/42--5-119-2009/582-2010-01-25-12-38-47.html

AP-12: *Вырыть яму – не поле перейти!* (Digging a pit is not like crossing a meadow!)
How to correctly dig a foundation pit for a building.
New lexical content.
http://www.domup.ru/article/39

AP-13: *Сдать квартиру – не поле перейти* (Renting out an apartment is not like crossing a meadow).
Problems when renting out an apartment in Moscow.
New lexical content.
http://www.kvadroom.ru/journal/stat_239.html

AP-14: *Родить не поле перейти!* (Giving birth is not like crossing a meadow!).

Problems of women expecting babies.
New lexical content.
http://velnovgorod.aif.ru/issues/1343/17

AP-15: *Лето прожить не поле перейти* (Living through summer is not like crossing a meadow).
How to spend summer vacations, depending on the amount of money you have.
New lexical content.
http://www.tri.md/articles/305.html

AP-16: *Ранец собрать – не поле перейти* (Packing the back-pack is not like crossing a meadow).
How to correctly pack your child's backpack for school.
New lexical content.
http://www.rg.ru/2005/08/31/tetradki.html

(There are many other anti-proverbs utilizing the same pattern)

Comments: This group of anti-proverb is unique in several aspects. First of all, this is one of very few cases where I simply had to stop: there were many more similar examples, but since they all used the same pattern (new lexical content), I saw little use in simply accumulating more of the same. Secondly, they all use the same linguistic mechanism: substitute the first part of the original proverb (Living a life) by something else. Thirdly, they all preserve the original message: some action mentioned in the first part is not as easy as it may seem. All these features show that the traditional proverb is doing very well in modern Russia, and that the second part (not like crossing a meadow) is enough for it to be recognized, which allows journalists and others to modify the first part as extensively as they want, as long as they leave the structure (*doing something*) intact. The most interesting example is #8, where the original noun *жизнь* (life) is preserved, as well; only instead of *прожить* (living) in the traditional proverb we have *издать* (publishing); this creates an interesting play on words, as the title talks about publishing the most comprehensive edition of works by the famous Russian writer (and Nobel prize winner) Boris Pasternak – that is, in a way, it is like living through all his life.

Не до жиру, быть бы живу (It is about survival, not about wealth).
When survival is at stake, one cannot think of anything beyond that.
Note: The Russian word *жир* is used here in its old meaning: profit, wealth.
English equivalent: Beggars can't be choosers.

AP-1: *Не до храма, быть бы живу* (When survival is at stake, one cannot think about the cathedral).
Czech government has no money for the reconstruction of a famous cathedral.
New lexical content.
http://www.radio.cz/ru/statja/119334

AP-2: *Не до ранжиру, быть бы живу* (When survival is at stake, one cannot think about ratings).
Secondary education reform in Russia.
Hidden rhyme, internal rhyme.
http://abiturcenter.ru/kompas/index.php?section=1&cont=long&id=660&year=2005&today=06&month=06

AP-3: *Пассажиру — быть бы живу* (For passengers– survival is at stake).
Danger of travelling by suburban trains in the Moscow region.
Hidden rhyme; internal rhyme.
http://www.mk.ru/social/article/2009/10/20/371010-passazhiru-byit-byi-zhivu.html

Comments: While the first two anti-proverbs repeat the original message, only adjusting it to a narrow context (no money for the reconstruction of a famous cathedral, or for secondary education reform) the third one, using the word *пассажиру* (for passengers) creates a perfect (linguistically) new coinage: not only does it rhyme with the original wording (*не до жиру – пассажиру*), but it also preserves both the rhythm (four syllables in both proverbs) and the internal rhyme of the traditional proverb. Its message, of course, has very little to do with the original proverb, as it talks not about being poor, but about the literal physical danger of riding a suburban train in the Moscow region.

З

Закон что дышло – куда повернул, туда и вышло (Law is like a shaft – you can turn it any way you like).
Law can be interpreted arbitrarily, depending on somebody's interests. Said when a law has been applied incorrectly, from the point of view of the person speaking.

AP-1: *"Э" оборотное что дышло* (Letter "Э" is like a shaft).
Department of the Ministry of Interior on the fight with extremism, and how this department constantly increases the number of political convicts in Russia.
Note: The Russian word "extremism" starts with letter "Э".
New lexical content.
http://www.grani.ru/Politics/Russia/Politzeki/m.161433.html

AP-2: *Язык что дышло* (Language is like a shaft).
The decree of the Ministry of Education of RF that defines the list of dictionaries, grammars, and references that contain the norms of modern Russian language.
New lexical content.
http://www.inosmi.ru/russia/20090904/252264.html

AP-3: *Диаграмма что дышло, как повернул — так и вышло* (A diagram is a like a shaft – you can turn it any way you like).
The importance of presenting figures by means of diagrams when doing presentations.
New lexical content.
http://habrahabr.ru/blogs/presentation/51175/

AP-4: *Патриотизм что дышло...* (Patriotism is like a shaft…)
Using patriotism for political purposes in modern Russia, in particular, in the celebration of Victory Day.

New lexical content.
http://www.rian.ru/authors/20060510/47906725.html

AP-5: *Конституция что дышло...* (Constitution is like a shaft…)
A new law on political parties and the discrimination of some parties, based on this law.
New lexical content.
http://www.russia-talk.com/rf/rons.htm

AP-6: *Регламент что дышло* (Rules of procedure are like a shaft).
Violations of rules during Cup of Russia in soccer.
New lexical content.
http://www.spbvedomosti.ru/article.htm?id=10257863@SV_Articles

AP-7: *Бюджет что дышло…* (Budget is like a shaft…)
Budget problems in Ukraine.
New lexical content.
http://www.zn.ua/2000/2080/67652/

AP-8: *История, что дышло...* (History is like a shaft…)
The history of wars in the Caucasus as described by pre-revolutionary Russian historians.
New lexical content.
http://objectiv.narod.ru/history.html

AP-9: *Устав — что дышло…* (The charter is like a shaft…)
Public hearings about changing the Charter of the city of Lipetsk.
New lexical content.
http://gazeta.aif.ru/_/online/lipeck/741/02_01

AP-10: *Счетчик, что дышло…* (Meter is like a shaft…)
A person in the city of Odessa had a gas meter with a broken seal; the gas company wants the owner of the apartment to pay for testing of the meter and recalculation.
New lexical content.

http://www.odvestnik.com.ua/issue/469/9338/

Comments: With one exception (#3), all new proverbs use only the first part of the traditional phrase (Law is like a shaft), which means it is enough to create an association with the original proverb. Next, they all use the same device – substituting the word *закон* (law) in the original proverb by something else, which is also subject to arbitrary interpretation, be it history, rules of procedure, or the Russian Constitution. Anti-proverb #3 is exceptional not only in its extended (full) form, but also in its meaning, as its message has nothing to do with the message of the traditional proverb, or, at least, interprets it literally.

Слышал звон, да не знает где он (He's heard the ringing but doesn't know where it's coming from).
Said about a person who judges about something that he or she has no real knowledge about.

AP-1: *Гришковец слышал звон, да сделал вид, что не знает, где он* (Grishkovest heard the ringing but pretended that he did not know where it was coming from).
A famous theater producer did not react to a cell phone ringing in the audience during his performance of a new play "+1" in Vologda.
New lexical content.
http://vologda.kp.ru/daily/24503/655845/

Comments: This proverb is an interesting case, but for a different reason as compared with the previous ones. There are a lot of instances when this particular traditional proverb is used in its original form, without any changes, and very few cases of any modifications. The only example I have also confirms that, as the only change is the insertion of the subject (the original phrase has no subject) and another verb (pretended); the rest is repeated exactly as it is in the original proverb. This fact – very few changes and a lot of instances of the use of the traditional proverb – may be explained by the abundance of situations where people judge about something they do not really know; that is why no changes to the traditional proverb are needed.

Слухами земля полнится (The earth gets filled with rumors). News spreads quickly, whether one wants it or not. Usually said as an answer to the question, *How do you know?* when one does not want to give a concrete answer; in this way, it is very similar to the English proverb below.
English equivalent: A little bird told me.

AP-1: *Ухами земля полнится* (The earth gets filled with ears).
Wiretapping of cell phones and how to prevent it.
Hidden rhyme.
http://www.atyraunews.com/showNews1891.html

AP-2: *Земля слухами полнится, а лето – ароматами!* (The earth gets filled with rumor, and summer – with different scents!)
Different types of perfume.
Syntactic extension.
http://www.womenclub.ru/perfumery/648.htm

AP-3: *Земля трупами полнится* (The earth gets filled with corpses).
A review of the thriller movie "Yulenka."
Hidden rhyme.
http://www.kinonews.ru/article_1911/

AP-4: *"Мирянами" земля полнится* (The earth gets filled with "Miryane").
Dating service "Miryane" for persons with disabilities in Yekaterinburg.
New lexical content.
http://ekaterinburg.bezformata.ru/listnews/miryanami-zemlya-polnitsya/89284/

AP-4: *Тезками земля полнится* (The earth gets filled with namesakes).
Four famous soccer players whose first name is Ronaldo.
New lexical content.
http://goal.ucoz.kz/news/2009-06-21-643

AP-5: *Слухами земля полнится...А также ваш счет!* (The earth gets filled with rumors… So is your account!)
Using word-of-mouth to promote a certain brand.
Syntactic extension.
http://leader.at.ua/news/2009-7-23-14-0-

AP-6: *Талантами, как известно, земля полн*ится (The earth, as is known, gets filled with talents).
Sayan Andriyanov, inventor of the tonal jaw harp.
New lexical content.
http://knobster.org/

AP-7: *Добротой земля полнится* (The earth gets filled with kindness).
A letter of thanks to the newspaper about a social worker who helps an elderly woman with her everyday life.
New lexical content.
http://smi.lanta-net.ru/pressa/znamya/20460-dobrotojj-zemlja-polnitsja.html

AP-8: *Слухами афганская земля полнится...* (Afghan earth gets filled with rumor).
Are President Karzai's brothers involved in drug trafficking?
New lexical content.
http://www.centrasia.ru/newsA.php?st=1223444280

AP-9: *Боеприпасом земля полнится* (The earth gets filled with ammunition).
An artillery shell was found near a parking lot in one of the cities in the Russian Far East.
New lexical content.
http://www.myvostok.ru/vostnov/2832

AP-10: *Схемами земля полнится* (The earths gets filled with schemes).
New fraudulent transactions with agricultural land.
New lexical content.
http://www.develop.com.ua/index.php?lang_id=1&content_id=835

AP-11: *Земля миллионами полнится!!!* (The earth gets filled with millions!)
Foreign investors are very interested in Ukrainian agricultural companies.
New lexical content.
http://lugastroy.com/index.php?name=mnews&op=detalis&id=240&pagenum=232®ion=16

AP-12: *"Фиатами" земля полнится* (The earth gets filled with Fiats).
New models of Fiat shown at an international exhibition in Frankfurt.
New lexical content.
http://www.zavedi.ru/worldnews/?id=3536

Comments: Most new proverbs completely ignore the original message, and interpret it, if at all, at its face value. This seems to be enough to create a catchy title. The only exception is #8, which indeed asks the question whether this rumor (about the brothers of the Afghan president) is just a rumor, or if there are real facts behind it. Linguistically, the most interesting coinage is #1, where the new word *ухами* (with ears) rhymes perfectly with the original word *слухами* (rumors). Interestingly, the form of the word is ungrammatical (the correct form of the instrumental case would be *ушами*), but this is done on purpose: violation of grammar rule only makes the new phrase even catchier; besides, the correct form would not rhyme with the original proverb.

Неча на зеркало пенять, коли рожа крива (Don't blame the mirror if your face is crooked).
Do not look for the cause of your problems in other people – look for it in yourself.

AP-1: *Неча на «Кривое зеркало» пенять, коли рожа крива* (Do not blame the "Crooked Mirror" [a popular TV show] if your face is crooked).
If there are enough viewers for a certain TV show it will run.
New lexical content.
http://timeua.info/010410/17523.html

AP-2: *Неча на Украину пенять, коли рейтинг кривой* (Do not blame Ukraine if your rating is crooked).
The chairman of the board of the national bank of Ukraine Pyotr Poroshenko finds it biased that Standard&Poor lowered its rating for Ukraine.
New lexical content.
http://obkom.net.ua/news/2009-02-26/1345.shtml

AP-3: *Великобритания: неча на босса пенять, коли рожа крива?* (Great Britain: Do not blame your boss if your face is crooked?)
A British boss has to pay a compensation to his employee for calling her "ugly and old."
New lexical content.
http://www.magicnet.ee/news+index.storytopic+4+start+839.htm

AP-4: *На Кремль неча пенять, коли рожа крива* (Do not blame Kremlin if your face is crooked).
Attitude to conflict with Georgia among Russian citizens who support actions of the government; they should not blame leaders for the conflict, as they are to blame themselves.
New lexical content.
http://www.globalrus.ru/opinions/783205/

AP-5: *Неча на PR пенять, коли рожа крива* (Do not blame PR if your face is crooked).
Political technologies and their influence on the elections; still, appearance remains one of the leading factors when voters chose their candidates.
New lexical content.
http://www.pronline.ru/read.php?type=news&id=1097

Comments: This is rather a diverse, though small, group of anti-proverbs. Once again, some of them keep the message of the original proverb: look for reasons of some problems in yourself (#2, 4). Others (#1, 3, and 5) literally talk about appearance: the first about an "ugly and old" person and the other – about the importance of good looks for political figures. Linguistically, anti-proverb #1 stands apart; it uses a play on words, based on the similarity of the wording of the original proverb and the name of a popular TV show that many viewers consider to be of low quality, but as long as people watch it, will continue on the air. The wordplay is further emphasized by another coincidence: the title of the show has the word *кривой* (crooked) in it, which is also used in the original proverb.

Из двух зол выбирают меньшее (Out of two evils choose the least).
Out of two or more problems, troubles, dangers – if they cannot be avoided – people should choose that one the consequences of which seem to be less dire.

AP-1: *Из двух зол Украина выбирает мужчину* (Out of two evils, Ukraine chooses the man).
Victor Yanukovich won presidential elections in Ukraine in the second round and got more votes than Yulia Timoshenko.
New lexical content.
http://www.aif.ru/politic/article/32534

AP-2: *Из двух зол и выбирать не стоит* (There is no point choosing out of two evils).
Fights and unions between various political parties in Ukraine in 2008, and what might be the result of these fights and unions.
New lexical content; syntactic extension.
http://4vlada.net/partii-lidery/iz-dvukh-zol-i-vybirat-ne-stoit

AP-3: *В Росии из двух зол выбирают оба* (In Russia, out of two evils they choose both).
Grigory Yavlinsky, Chairman of the Russian United Democratic Party Yabloko, talking about the current (1998) political situation in Russia and how we chose "both evils" in 1996.
New lexical content.
http://www.yabloko.ru/Publ/Articles/yavl-31.html

AP-4: *Из двух «зол» кое-где придется выбирать дважды* (Out of two evils, in some places they will have to choose twice).

Local elections in Permsky krai; in some cases there will be a second round.
New lexical content.
http://www.nk.perm.ru/articles.php?newspaper_id=790&article_id=20725

AP-5: *Улитки выбирают из двух зол большее* (Snails out of two evils choose the largest).
Snails develop means of defense against the bigger enemy, if both enemies are present: crabs and starfish.
Antonym.
http://deyerler.org/ru/27485-ulitki-vybirajut-iz-dvukh-zol-bolshee.html

AP-6: *Финансовые власти выбирают из двух зол: кризис ликвидности или разгон инфляции* (Financial authorities choose out of two evils: crisis of liquidity or speeding up inflation).
Syntactic extension.
http://news.zakon.kz/engine/print.php?page=1&newsid=109405&show_comm=1

Comments: All new proverbs develop and adjust the message of the traditional proverb about choosing out of two evils. Thus, some of them claim that it makes no difference (#2); others claim that for better or worse both are chosen (#3); still others, contrary to the original proverb, state that snails choose the bigger evil (#5); finally, some restate the traditional message (#1), while others are not even sure which evil is less dangerous (#6). The proverb about elections (#4) uses the association with the traditional phrase mostly to catch readers' attention and to say that not only are both candidates bad, but the voters will have to go through the procedure twice, since no one will be chosen in the first round.

Мал золотник, да дорог (Zolotnik is small but expensive/valuable/precious) .
Said to emphasize valuable qualities of something that is small, or seems insignificant, but in reality is important, or of somebo-

dy who is young but has great potential.
Note: Zolotnik is an old Russian unit of weight, equal to 4, 266 grams. This was the smallest weight piece and hence was used mostly to weigh gold and silver.
English equivalent: Good things come in small packages.

AP-1: *Мал первоклассник, да дорог* (First grader is small but expensive).
The cost of buying everything necessary for school.
Hidden rhyme; polysemy.
http://www.newizv.ru/news/2010-05-18/126592/

AP-2: *Мал союзник, да дорог* (An ally is small but valuable).
The role of Tuva [a small region in Russia] in fighting fascism during World War II.
Hidden rhyme.
http://www.stoletie.ru/territoriya_istorii/mal_sojuznik_da_dorog_2010-05-12.htm

AP-3: *Мал аппарат, да дорог* (The device is small, but valuable).
A new device in the Dnepropetrovsk hospital for rehabilitation of patients after strokes.
New lexical content.
http://dv-gazeta.info/zdorovje/mal-apparat-da-dorog.html

AP-4: *Мал скутер, да дорог* (Scooter is small but expensive).
More and more well-to-do persons in Amur oblast buy water scooters.
New lexical content.
http://www.ampravda.ru/2009/05/22/021595.html

AP-5: *Мал дефицит, да дорог* (Deficit is small but expensive).
A trillion rubles deficit in Russian budget (2009) .
New lexical content.
http://www.rbcdaily.ru/2009/08/13/focus/426563

AP-6: *Мал налог, да дорог!* (The tax is small but expensive!)
How to correctly calculate the amount of tax using a simplified

formula in Russia.
New lexical content.
http://www.vkursedela.ru/article684/

AP-7: *Мал сокол, да дорог* (Pigeon hawk is small but valuable).
The first in the world monument to pigeon hawk was opened in Vitebsk oblast.
New lexical content.
http://www.ng.by/ru/issues?art_id=48237

AP-8: *Мал пятачок, да дорог* (The snout of a pig is small but expensive).
The latest trend in pets in Russia – mini pigs.
New lexical content.
http://www.runewsweek.ru/society/7884/

AP-9: *Мал офис, да дорог* (The office is small but expensive).
The price of renting office space in Moscow.
New lexical content.
http://www.lbudget.ru/rubrics/?tid=23&rubric=plan&rid=710

AP-10: *Мал элемент, да дорог* (The mineral is small but valuable).
Importance of a diet rich in minerals.
New lexical content.
http://gazeta.aif.ru/online/health/513/07_01

AP-11: *Мал злотый, да дорог* (Zloty [monetary unit of Poland] is small but dear).
The Poles are in no hurry to join the euro zone.
Paronymy.
http://gazeta.24.ua/news/show/id/53060.htm

AP-12: *Мал капилляр, да дорог* (Capillary vessel is small but valuable).
The importance of capillary vessels for the overall wellness of the human body.
New lexical content.
http://z0j.ru/article/a-298.html

AP-13: *Мал кредит, да дорог* (The loan is small but expensive).
Small business problems with getting loans in Russia.
New lexical content.
http://www.banki.ru/news/daytheme/?id=260857

AP-15: *Мал кварцит, да дорог* (Quartz rock is small but expensive).
Plans to build a new plant producing ferrous alloys in Russia.
New lexical content.
http://www.izvestia.ru/economic/article25529/

AP-16: *Мал зал, да дорог* (The hall is small but dear).
The small hall of the Philharmonic opened to the public after restoration.
New lexical content.
http://www.vedomosti.ru/newspaper/article/2007/02/06/120203

AP-17: *Мал ноутбук, да дорог* (The notebook is small but expensive/valuable).
New Sony Vaio notebooks.
New lexical content.
http://www.rosinvest.com/news/666413/

Comments: In the traditional proverb, the key word is the last one: *дорог*. This adjective can have quite different meanings: expensive, valuable, precious, dear, etc. This vagueness (out of the context) of its meaning explains why modern versions of this proverb are able to utilize various meanings while preserving the same structure and only change the word *zolotnik* (by the way, few Russians will know what it means) by something else, be it Sony notebooks or a capillary vessel. More than that, many of these anti-proverbs utilize several of the meanings simultaneously, thus creating an interesting case of a play on words, created by a single word; in other words, by deliberate vagueness of the meaning of the word *дорог* in their contexts. Let us have a look at the last one – about Sony Vaio. Are they valuable? Yes. Are they expensive? Yes. Which of these meanings is used in the title? Both. At the same time, the majority of the anti-proverbs choose one of the meanings: some choose "expensive" (#1, 4, 5, 6, 8, 9, 15); some others – valuable (2, 3, 7, 10, 12); still others – dear (emotionally) – # 11, 16. Linguistically, the most interesting case is #11, based on the paronymy between the original word *золотник* (zolotnik) and the new word *злотый* (zloty). Also, those anti-proverbs that preserve the original rhythm while substituting the word *zolotni*k by one rhythmically similar (that is, a three-syllable word with the stress on the last syllable), make up better structures because rhythm is another important feature of the traditional proverbs, and preserving it helps to establish better association with the original phrase; these are anti-proverbs # 3, 5, 8, 10, 12, 17.

Не все то золото, что блестит (All is not gold that glitters).
Not everything that has an attractive appearance is really valuable.
This is an international proverb, found in many languages. The *English version* is: All that glitters is not gold.

AP-1: *Не все та Золушка, что блестит* (All is not Cinderella that glitters).
A new production of the play "Cinderella" in Irkutsk youth theater.
Paronymy.
http://www.ogirk.ru/news/2010-05-31/zolushka.html

AP-2: *Не все то стекло, что блестит* (All is not glass that glitters).
Glass wall paper.
New lexical content.
http://www.idh.ru/jornal/archive/article100000245.html

AP-3: *«Домашняя» химия: не все то полезно, от чего блестит* (Home care: all is not useful which makes things glitter).
The market of synthetic detergents.
New lexical content; syntactic restructuring.
http://tvplus.dn.ua/pg/news/14/full/id=3148

AP-4: *Не все то чешуя, что блестит* (All is not scale that glitters).
The program of developing the fishing industry in 2006-2010 in Belorussia.
New lexical content.
http://www.ng.by/ru/issues?art_id=48216

AP-5: *Не всё салон, что блестит* (All is not a [hairdressing] saloon that glitters).
Hairdressers charge too much for their services in Belorussia.
New lexical content.
http://pda.sb.by/post/vsyo_salon_chto_blestit/

AP-6: *Не все бриллиант, что блестит* (All is not diamonds that glitters).
Different types of precious stones.
New lexical content.
http://www.jewellerynews.ru/process/news.html?id=9901

Comments: All new coinages preserve the core of the original idea: do not trust the appearance; thus, they mostly criticize something or somebody for poor quality, be it a theater performance or a hairdressing salon. Some of them, though, divert from this idea a little and not so much criticize something that has an attractive appearance and poor quality, but mostly state that things that look the same are in fact different (not necessarily worse) – #2 and 6. Linguistically, the best coinage is #1, where the Russian word *Золушк*а (Cinderella) is a paronym to the original word *золото* (gold).

И

Игра не стоит свеч (The game is not worth the candle).
Said as advice not to start something which will require a lot of effort, resources, and expenses.
This is a calque from *French*: Le jeu ne vaut pas la chandelle.

AP-1: *Игла не стоит свеч* (The needle is not worth the candle).
Rehabilitation center for drug-addicts in Belorussia.

Paronymy; hidden rhyme.
http://www.respublika.info/forum/viewtopic.php?t=1701&sid=8a840d6df80aa1deb56c7d95be18e484

AP-2: *Этот геморрой не стоит свеч. Проктология* (This hemorrhoid is not worth the candle/suppository. Proctology).
Polysemy.
http://www.wikiaion.ru/zdorove/etot-gemorroy-ne-stoit-svech.-proktologiya.html

AP-3: *Икра стоит свеч* (The caviar is worth the candle).
Record harvest of red salmon caused a 30% drop in the price of caviar. 22.10.09
Paronymy. Hidden rhyme.
http://news.ngs.ru/more/55114/

AP-4: *Капремонт стоит свеч* (Repairs are worth the candle).
Chelyabinsk city hall uses federal money to repair residential buildings.
New lexical content.
http://www.ugkh-chel.ru/site/index/Smi/kapremont/

AP-5: *Каких свечей стоит игра?* (What type of candle is the game worth?)
Different type of games.
Syntactic restructuring.
http://www.dengi-info.com/archive/article.php?aid=308

Comments: This is an interesting little group from the point of linguistic mechanisms that most of the new proverbs use. Thus, #1 and 3 use paronymy: the Russian words *игла* (needle) and *икра* (caviar) sound very similar to the original word *игра* (game); hence, hidden rhyme. #2 uses polysemy, as it has the word *свеч* (candle) in a different, medical meaning. Finally, #5 changes the original statement into a question, while #4 claims that the game (that is, repairs) is worth the candle (spending the money on it). It also interesting to note that none of the new proverbs continues the message of the original proverb (with the probable exception of #4); they use it simply as a catchy phrase to claim something completely different.

Не красна изба углами, а красна пирогами (A house is made red not by its corners but by its pies). A home is characterized by the hospitality of the hosts, not by its appearance.
Note: the Russian word *красна* (red) is used in its old meaning here: beautiful, good.

AP-1: *Красна изба не углами, а красна долгами* (The house is made red not by its corners, but by its debts).
New Russian law "On Enforcement Proceedings" (2008) gives new powers to bailiffs-court executives to collect debt.
Hidden rhyme, internal rhyme.
http://www.russianmontreal.ca/index.php?newsid=43

AP-2: *Не красна изба углами, а красна дверями* (The house is made red not by its corners, but by its doors).
Various types of doors for homes.
Hidden rhyme, internal rhyme.
http://kata-log.ru/stroyka/ne-krasna-izba-uglami-a-krasna-dverami.html

AP-3: *Красна площадь углами, а не пирогами* (The square is made red by its corners, but not by its pies).
Reporters analyze the quality of several restaurants in the center of Moscow.
Syntactic restructuring.
http://pskov.kp.ru/daily/23567.3/43618/

AP-4: *Красна страна углами* (The country is made red by its corners).
Day of the city in Tomsk, June 7.
Ellipsis; new lexical content.
http://tomsk.mn/index.php?menu=main&task=show&id=14

AP-5: *Изба красна углами, а библиотека – читателями* (The house is made red by its corners, and the library – by its readers).
Day of Libraries in Russia.

New lexical content.
http://kohma.ivanovoweb.ru/index.php?option=com_content&view=article&id=1306:2010-06-03-06-14-12&catid=34:2009-01-16-11-52-54

AP-6: *Изба красна углами, а офис – хозяйкой* (The house is made red by its corners, and the office – by its hostess).
Training courses for office managers in Samara.
New lexical content.
http://old.samara.ru/paper/41/568/9655/

AP-7: *Школа красна не углами, а своими учителями* (A school is made red not by its corners, but by its teachers).
A meeting of educators in Kazakhstan.
Hidden rhyme; internal rhyme.
http://www.e-kyzylorda.kz/rus/Events/news/regnews/Pages/180309_5.aspx

AP-8: *Красна "Стрела" углами...* ("Strela" is made red by its corners…)
"Krasnaya Strela" is a famous Russian night train between Moscow and Saint-Petersburg; compartments are fine, but the food was disappointing.
Ellipsis; new lexical content.
http://zdr-gazeta.ru/engine/print.php?newsid=6339&news_page=1

Comments: This is another very interesting group of anti-proverbs. First of all, those who coined some of them (#4, 5, 6) seem to have forgotten the original proverb, as their versions claim that the house is indeed made red (good) by its corners (that is, appearance), while in the traditional proverb is exactly opposite: appearance is not important. Secondly, many new coinages use traditional means of creating proverbs very well: internal rhyme and rhythm. Another way to create a stronger association with the traditional proverb is hidden rhyme (#1, 2, 7) between the anti-proverb and the original proverb: new lexical content in these proverbs – *долгами, дверями, учителями* (debts, doors, teachers) rhymes with *пирогами* (pies). Finally, some new proverbs use ellipsis, that is, only part of the traditional structure (#4), which proves that it is enough to establish an association with the traditional proverb. And lastly, #3 and 8 criticize Moscow restaurants and an express train, correspondingly, for low quality of food, thus reversing the traditional message.

К

Терпи, казак, атаманом будешь (Be patient, Cossack, and you will be ataman [hetman, leader]).
It is necessary to endure hardships patiently in order to achieve something in life.
English equivalent: Everything comes to him who is patient.

AP-1: *Терпи, абитуриент, студентом будешь* (Be patient, school leaver, and you will be a [college] student).
Entrance exam time in universities in Ukraine.
New lexical content.
http://www.stb.ua/newsv.php?item.39231

AP-2: *Терпи, проект, законом будешь!* (Be patient, bill, you will become law!)
A bill in the Russian parliament to simplify taxations for small businesses.
New lexical content.
http://www.klerk.ru/buh/news/1227/

AP-3: *Терпи, студент, лейтенантом будешь* (Be patient, student, and you will be lieutenant).
Reserve training – the last stage of completing military training for college students in Moscow and getting the rank of lieutenants.
New lexical content.
http://www.msn.kg/ru/news/10832/

AP-4: *Терпи, Козак, аппаратом будешь* (Be patient, Kozak, and you will become administration).

Dmitry Kozak was rumored to become new prime-minister after Michael Kasyanov, but Putin appointed Michael Fradkov instead.
Paronymy; new lexical content.
http://dlib.eastview.com/browse/doc/6010217

AP-5: *Терпи, Козак, прокурором будешь?* (Be patient, Kozak, and you will be prosecutor?)
The general prosecutor of Russia Ustinov and his contender Kozak; June 2000.
Paronymy, new lexical content.
http://novgaz.ru/data/2000/43/04.html

Comments: All new proverbs retain the message of the traditional proverb: one has to be patient, and endure a lot to achieve something in life. Obviously, every proverb adjusts this message to its own context; thus, school leavers will become college students (#1); students will become lieutenants (#3), a bill will become a law (#2). The most interesting coinages are the last two (#4 and 5): they use the last name of Dmitry Kozak, which is a paronym to the word *казак* (Cossack) in the original proverb, and discuss his chances to become either prime-minister or prosecutor general of Russia.
Note: Dmitry Kozak is deputy prime-minister of the Russian Federation (since 2008).

Под лежачий камень и вода не течет (Water does not flow under a stone that lies still).
If one does nothing, then nothing will happen. Said as a reproach of slackness, doing nothing.
English equivalent: No pains, no gains.

AP-1: *Маячок Power Flare: под лежачего полицейского вода не течёт* (Beacon light Power Flare: water does not flow under a lying policeman [speed bump]).
A new safety device invented by a policeman from Silicon Valley.
New lexical content.

http://www.membrana.ru/articles/simply/2004/04/07/220700.html

Comments: This is a perfect example of a situation when the original proverb has nothing to do with the new coinage, and is used by some writer simply to catch readers' attention. The only association – if any – with the traditional proverb is the adjective *лежачий* (lying) used in both versions, but the phrase *лежачий полицейский* (literally: lying policeman, that is, speed bump) has nothing to do with *лежачий камень* (lying stone).

Капля камень точит (A drop [of water] wears away stone).
One can achieve a lot, even if one does little at a time, but persistently and constantly.
The proverb has *Latin* origin and is attributed to Ovid, an ancient Roman poet (43-17 B.C.): Gutta cavat lapidem non vi, sed saepe cadendo (The drop hollows out the stone not by force but by frequent dropping).
English equivalent: Little strokes fell great oaks.

AP-1: *Российская «капля» точит «камень» эстонской экономики* (Russian "drop" wears away the "stone" of Estonian economy).
Cutting economic relations with Russia may become a much more serious problem for Estonia than Estonian politicians claimed.
New lexical content.
http://gadjet.clan.su/news/2007-07-12-28

AP-2: *Капли никотина камень точат* (Drops of nicotine wear away stone).
Expansion of tobacco companies in the markets of Central Asian countries, in spite of anti-tobacco legislation and unfavorable macro-economic conditions.
New lexical content.
http://www.sostav.ru/articles/2009/10/22/ko2/

AP-3: *Капля Бэтмена точит* (A drop wears away Batman).
Threat of three Russian hockey players – Malkin, Overchkin,

Kovalchuk to boycott N.H.L. if the league does not send its players to take part on Olympic Games in Sochi in 2014. Garry Bettman is the N.H.L commissioner.
New lexical content.
http://news.sport-express.ru/2009-01-27/281310

AP-4: *Капля точит камень, если он не обработан особыми смесями ATLAS...* (A drop wears away stone if it is not covered by special compound ATLAS).
An ad for water-proofing mixtures for basements and other parts of houses made of stone, concrete, etc.
Syntactic extension.
http://articles.stroybm.ru/articles/napravahreklamy/18491.html

AP-5: *Капля камень точит, а журналист — власть* (A drop wears away stone, and a journalist – those in power).
An interview with Tamara Kaleyeva, president of an international foundation for protection of freedom of speech about the necessity to make courts system more open.
Syntactic extension.
http://www.internews.kz/newsitem/16-11-2009/9621

AP-6: *Капля воды не только камень точит, но и мозг продолбит. Особенно когда вода капает из крана* (A drop of water not only wears away stone but will also batter the brain. Especially when it is coming from a leaking faucet).
How to repair an annoying leaking faucet yourself.
Syntactic extension. Wellerism.
http://akak.ru/recipes/6000-kak-pochinit-kran-na-kuhne

Comments: Once again, we have a very diverse group. In some anti-proverbs, the association with the original proverb is purely formal, and the new phrase has little to do with the original message (#1, 2, 3). In others, the proverb is interpreted literally, and is used either as an ad for water-proof compounds (#4), or as advice how to fix a leaking faucet (#6). In the last one, the addition of another sentence makes the whole structure a good example of wellerism: the second sentence changes the meaning of the first one completely. The only anti-proverb where the message of the original proverb is fully preserved, and is the basis for its continuation, is #4, which encourages journalists to protect the freedom of speech as persistently and methodically as drops of water wear away stones.

На чужой каравай рот не разевай (Do not open your mouth to somebody else's pie).
Do not try to get what does not belong to you.

AP-1: *На чужой насыбай рот не разевай* (Do not open your mouth to somebody else's naswar).
Ban in Azerbaijan to import smoking mixes from abroad; so people who like to smoke kalian can only have home-grown naswar, as all other smoking mixtures are prohibited.
Hidden rhyme; internal rhyme.
http://www.vecher.kz/?S=11-201001230550

AP-2: *На чужой Бакай рот не разевай!* (Do not open your mouth to somebody else's Bakay!).
Inventory of land plots in the village of Bakay in Kazakhstan led to fights between the owners of land; old-timers did not want to share land with the newcomers.
Hidden rhyme; internal rhyme.
http://i-news.kz/news/1224724

AP-3: *На чужой каравай рот... разевай* (Do open your mouth to somebody else's pie).
Singer Safura Alizade represented Azerbaijan at Eurovision 2010 contest.
New lexical content.
http://www.zerkalo.az/2010-05-26/culture/9744-safuraalizade-elarizmamedoglu-elzaseiddjahan

AP-4: *На чужой пай рот не разевай* (Do not open your mouth o somebody else's land plot).
Abuse and machinations with land plots in Ukraine.
Hidden rhyme; internal rhyme.
http://www.uc.kr.ua/fresh/1046/

Comments: The traditional proverb has a very rigid structure: clear-cut rhythm, and internal rhyme. That is why all new coinages follow the same criteria: all the new words also rhyme with the original word *каравай* (pie) and as a result, with the verb *разевай* (open). Anti-proverb #3, by omitting negation, encourages you to open your mouth to somebody else's pie, which in the context is a form of support for the singer.

Кашу маслом не испортишь (Too much butter won't spoil the porridge).
Something good or pleasant can do no harm, even if there is too much of it.
English equivalent: Plenty is no plague.

AP-1: *Здоровье маслом не испортишь?* (Too much butter won't spoil your health?)
A topic of a popular TV show on Russian TV, dedicated to healthy life style; this particular episode was dedicated to butter.
New lexical content.
http://malahov-plus.com/main/synopsises/1952-zdorove-maslom-ne-isportish.html

AP-2: *Мотор маслом не испортишь* (Too much butter/oil won't spoil the engine).
Modern types of engine oil.
New lexical content.
http://www.mrmz.ru/article/v23/article2.htm

AP-3: *«Тачку» маслом не испортишь* (Too much butter/oil won't spoil "wheels" [car])
The importance of correct engine oil for the car.
New lexical content.
http://www.autostart.ru/chemical/maslo/

AP-4: *Ванну маслом не испортишь* (Too much butter/oil won't spoil your bath).
Aromatic oils for baths.
New lexical content.
http://aktualii.org/content/social/110

AP-5: *Салаты маслом не испортишь* (Too much butter/oil won't spoil salads).
Different types of vegetable oil.
New lexical content.
http://www.oede.by/item/845/

AP-6: *Праздник маслом не испортишь* (Too much butter/oil won't spoil the festivities).
Oil in the celebration of the eight days of Hanukkah holiday.
New lexical content.
http://www.ru.chabad.org/library/article_cdo/aid/794792

AP-7: *Фильтром масло не испортишь* (Filter won't spoil the butter/oil).
Choosing oil filters for the car engine.
Syntactic restructuring.
http://www.zr.ru/articles/41704/

AP-8: *Маслом кожу не испортишь* (Too much butter won't spoil your skin).
Different types of massage oil, and how to choose the right oil depending on the type of massage.
New lexical content.
http://cosmetics.saleone.ru/article.php?id_article=183&a=1

AP-9: *Рынок маслом не испортишь* (Too much butter/oil won't spoil the market).
Production of vegetable oils in Russia.
New lexical content.
http://www.rosinvest.com/dir/analysis/40/34/

AP-10: *Фигуру маслом не испортишь* (Too much butter won't spoil your figure).
Interview with Nina Bogdanova, a Belorussian singer, and how she uses butter.
New lexical content.
http://www.ng.by/ru/issues?art_id=41955

AP-11: *Масло кашей не испортишь* (Porridge won't spoil your

butter/oil).
Description of different types of vegetable oils.
Syntactic restructuring.
http://www.lecitinplus.ru/p0023.htm

AP-12: *Хумус маслом испортишь* (Too much butter will spoil hummus).
An interview with the chef of a Lebanon cuisine restaurant in Moscow.
New lexical content.
http://www.kommersant.ru/doc.aspx?DocsID=578101

AP-13: *«Маслом» Хью Джекмана не испортишь* (Too much "Butter" won't spoil Hugh Jackman).
Hugh Jackman to play in the political satire movie "Butter."
New lexical content.
http://video.ru/news/entry/3876

AP-14: *Дизель рапсом не испортишь* (Too much rape oil won't spoil the diesel).
Plans to build several plants producing bio fuel from rape in Russia.
http://www.bioethanol.ru/biodiesel/news/dizel_rapsom_ne_isportish/

AP-15: *Долг маслом не испортишь* (Too much butter/oil won't spoil your debt).
About a company in Ukraine specializing in oil/butter and grain business: even though its debt grows, it pays its bills regularly.
New lexical content.
http://www.investgazeta.net/kompanii-i-rynki/dolg-maslom-ne-isportish-157911/?rb

AP-16: *Праздник маслом не испортишь* (Too much butter/oil won't spoil the holiday).
On the eve and during winter holidays, consumption of vegetable oils increases.
New lexical content.

http://prodinfo.com.ua/index.php?option=com_content&task=view&id=616&Itemid=108

AP-17: *Уголь маслом не испортишь* (Too much butter/oil won't spoil coal).
Covering with oil cargo cars used to transport coal saves railroads a lot of trouble, especially during winter: coal used to freeze to the floor and walls of cars; Russian Eastern Siberia.
New lexical content.
http://zdr-gazeta.ru/index.php?newsid=56770

AP-18: *Кашу спрэдом не испортишь* (Too much spread won't spoil the porridge).
Ukrainian authorities tested 23 samples of butter from various producers; it turned out that half of the "butter" was a mixture of vegetable oil and butter, so it should be correctly called spread, not butter.
English word with a Russian morphological ending.
http://www.epravda.com.ua/press/2010/06/15/238616/

Comments: This group is interesting for several reasons. First of all, it is much larger than average; secondly – and more importantly – all new coinages preserve the original "butter" in them. This is explained mostly by the fact that the Russian word *масло* can mean both "butter" and "oil"; and this polysemy is used by the majority of the new proverbs: they talk about vegetable oil or aromatic oils, or engine oil, or rape oil, or even butter – and in all these cases the Russian word is the same – *масло.* Besides, most of them confirm the message of the traditional proverb (even if adjusted to some context): too much butter/oil can do no harm. There are exceptions to this rule: #12 in fact says that too much butter is bad for hummus, while # 7 and 11 reverse the original structure and talk not about the influence of butter on something, but the other way round: how something (filter or porridge) influences butter/oil. Finally, anti-proverb #13 has nothing to do with either butter or the original message of the traditional proverb; once again, it is simply a catchy title based on the fact that the title of the movie happens to be "Butter."

Клин клином вышибают (A wedge is removed with a wedge). Bad consequences of something are dealt with by the same means that were the reason for these consequences.
English equivalent: Fight fire with fire.

AP-1: *Клин пробкой вышибают* (Klin is removed by a cork).
Traffic jams in Moscow and Moscow region; an example – the city of Klin in Moscow oblast.
Homonymy.
http://www.mk.ru/auto/article/2010/07/08/515194-klin-probkoy-vyishibayut.html

AP-2: *«Клик» клином вышибают* (Click is removed by a wedge).
Hackers' attacks in Belorussia.
Paronymy.
http://sb.by/print/post/83693/

AP-3: *"КиН" клином вышибают* (KiN is removed by a wedge).
Tax inspectors of Moscow searched the premises of the cognac factory KiN.
Paronymy.
http://www.kommersant.ru/doc.aspx?fromsearch=f1d75ec5-efd1-4cce-8524-fb0349919a1a&docsid=789877

AP-4: *Лом клином вышибают* (Scrap metal is removed by a wedge).
In the Kustanai region of Kazakhstan, all collecting stations of scrap metal were closed, because of the numerous cases of theft of these metals.
New lexical content.
http://www.izvestia.kz/news.php?date=19-09-05&number=9

AP-5: *Клин кленом вышибают* (A wedge is removed by a maple).
Russian hockey clubs buy Canadian players to play in the Russian national championship.
Paronymy.

http://www.novayagazeta.ru/data/2000/9/21.html

Comments: Three of the new coinages use paronymy in their wording (and one uses homonymy) to create a clear association with the original proverb. At the same time, from the point of view of their meaning, all of them depart from the original proverb and in fact have nothing to do with its idea ("same means"), even though they do preserve the part about dealing with some problem. Linguistically, the most interesting case is #1, where the name of the town – Klin – is a homonym with the Russian word for wedge. At first, it seems that the article will be about a wedge (either literally or figuratively), but it turns out to be about the town of Klin and traffic jams. Another interesting part creating a unique play on words is the Russian word *проб-ка* (cork), because the Russian expression for traffic jam is the word "cork" used metaphorically.

Куда ни кинь, всюду клин (No matter where you cast lots – everywhere there is a narrow plot).
No variant of solving a problem seems to work; said when one is in a desperate, hopeless situation.
Note: *Клин* in this context means a narrow land plot, unsuitable for agriculture (it is a homonym to the word used in the previous proverb – *клин* which means "wedge"). In old times, when land was distributed between peasants, it was decided by casting lots. Thus, no matter where one casts lots, one will get a bad plot of land.

AP-1: *Куда деньги ни кинь – всюду минус* (No matter where you cast money – everywhere there is a loss).
Bank deposits did not bring any profit to their owners in 2004; only losses.
New lexical content.
http://www.rg.ru/2005/02/08/pribyl.html

AP-2: *Куда ни кинь – всюду... спонсор!* (No matter where you cast lots… everywhere there is a sponsor!)
Chief of police of the city of Kohma, Ivanovo oblast, did not fine entrepreneurs for violations, provided they would be sponsors to

the police.
http://iv-hronometr.ru/156-kuda-ni-kin-vsyudu-sponsor.html

AP-3: *Куда ни кинь, всюду блин!* (No matter where you cast lots, everywhere there is a pancake!)
Museum of history in Yekaterinburg organizes a culinary event "No matter where you cast, everywhere there is a pancake!" It is dedicated to Maslenitsa [traditional Pancake festival].
Paronymy; internal rhyme; hidden rhyme.
http://prazdnik-land.e-burg.ru/news/regionalnyie-novosti/2010/2/9/akciya-kuda-ni-kin-vsyudu-blin-v-ekaterinburge/

AP-4: *Так что, куда ни кинь, всюду клинТОН или БУШ* (No matter where you cast lots, everywhere there is KLINton or Bush).
Foreign advisors at the post-soviet Russian government.
Homonymy.
http://rusyouth.ru/

AP-5: *Куда ни кинь, всюду китайский линь да карась* (No matter where you cast lots, there is a Chinese tench or crucian).
Absence of quality and cheap fish in Moscow.
Paronymy; internal rhyme.
http://www.vmdaily.ru/article/85359.html

AP-6: *Куда ни кинь — всюду прикуп* (No matter where you cast – everywhere there is a bribe).
Colonel Kvachkov who was found not guilty in the attempt to assassinate Anatoly Chubais. The political and economic situation created by Putin, including necessity of bribes to get anything done.
New lexical content.
http://www.novayagazeta.ru/data/2008/41/04.html

Comments: The original proverb has internal rhyme (*кинь – клин*); three of the anti-proverbs (#3, 4, 5) using paronymy, and thus creating hidden rhyme, preserve this quality of the original proverb and as a result, look and sound much better than the other three, where this quality is lost. Linguistically, the most interesting case is #4, where the wordplay is based on the coincidence between the Russian word *клин* (klin) and the first syllable of the last name of president CLINton.

Черного кобеля не отмоешь добела (A black dog cannot be washed so as to make it white).
Some negative qualities of a person cannot be changed.
English equivalent: *The leopard cannot change his spots.*

AP-1: *Преступные деньги не отмоешь доб*ела (Criminal money cannot be washed so as to make it white).
Money laundering in the Far East of Russia.
New lexical content.
http://toz.khv.ru/page.php?page=24949&date_id_num=2006-01-28&year=2006&month=01&day=28

AP-2: *Черного воробья не отмоешь добела* (A black sparrow cannot be washed so as to make it white).
The deputy in the Shuya oblast duma from "United Russia" party O. Vorobyev [his last name means "sparrow" in Russian].
Hidden rhyme; internal rhyme.
http://gazeta.shuyanet.ru/index.php?option=com_content&task=view&id=1020&Itemid=143

AP-3: *Черного Лернера не отмоешь добела* (Black Lerner cannot be washed so as to make him white).
Financial machinations of Grigory Lerner.
New lexical content.
http://www.compromat.ru/page_21924.htm

AP-4: *Как отмыть добела черного сибирского кобеля?* (How to wash a black Siberian dog so as to make it white?)
How to market Novosibirsk oblast to tourists.
Syntactic restructuring; new lexical content.
http://megansk.ru/partanalitics/1281087063

Comments: The most interesting example is #2, where the wordplay is based on the fact that the last name of the deputy in question is *Воробьев* (sparrow in Russian). Besides, since the

Russian word *воробья* (sparrow in Genitive case) rhymes with the original word *кобеля* (dog) the anti-proverb both preserves the internal rhyme and establishes a clear association with the traditional proverb. While three new proverbs preserve the original message (#1, 2 and 3), #4 is the farthest from the traditional proverb, as it has nothing to do with changing or critisizing "negative qualities" of somebody or something.

Коготок увяз – всей птичке пропасть (If one claw is caught, the whole bird is lost). Once a person sacrifices some principles, there is no coming back.

AP-1: *Мембер увяз — всей птичке пропасть* (If a member is caught, the whole bird is lost).
A review of the movie "Austin Powers in Goldmember."
Neologism.
http://www.film.ru/article.asp?id=3480

Comments: This lonely example features the English word *member* (from Goldmember) written in Cyrillic – *мембер*. This, in itself, catches readers' attention, but it is also the only thing that can be said about this anti-proverb. There is hardly any connection with the original proverb.

Не плюй в колодец – пригодится воды напиться (Do not spit into the well—it may be useful to drink water).
Do not do harm to others, as by doing so you can deprive yourself of their help in the future.
English equivalent: A bad penny always comes back. Don't bite the hand that feeds you.

AP-1: *Агента слушай, но в колодец не плюй* (Listen to the agent, but do not spit into the well).
Russian hockey players who are drafted to play in North American clubs.
New lexical content.
http://www.fhr.ru/content/news/6271.html

AP-2: *Не плюй в угольный колодец* (Do not spit into the coal

well).
Disputes about coal mines in Kemerovo oblast between the owners of the mine and governor Aman Tuleev.
New lexical content; ellipsis.
http://www.nakanune.ru/articles/14162

AP-3: *Не плюй в колодец, ведь можно аммиаком захлебнуться* (Do not spit into the well, you can get drowned in ammonia).
Competition to export ammonia among Russian oligarchs.
New lexical content.
http://www.pravda.ru/news/economics/13-01-2005/52573-2/

AP-4: *Не плюй в колодец, даже если власти позволяют...* (Do not spit into the well, even if authorities allow you to…)
Problems of the sewage treatment plant and water discharge into Irkutsk reservoir.
New lexical content.
http://baikalarea.ru/pribaikal/reki/angara/neplluy.htm

Comments: All new coinages preserve, to some extent, the original message: do not do something in haste without thinking, as it can do harm to you in the future. At the same time, three anti-proverbs follow the traditional phrase in using the idea of spitting into the well figuratively, while the last one (#4) treats it literally, as it is concerned with the quality of water.

Старый конь борозды не испортит (An old horse will not spoil the furrow).
There is no doubt that an experienced person will do the job excellently.

AP-1: *Rally del Corallo: Старый Porsche борозды не испортит* (Rally del Corallo: an old Porsche will not spoil the furrow).
Porsche 911 won the rally for historic cars.
New lexical content.
http://www.carclub.ru/new_19_03_2009_Rally_del_Corallo_Staryijj_Porsche_borozdyi_ne_isportit.html

AP-2: *Старый «Завет» борозды не испортит* (Old "Zavet" [Testament" in Russian] will not spoil the furrow.)
Thrash metal group "Zavet."
New lexical content.
http://www.zvuki.ru/R/P/18373

AP-3: *Старый премьер борозды не испортит* (An old prime-minister will not spoil the furrow).
Will Michael Kasyanov be reappointed prime-minister for the second presidential term of Vladimir Putin?
New lexical content.
http://dlib.eastview.com/browse/doc/5795080

AP-4: *Старый трактор борозды не испортит* (An old tractor will not spoil the furrow).
Tractors made in Kharkov tractor plant during soviet times are still used abroad.
New lexical content.
http://dozor.kharkov.ua/city/promyshlennost/1053713.html

AP-5: *Старый тяжеловес борозды не испортит?* (Old heavy-weight will not spoil the furrow?)
Eduard Rossel, who was governor of Sverdlovsk oblast for many years, is stepping down.
New lexical content.
http://www.lentachel.ru/articles/377

AP-6: *Старый рокер борозды не испортит* (An old rocker will not spoil the furrow).
Deep Purple concert in Moscow in 2008.
New lexical content.
http://kp.ru/daily/24189/396679/

AP-7: *"Робин Гуд": старый Скотт борозды не испортит* ("Robin Hood": old Scott will not spoil the furrow).
A new version of Robin Hood in the movie directed by Ridley Scott.
New lexical content.
http://mors.sibnet.ru/nsk/article/489/&rubid=1

AP-8: *Старый СНиП борозды не испортит* (An old SNiP [Construction Norms and Regulations] will not spoil the furrow).
A new law on regulations in construction.
New lexical content.
http://www.beton.ru/news/detail.php?ID=314822

AP-9: *Старый лис борозды не испортит* (An old fox will not spoil the furrow).
Analysis of vice-presidential candidate in US elections-2008.
New lexical content.
http://www.demographia.ru/articles_N/index.html?idR=24&idArt=1216

AP-10: *Старую борозду горводоканал не испортит* (An old furrow will not be spoiled by the city water agency).
Prosecutors' office charged the city water agency of Pskov in destroying the historical cultural layer while conducting their work.
New lexical content; syntactic restructuring.
http://pravdapskov.ru/rubric/25/5361

AP-11: *Старый комп борозды не испортит* (An old computer will not spoil the furrow).
A virtual flee market of used computers.
Paronymy.
http://www.yeisk.ru/fender/

AP-12: *Говорила я американцам: выбирайте Маккейна, старый президент борозды не испортит* (I was telling Americans: elect McCain, an old president will not spoil the furrow).
Valeria Novodvorskaya [a prominent Russian dissident] about Obama and US-Russia relationships.
New lexical content.
http://mnenia.obozrevatel.com/info/19.htm

Comments: With one exception (#10) all new proverbs confirm the traditional wisdom: someone (or something) with experience will do an excellent job, be it an old soviet tractor, or an antique

car, a vice-presidential candidate or an aging rock musician; so in that aspect, they all are the same and use the same device – substitute the word *horse* by something new. In #10, we have a different situation: it talks about the city water agency, while doing their job (laying water pipes) should not destroy the old historic cultural layer of the city of Pskov. Thus, it is not about an old horse anymore, but – literally – about an old furrow.
Note: Pskov is one of the oldest Russian cities; it is first mentioned in the Russian chronicle of 903 A.D.

Дареному коню в зубы не смотрят (Don't look a gift horse in the mouth).
One should not discuss a gift, but accept it with gratitude, even if it is not something that one would like.
This is an international proverb, known in many languages, including English.

AP-1: *Дарёному Гусю в зубы не смотрят* (Don't look a gift goose in the mouth).
A journalist made a gift – a clay goose – to the then-head of Administration of the President of Russia, Alexander Voloshin.
Homonymy.
http://www.compromat.ru/page_24833.htm

AP-2: *Дареному Кони в зубы не смотрят: необычные подарки Путину* (Do not look a gift Koni in the mouth: unusual presents given to Putin).
Koni is the name of Putin's dog that he received as present in December 2001 as a New Year gift from Sergey Shoigu, Minister of Emergency Situations.
Paronymy.
http://www.glomu.ru/smi/20081010/67899161.html

AP-3: *Дарёному Быку в зубы не смотрят* (Do not look a gift bull in the mouth).
The problem of choosing New Year gifts in 2008, the next year being the year of the Bull.
New lexical content.
http://www.vecherniyorenburg.ru/arhiv/677/11099/

AP-4: *Дареному коню смотрят в зубы, в хвост и в гриву* (Do look a gift horse in the mouth, as well as tail and mane).
Choosing New Year presents, December 2001.
Syntactic extension.
http://www.dp.ru/a/2001/12/24/Darenomu_konju_smotrjat_v_z

AP-5: *Дарёному коню в ценник смотрят* (Do look in the price tag of the gift horse).
Government officials in the city Kursk about gifts that they get: within the law; although Kursk businessmen state the opposite.
New lexical content.
http://gazeta.aif.ru/_/online/kursk/778/02_01

AP-6: *Дареному коню на таможне в зубы смотрят* (Customs officials look in the mouth of the gift horse).
Russian customs authorities in the Far East did not allow a sailor to bring into the country a toy horse that he bought in Japan for his newborn son; 2006.
New lexical content.
http://www.toz.khv.ru/page.php?page=28506&date_id_num=2006-09-28&year=2006&month=09&day=28

AP-7: *Дареному медведю в зубы не смотрят* (Do not look a gift bear in the mouth).
Gifts to government officials and members of the Russian parliament.
New lexical content.
http://www.newizv.ru/news/2006-05-12/46028/

Comments: This is a pretty diverse group, even though on the surface they all look the same and talk about gifts. At the same time, some of them contradict the message of the original proverb (#4), while others discuss the problem of gifts to government officials and members of the Russian parliament (#2, 5, 7). One proverb treats the original phrase literally and indeed talks about a gift horse (#6). Linguistically, the most interesting coinages are #1 and 2. In the first one, there is a play on words between the Russian word *гусь* (goose) and the abbreviated last name of the famous Russian oligarch – *Гусинский* (Gusinsky).

Thus, by presenting the head of administration the gift of a clay goose, the journalist hinted to Gusinsky (incidentally, the clay goose was money box, which only made the allusion more obvious, as by persecuting Gusinsky, the government literally killed the goose who was laying golden eggs). In #2, the name of the dog given to Putin – Koni is a paronym to the word in the traditional proverb – *коню* (horse in Dative case); thus, the wordplay underlines the message of the title – unusual gifts given to Putin.

Копейка рубль бережет (A kopeck saves a ruble).
Advice to be thrifty, not waste money.
English equivalent: Take care of the pence and the pounds will take care of themselves.

AP-1*: Копейка рубль бережет, цент приносит тысячи* (A kopeck saves a ruble, a cent brings thousands).
People who gambled in Italian casinos got huge amounts of money, even though they initially had very little money.
Syntactic extension.
http://www.italynews.ru/material_3242.html

AP-2: *Копейка рубль не бережет* (A kopeck does not save a ruble).
The Russian parliament discusses the question of discontinuing minting coins of 1 kopeck and some others. 2010.
New lexical content.
http://www.chas-daily.com/win/2010/08/13/v_049.html?r=3

AP-3: *"Копейка" рубль бережет!* ("Kopeika" saves a ruble!)
A sale event in the chain grocery store "Kopeika" [kopeck].
Polysemy.
http://cenorez.ru/?p=237

AP-4: *Гривня рубль бережет* (A hryvnia [a monetary unit of Ukraine since 1996] saves a ruble).
Devaluation of hryvnia to ruble may improve the trade balance of Ukraine.
New lexical content.

http://www.expert.ua/articles/9/0/6532/

AP-5: *Киловатт рубль бережет* (A kilowatt saves a ruble). Electricity is a major expense in metallurgical plants; ways to reduce the overall cost of metal production.
New lexical content.
http://www.kommersant.ru/doc.aspx?DocsID=607221

AP-6: *Нефть рубль бережет или как сохранить деньги во время кризиса* (Oil saves a ruble, or how to save your money during a crisis).
A conference dedicated to the world economic crisis, organized by the Russian newspaper "Vedomosti"; June 2009.
New lexical content; syntactic extension.
http://www.kapital-rus.ru/articles/article/42659/

AP-7: *Полтинник рубль бережет* (50 kopecks save a ruble).
Gas prices fell 50 kopecks in Barnaul; October 2006.
New lexical content.
http://altapress.ru/story/11039/

AP-8: *Доллар рубль бережет* (A dollar saves a ruble).
Landlords would like to get rent in dollars or euros, while most people who rent get their pay in rubles. 2009.
New lexical content.
http://www.bestrealtor.ru/useful_info/30/dollrublevarena

AP-9: *Закупка рубль бережет* (A purchase saves a ruble).
How businesses can save on office expenses.
New lexical content.
http://www.kommersant.ru/doc.aspx?DocsID=859636

AP-10: *Ноутбук рубль бережёт* (Notebook saves a ruble).
Deputies of city council in Blagoveshchensk will use notebook computers and electronic documents instead of paper.
New lexical content.
http://tvgorod.ru/2010/03/17/v-gorodskoj-dume-gryadut-texnologicheskie-izmeneniya.html

AP-11: *Каталог рубль бережёт* (A catalog saves a ruble).
A special catalog of periodicals with discounted prices for veterans dedicated to the 65th anniversary of the victory in WWII.
New lexical content.
http://www.newworldnews.ru/index.php?option=com_content&task=view&id=11203

AP-12: *Ленин рубль бережет* (Lenin saves a ruble).
A taxi company in Yekaterinburg, on April 22, 2008, accepted bills of the soviet period when people were paying for the ride.
Note: April 22 (1870) is Vladimir Lenin's birthday.
Metonymy.
http://news.taxopark.com/content/view/29/16/

AP-13: *Тарифный рубль сотню бережет* (Tariff ruble saves a hundred).
Strong demand among citizens of Perm to have water and heat meters in their apartments.
New lexical content.
http://www.metrosphera.ru/market/construction/news/?pub=10339

AP-14: *Бюджетный рубль миллионы бережет* (Budget ruble saves millions).
The budget of the republic of Chuvashia for 2004.
New lexical content.
http://www.gov.cap.ru/hierarhy.asp?page=./24/17478/48014/87429/87436/87437

AP-15: *Рубль нервы бережет* (A ruble saves your nerves).
Volatility in the dollar/ruble rate and measures of the Russian government to decrease it.
New lexical content.
http://xn--80av.com

AP-16: *Юань рубль не бережет* (Yuan [Chinese monetary unit] does not save a ruble).
Because of the sharp fall of the ruble to dollar Chinese shops close to the border refused to accept rubles from Russian tour-

ists, as they used to do before that; September 2008.
New lexical content.
http://www.rg.ru/2008/09/09/yuan.html

AP-17: *Копейка доллар бережет* (A kopeck saves a dollar).
Russian citizens who invest their money in coin collections get richer ever year.
New lexical content.
http://www.itogi.ru/archive/2004/7/68876.html

AP-18: *Советская копейка рубль бережет?* (A soviet kopeck saves a ruble?)
Rare coins of the soviet period can be sold for good prices today.
New lexical content.
http://kp.ru/daily/24506/657991/

AP-19: *Рубль семейный бюджет бережет* (A ruble saves family budget).
Tax refunds in Russia: eligible expenses, applicable law, procedure, necessary documents, examples.
New lexical content.
http://www.ug.ru/issues/?action=topic&toid=6175

AP-20: *Копейка рубль бережёт, а цент – евро* (A kopeck saves a ruble, while a cent saves a euro).
Coins of 1 and 2 cents in euro zone: some countries decided to stop using them; September 2004.
Syntactic extension.
http://news.numizmatik.ru/kopeika-rubli-bereget_-a-cent---evro_n1411.html

Comments: The majority of the 20 new coinages develop the basic idea of the traditional proverb: saving money, even though they adjust it to their contexts, and do not necessarily talk about kopecks – it can be rubles, or oil, or electricity, or water meters. As usual, some proverbs use the traditional phrase at its face value, and literally talk about coins of one kopeck (or one cent) – #2, 18, and 20. Linguistically, the most interesting cases are #3, which talks about a sale event in a chain of supermarkets whose name is “Kopeika” (kopeck in Russian), and #12, where we have metonymy: the soviet paper money had the portrait of Lenin; thus, when the anti-proverb says “Lenin saves a ruble,” it means that old soviet paper bills with the portrait of Lenin were accepted during that day, which allowed people to save their real money for some other expenses.

Большому кораблю – большое плавание (A big ship needs a big sea).
A gifted, outstanding person needs a lot of space, freedom for fruitful activity. Often said to express one’s good wishes to someone who is entrusted with an important task.

AP-1: *Большому порту — большое плавание* (A big port needs a big sea).
Plans for reconstruction of Saint-Petersburg sea port.
New lexical content.
http://www.kommersant.ru/doc.aspx?DocsID=889356

AP-2: *Большому теннису — большое плавание* (Big tennis needs big sea).
Development of lawn tennis in the city of Krivoy Rog.
New lexical content.
http://www.krivbass.in.ua/content/view/1406/31/

AP-3: *Большому "Аквариуму" — большое плавание* (Big “Aquarium” needs a big sea).
A new album by the Russian rock group “Aquarium.”
New lexical content.
http://nestanda.com/se/news/6161.html

AP-4: *Большому стенду – большое плавание* (A big booth needs a big sea).
The booth of State Maritime Academy in S-Petersburg at the exhibition “Neva-2009.”
New lexical content.
http://www.rwr.ru/news/design/design_4246.html

AP-5: *Большому дому – большое плавание* (A big house needs

a big sea).
An article about houses on water in different countries, including Russia.
New lexical content.
http://vsedoma.km.ru/view/?mode=article&id=6c01c4e8-e722-4b20-90e0-192b47f764f4

AP-6: *Большим компаниям – большое плавание!* (Big companies need a big sea!)
An advertisement of fitness clubs for companies who care about their employees.
New lexical content.
http://www.infit.ru/news/club/Bolshim_kompaniyam_-_bolshoe_plavanie.html

AP-7: *Большому забору – большое плавание* (A big fence needs a big sea).
Thieves stole 400 metal sheets for the future fence in the town of Serpuhov in Moscow oblast.
New lexical content.
http://www.mk-serp.ru/index.php?option=com_content&view=article&id=139:2009-03-11-10-09-22&catid=33:11-04032009-11032009

AP-8: *Большому По – большое плавание!* (A big Po needs a big sea!)
German soccer club “Stuttgart” bought a Russian player Pavel Pogrebnyak.
New lexical content.
http://www.championat.ru/football/article-37141.html

AP-9: *Большому Большакову – большое плавание* (Big Bolshakov needs a big sea).
Russian swimmer from Izhevsk will take part in the world championship in Rome.
Paronymy.
http://izvestiaur.ru/society/391896.html

AP-10: *Большому региону — большое «плавание»?* (A big re-

gion needs a "big sea"?)
The rising water level in Cheboksary reservoir will be good for Chuvashia, but it will mean ecological disaster for other regions of Russia which will be affected by this; many settlements will be under water.
New lexical content.
http://www.pravda-nn.ru/archive/number:552/article:8625/

AP-11: *Большому Филу – большое плавание?* (Big Fil needs a big sea?)
About the coach of the Brazilian national soccer team, Lois Filippe Scolary (big Fil).
New lexical content.
http://www.sovsport.ru/gazeta/article-item/63488

Comments: Most new coinages continue the message of the traditional proverb – wishing well to somebody or something in their future endeavors, be it the development of lawn tennis or a new album by a famous rock group. The only exception is #10, which literally talks about a "big sea" being created in one of the regions of Russia, and what effect it will have on its neighbors. Linguistically, we do not have any interesting coinages, with the exception of #9, where the last name of the athlete and the Russian word "big" have the same root: *Большаков – большой* (Bolshakov – big).

Нашла коса на камень (The scythe struck a stone).
Two stubborn persons confront each other, no one wants to yield.

AP-1: *Нашла рука на камень* (The hand struck a stone).
Archeological discoveries in Kharkov.
New lexical content.
http://www.interesno.name/node/129

AP-2: *Нашла краса на камень* (The beauty struck a stone).
Husband and wife, professional geologists, created a museum of stones on their summer cottage land plot.
Hidden rhyme.

http://www.mk.ru/social/article/2009/11/24/391097-nashla-krasa-na-kamen.html

AP-3: *Политическая «коса» нашла на таможенный «камень»* (Political “scythe” struck a customs “stone”).
Problems with the implementation of the customs union of Russia, Belorussia, and Kazakhstan.
New lexical content.
http://www.respublika-kaz.info/news/politics/7543/

AP-4: *Австрийская коса нашла на чешский камень* (Austrian scythe struck a Czech stone).
Austria does not like that the Czech republic built a nuclear power plant 70 km from the border.
New lexical content.
http://www.ng.ru/world/2000-10-17/6_chehstone.html

AP-5: *Нашла Каса на камень* (Kasa struck a stone).
A court case in Yaroslavl about the lawfulness of the construction of a new hotel, which was built by the Turkish firm “Casa Story.”
Homonymy; hidden rhyme.
http://www.goldring.ru/index.php?option=com_content&task=view&id=96394&Itemid=1&date=0

AP-6: *Нашла пила на камень* (The saw struck a stone).
Co-owners of the metallurgic plant in Nizhny Novgorod dispute about its future; representatives of the new owner sawed the machinery.
New lexical content.
http://www.kommersant.ru/doc.aspx?DocsID=1368085

AP-7: *Прокурорская коса нашла на генеральский камень* (Prosecutor’s scythe struck general’s stone).
A district court in Volgograd found general Mihail Tsukruk guilty of abuse of office.
New lexical content.
http://www.wek.ru/articles/obsh/236326/index.shtml

AP-8: *Их коса нашла на наш камень* (Their scythe struck our stone).
Eduard Limonov [one of the leaders of the opposition in Russia] about a court hearing: Moscow city hall did not permit the opposition meeting on December 31, 2009 and January 31, 2010.
New lexical content.
http://www.ehorussia.ru/new/book/export/html/150

Comments: A peculiar feature of this group of anti-proverbs is the fact that half of them use the exact wording of the traditional proverb and only add adjectives to narrow down the context (thus, we have *political* scythe, *Austrian* scythe, *prosecutor's* scythe, and *their* scythe; the same is true for the other key word – stone: *Czech* stone, *general's* stone, *customs* stone, and *our* stone). All of these four anti-proverbs retain the original message, too, about a clash of two opposite positions. Among the other half, #1 and 2 have nothing to do with the meaning of the original proverb, and use it simply as a catchy phrase; while #5 and 6 do preserve this message. Both of these proverbs are also interesting in their own way; thus, in #5 the name of the firm – *Casa* – is a homonym to the Russian word *коса* (scythe); thus, an interesting wordplay is the result of it, based on the hidden rhyme (it is also present in #2: *краса – коса*, that is *beauty – scythe*). In #6, though it also talks about a conflict between two parties (co-owners of the plant), the word *пила* (saw) is used here in its literal sense, as one of the co-owners literally sawed the machinery, thus effectively destroying it.

Ночью все кошки серы (All cats are grey at night).
In unfavorable situations it is difficult to understand who is right and who is wrong. The proverb is used as an excuse for wrong judgements or actions.

AP-1: *Ночью все елки серы* (All spruce trees are grey at night).
Illegal sale of trees on New Year's eve in Belorussia; December 2007.
New lexical content.
http://sb.by/post/62986/

AP-2: *Ночью не все кошки серы* (Not all cats are grey at night).
Night clubs' business in Kazakhstan.
New lexical content.
http://www.izvestia.kz/news.php?date=03-11-05&number=8

AP-3: *Ночью не все кошки серы* (Not all cats are grey at night).
Drug addiction among young people in Tatarstan – police raids at night clubs.
New lexical content.
http://webcache.googleusercontent.com/search?q=cache:CGFZAmPoFTsJ:ufskn.tatar.ru/rus/file/pub/pub_8118.doc

AP-4: *Когда все кошки серы, пора в "ветеринарку"* (When all cats are grey, it is time to visit a veterinary clinic).
Night veterinary clinics in Moscow.
Syntactic extension; contextual synonym.
http://week.izvestia.ru/reportings/article4825

Comments: Judging by these – very few – examples, it seems that the original meaning of the traditional proverbs is pretty much lost, and in most cases the new proverbs are used simply as a catchy phrase, and have nothing to do with the idea that was present in the traditional proverb. Linguistically, most interesting is #4: the phrase "when all cats are grey" is a contextual synonym for the word "night" and describes night animal clinics.

Страшнее кошки зверя нет (There is no scarier animal than a cat).
Said, often ironically, as a reaction to somebody's fear, when someone is scared of something which in reality is not scary at all.

AP-1: *Страшнее мухи зверя нет* (There is no scarier animal than a fly).
Insect pests in vegetable gardens.
New lexical content.
http://www.floraprice.ru/2010/04/strashnee-muxi-zverya-net/

AP-2: *Страшнее кокера-спаниеля зверя нет* (There is no scar-

ier animal than a cocker spaniel).
English cocker spaniel is the most aggressive dog breed, based on the research of scientists from the Autonomous University of Barcelona.
New lexical content.
http://www.newizv.ru/lenta/109547/

AP-3: *Страшнее зайца зверя нет?* (There is no scarier animal than a rabbit?)
Rabbits and other rodents damage plants in winter.
New lexical content.
http://sb.by/print/post/78567/

AP-4: *Страшнее мыши зверя нет* (There is no scarier animal than a mouse).
Diseases of people who spend too much time in front of computer screens.
Polysemy.
http://medobzor.net/index.php?option=com_content&task=view&id=115&Itemid=65

AP-5: *Страшнее хама зверя нет* (There is no scarier animal than a rude person).
How to deal with rude people.
New lexical content.
http://www.marusia.ru/style1999/06-01.html

AP-6: *Страшнее боли зверя нет* (There is no scarier animal than pain).
The nature, origin and function of pain in the human body.
New lexical content.
http://www.provisor.com.ua/archive/1999/N21/lvova.php

AP-7: *Страшнее слизня зверя нет?* (There is no scarier animal than a slug?)
How to fight slugs.
New lexical content.
http://www.kp.ru/daily/23536.3/41455/

AP-8: *Страшнее каракаmа зверя нет* (There is no scarier animal than karakat).
Hunting in tundra in Komi Republic using karakat.
Note: Karakat is a special vehicle for hunting in tundra in Komi Republic; the name is derived from the Russian word for cuttlefish – *каракатица*.
New lexical content.
http://www.inkomi.ru/articles/2005/11/17/karakat/

AP-9: *Страшнее крысы зверя нет* (There is no scarier animal than a rat).
The year of the rat – 2008; rats spreading dangerous diseases.
New lexical content.
http://www.tovarish.com.ua/rus/print/Strashnee_4670.html

AP-10: *Страшнее утренней зарядки зверя нет* (There is no scarier animal than morning exercises).
The best time for physical activity is not mornings, but evenings.
New lexical content.
http://www.notablets.ru/archives/1385

AP-11: *Страшнее «зебры» зверя нет* (There is no scarier animal than "zebra").
Cars hit pedestrians most often on pedestrian crossings – "zebras" in Russian.
Polysemy.
http://www.mr7.ru/story/top/story_3706.html

AP-12: *Страшнее гастарбайтера зверя нет* (There is no scarier animal than migrant workers).
Russian parliament passed the Code on Administrative Violations, which includes provisions prohibiting employment of illegal immigrants, and raising fines for the employers and even private citizens who employ illegal workers.
New lexical content.
http://www.rabota.ru/vesti/career/strashnee_gastarbaitera_zverya_net.html

AP-13: *Страшнее прессы зверя нет* (There is no scarier ani-

mal than the press).
A new law in Kazakhstan that limits freedom of the press; 2009.
New lexical content.
http://www.zakon.kz/58868-strashnee-pressy-zverja-net.-kak-i.html

AP-14: *Страшнее таксы зверя нет* (There is no scarier animal than a badgerer).
The article claims that the badgerer is the most aggressive dog.
New lexical content.
http://www.gzt.ru/topnews/science/-strashnee-taksy-zverya-net-/186338.html

AP-15: *Страшнее Барби зверя нет* (There is no scarier animal than a Barbie).
Russia may prohibit the sales of sexy-looking dolls; 2005.
New lexical content.
http://www.mk-piter.ru/2005/05/11/031/

AP-16: *Страшнее коровы зверя нет* (There is no scarier animal than a cow).
Cows in the center of the Russian city of Kachkanar cause traffic accidents and attack pedestrians.
New lexical content.
http://horoscopes.trud.ru/article/26-07-2007/118817_strashnee_korovy_zverja_net.html

AP-17: *Нет зверя страшнее человека* (There is no scarier animal than a man).
People have aggressive breeds of dogs as pets; these dogs attack other people and kids.
New lexical content.
http://www.russian-bazaar.com/Article.aspx?ArticleID=9111

AP-18: *Страшнее моды зверя нет?* (There is no scarier animal than fashion?)
Fashion for children and teens; peer pressure; advice for parents.
New lexical content.

http://www.nashideti.info/topic/nashi_modniki/strashnee_modi_zverja_net/

AP-19: *Страшнее пьяной зверя нет* (There is no scarier animal than a drunken woman).
A drunken female driver in Yekaterinburg made quite a show for traffic police who stopped her.
New lexical content.
http://www.e1.ru/news/spool/news_id-323570-section_id-107.html

AP-20: *Страшней отметки зверя нет* (There is no scarier animal than a [bad] grade).
Do failing grades motivate students to do better?
New lexical content.
http://zdd.1september.ru/articlef.php?ID=200601810

AP-21: *Страшней чиновника зверя нет* (There is no scarier animal than a government official).
A survey of migrant workers in Russia: what they are afraid of most of all: police, migration services, and government officials in general (53.3% of respondents).
New lexical content.
http://dlib.eastview.com/browse/doc/12542623

AP-22: *Страшнее стресса зверя нет* (There is no scarier animal than stress).
How to cope with stress and seek help.
New lexical content.
http://www.rokf.ru/carera/2009/08/24/072309.html

Comments: The first thing that strikes in this large group of anti-proverbs is that none of them (with the probable exception of #20) confirms the original message about groundless fear. In fact, they all claim exactly the opposite: the animal (someone, or something else) in question is indeed the scariest. Linguistically, #11 is the most interesting example: it is based on the wordplay between two meaning of the word *zebra* in Russia: an animal and a pedestrian crossing (that looks like a zebra because of its white stripes on the road).

Не родись красивым, а родись счастливым (It is better to be born happy than to be born beautiful).
Luck and happiness are much more important than beauty.

AP-1: *Не родись красивой, а найди хирурга* (It is better to find a surgeon than to be born beautiful).
Cosmetic surgeries of Russian movie stars.
New lexical content.
http://www.kp.ru/daily/24378/559354/

AP-2: *Не родись красивой, а родись Шосиной* (It is better to be born Shosina than to be born beautiful).
A single mother called her new born baby Shosina – after the summit of ШОС (SCO) that took place in Yekaterinburg; she was born on June 15 – when the summit started.
Note: the name *Шосина* (Shosina) is derived from the Russian abbreviation ШОС – which is The Shanghai Cooperation Organization (SCO).
Neologism.
http://www.izvestia.ru/russia/article3129787/

AP-3: *Не родись красивой, а роди и стань красивой!* (It is better to give birth and become beautiful than to be born beautiful!)
Advice to women: how to preserve good figure after giving birth to a baby.
New lexical content.
http://bt-lady.com.ua/?articleID=3510

AP-4: *Не родись красивой, а родись в России* (It is better to be born in Russia than to be born beautiful).
Car fleet of the richest woman in Russia, Elena Baturina, who is the wife of the former Moscow mayor Yury Luzhkov.
New lexical content.
http://www.today.kz/ru/news/business/2010-08-05/28061

AP-5: *Не родись солдатом, а родись миллионером* (It is better

to be born a millionaire than to be born a soldier).
A bill submitted to the Russian parliament to pay one million rubles to be excused from military draft.
New lexical content.
http://www.chaskor.ru/article/ne_rodis_soldatom_a_rodis_millionerom_17816

AP-6: *Не родись красивой, а сходи к стоматологу* (It is better to visit a dentist than to be born beautiful).
Cosmetic dentistry; consultation by orthodontic specialists about bite correction.
New lexical content.
http://www.dentoprofile.ru/php/content.php?id=639

Comments: Unlike the previous group, all these anti-proverbs confirm the message of the traditional proverb: something else is better, or more important than to be born beautiful, be it cosmetic surgery, or being the wife of Moscow mayor, or having enough money to pay for not being drafted. The most interesting example is #2, where a single mother created a name for her daughter based on the Russian abbreviation for the Shanghai Cooperation Organization (SCO); since this abbreviation is *ШОС* (SHOS), the girl's name is *Шосина* (Shosina). This trend – creating new names based on popular abbreviations – was very popular after the revolution of 1917; a lot of "revolutionary" names were created; for example, *Вилор* (Vilor) is comprised of the first letters of the Russian phrase "Vladimir Ilyich Lenin – organizer of revolution."

Всякий кулик свое болото хвалит (Every sandpiper praises its own swamp).
Said about people who overestimate their capability, and exaggerate their importance.
English equivalent: Every cook praises his own broth.

AP-1: *Всяк футболист своё болото хвалит* (Every soccer player praises his own swamp).
World soccer cup in Finland in swamp football; 340 teams.
New lexical content.

http://www.vmdaily.ru/article/101109.html

AP-2: *Всякий Шрэк свое болото хвалит* (Every Shrek praises his own swamp).
A review of the last Shrek movie – *Shrek Forever After*.
New lexical content.
http://www.shpil.com/content/shrek-nazavzhdi-vsyakii-shrek-svoe-boloto-khvalit

Comments: Both new coinages are interesting for treating the traditional proverb at its face value, as both of them do talk about swamps. This creates an unusual effect – a sort of defeated expectancy, as the readers are familiar with the proverb and expect to interpret the word *swamp* metaphorically, while in reality both articles talks about a real swamp – one is where soccer is played and the other is where Shrek lives.

Курица не птица, баба не человек (Польша не заграница).
(A hen is not a bird; a woman is not a human being (Poland is not abroad). The second part of the proverb varies.
Said about something very common and not worth paying attention to. The emphasis is always on the second part of the proverb.

AP-1: *Курица – не птица, индейка – не заграница* (A hen is not a bird, a turkey is not abroad).
A new poultry farm in Chelyabinsk oblast producing turkey.
New lexical content.
http://chel.ru/news/297952.html

AP-2: *Курица не птица, насморк не болезнь?* (A hen is not a bird, a cold is not a disease?)
Long lasting colds and how to cure them.
New lexical content.
http://www.kazved.ru/article/29716.aspx

AP-3: *Курица – не птица, женщина – не бизнесмен!* (A hen is not a bird, a woman is not a businessman!)
How difficult it is to be a business woman in Russia.

New lexical content.
http://digest.subscribe.ru/business/school/n326066922.html

AP-4: *Курица не птица, Йоханнесбург не Африка* (A hen is not a bird, Johannesburg is not Africa).
The city is very civilized and looks like any European city; the tourists do not have the impression that they are in Africa.
New lexical content.
http://www.saparov.ru/blog/30.html

AP-5: *Курица – не птица, Россия – не заграница* (A hen is not a bird, Russia is not abroad).
An article from Polish press (Kurica nie ptica, Rosja nie zagranica) about similarities in the political regimes in Poland and Russia in 2007.
Contextual antonyms.
http://www.inosmi.ru/world/20071212/238363.html

AP-6: *Курица не птица, Батуми не Ницца* (A hen is not a bird, Batumi is not Nice).
Very few tourists in Adjaria in 2009 tourist season, because of not only economic crisis, but instability in the region.
Hidden rhyme; internal rhyme.
http://analitika.at.ua/news/2009-05-28-8930

AP-7: *Курица не птица, фура – не самолет* (A hen is not a bird, a truck is not a plane).
A traffic accident with a huge truck that hit the railing on the bridge and was hanging for several hours over a busy road threatening cars below.
New lexical content.
http://www.kolesa.ru/news/2010/01/25/kuritsa_ne_ptitsa_fura_-_ne_samolet_video

AP-8: *Курица все еще не птица, а вот Болгария уже заграница* (A hen is still not bird, while Bulgaria is already abroad).
Russian tourists describe their vacations in Bulgaria.
Antonyms.
http://bulgaria.ayda.ru/stories.php?t=6861

AP-9: *Курица – не птица, а Польша – заграница* (A hen is not a bird, while Poland is abroad).
Belorussian architects describe their visit to their Polish colleagues.
Antonyms.
http://bsa.by/sobyitiya/kuritsa-%E2%80%93-ne-ptitsa-a-polsha-%E2%80%93-zagranitsa.html

AP-10: *Курица не птица, Биарриц не заграница* (A hen is not a bird, Biarritz is not abroad).
A meeting in Moscow with the writer Vasily Aksenov who lives in the town of Biarritz in France. 2002.
Metonymy.
http://www.liter.net/club/Duma/020710_Aksenov/press.htm

AP-11: *Курица – не птица, аренда – не услуга* (A hen is not a bird, a lease is not a service).
Tax agency insists that leasing is a service; thus, firms who are leasing out their space, are required to use cash registers when getting paid from the lessees.
New lexical content.
http://legalru.ru/document.php?id=31998

AP-12: *Курица не птица, Польша – заграница!* (A hen is not a bird, Poland is abroad!)
On October 1, 2003 Poland introduced visas for Russian citizens, as a requirement for its membership in the EU.
Antonym.
http://www.kp.ru/daily/23126/23658/

AP-13: *Курица – не птица, женщина – не матрос* (A hen is not a bird, a woman is not a sailor).
A woman sailor was fired because she was a woman.
New lexical content.
http://www.xronometr-ast.ru/index.php?newsid=537

AP-14: *Курица не птица, Москва не столица* (A hen is not a bird, Moscow is not a capital).
New lexical content.

wap.gazeta.kz/article/140148

Comments: There are two types of anti-proverbs here: one reaffirms the message of the original phrase about something being very ordinary (unlike what is expected or said) and not worth paying attention to. In this group, the most striking example is #5, where the tables are turned: it is a Polish author that claims that Russia is nothing different as compared to Poland, contrary to the traditional wording but preserving the core message. The other group, much more interesting, defies the original wisdom and states the opposite. Among this latter group, the most interesting examples are #8, 9, and 12, which are in fact antonymous to the traditional proverb and claim that Poland (Bulgaria) is indeed abroad now.
Note: To understand the original wording, one has to keep in mind that during Soviet Union time, travelling abroad was severely restricted for the majority of the soviet people. One could visit, as a tourist, one of the socialist countries (Poland, Bulgaria), but since their way of life and political structure were very much the same as the ones of the Soviet Union, soviet tourists did not see anything new, hence the conclusion, "Poland is not abroad." To visit a capitalist country, that is to see something that was really "abroad," was not an option.

Л

Одна ласточка весны не делает (One swallow does not make a spring).
First signs of something new do not yet mean a new quality.
English equivalent: One swallow does not make a summer.

AP-1: *Одна «белуга» весны не делает* (One beluga does not yet make a spring).
The first two German cargo ships, *Beluga Fraternity* and *Beluga Foresight*, went through Northern trade route without the help of ice-breakers. Still, it is too early to say that this route can really compete with the traditional ones.
New lexical content.
http://www.ej.ru/?a=note&id=9518

Comments: This lonely anti-proverb continues the message of the traditional proverb: it is too early to say whether this means a breakthrough in transporting cargo. An interesting feature of this new version is a certain play with the word *spring*: traditionally, one had to wait till spring (warm season) comes in order to reach northern route territories, while these two ships did not have to, and in that sense, did make spring come early.

Лес рубят – щепки летят (When they chop down wood, woodchips will fly).
In a big undertaking, it is inevitable that one makes mistakes, or expenses, or sacrifices. Said to justify some less important, from the point of view of the speaker, losses which do not diminish the overall positive value.
English equivalent: You can't make an omelet without breaking eggs.

AP-1: *Лес не рубят, а «щепки» летят* (They do not chop wood, while "woodchips" fly).
Unemployment in the village of Novaya Igirma, Irkutsk oblast, after local logging company went bankrupt.
Antonym.
http://www.irk.aif.ru/money/article/11597

AP-2: *Щепки все летят* (Woodchips still fly).
Cutting trees in Khimki forest in Moscow region; the forest is a national reserve, but in spite of that the construction of the highway on its territory continues.
Ellipsis.
http://www.gazeta.ru/comments/2010/07/26_e_3401506.shtml

AP-3: *Спирт "рубят", щепки летят* (They "chop" alcohol, woodchips fly).
Sale of alcohol as one of the major sources of revenues in the Russian budget; 2009.
Polysemy.
http://www.mk.ru/politics/article/2009/06/28/309610-spirt-rubyat-schepki-letyat.html

AP-4: *Лес уже не рубят, а щепки летят*... (They do not chop wood any more, but the wood chips still fly…)
Economic consequences of the ban to harvest forest in Kazakhstan.
Antonym.
http://articles.gazeta.kz/art.asp?aid=56636

AP-5: *Лес не рубят, а щепки (защитники Химкинского леса) летят*... (They do not chop wood, but woodchips (defenders of Khimki forest) fly…)
People protesting against cutting the forest were detained and taken to police station.
Metaphor.
http://www.vmdaily.ru/article/101638.html

AP-6: *Лес рубят — щепки в дело летят* (They chop wood – woodchips fly for a purpose).
Using woodchips as fuel for power stations, Belorussia.
Syntactic extension.
http://minpriroda.by/ru/ecosreda?id=454

AP-7: *Сибирский лес рубят, щепки по всей России летят* (When they chop wood in Siberia, woodchips fly all over Russia).
Deep timber processing in Buryatia (a subject of the Russian Federation] has been approved by the Ministry of Industry and Commerce of Russia.
New lexical content.
http://www.zabinfo.ru/modules.php?op=modload&name=News&file=article&sid=49781

AP-8: *Лес рубят — щепки в летят. А деньги уплывают* (When they chop wood, woodchips will fly. And money will flow away).
Forests, if managed properly, are a potential source of profit.
Syntactic extension.
http://infoart.udm.ru/money/press/digest/00/12/22_015.htm

AP-9: *Лес рубят – погоны летят* (When they chop wood –

shoulder straps will fly).
Reform of the Russian Ministry of the Interior.
New lexical content. Metonymy.
http://svpressa.ru/society/article/21389/

AP-10: *Тимошенко «рубят» – экс-министры «летят»* (When they “chop” Timoshenko – former minister will “fly”).
Criminal charges against former ministers in the government of Yulia Timoshenko, when she was prime-minister of Ukraine.
New lexical content; polysemy.
http://www.from-ua.com/politics/a405336c70b27.html

AP-11: *ГЭС рубят — щепки летят* (When they chop the hydro-electric power station, woodchips will fly).
Building Boguchansky reservoir for a hydro-power station in Siberia.
New lexical content.
http://www.runewsweek.ru/country/33326/

P-12: *Лес рубят – миллионы летят* (When they chop wood, millions will fly).
Illegal forest harvesting in Russia.
New lexical content.
http://www.sovsekretno.ru/magazines/article/1073

AP-13: *Закон рубят – скверы летят!* (When they chop a law, parks will fly!)
A new ordinance in Saint-Petersburg, according to which the number of protected parks in the city got 1/3 smaller.
New lexical content; polysemy.
http://www.smena.ru/news/2010/07/05/17481/

AP-14: *Губернаторов рубят — спикеры летят* (When they chop governors – speakers will fly).
An alleged connection between the arrest of the governor of Nenets national okrug and criminal investigation against the speaker of Nenets parliament.
New lexical content; polysemy.
http://www.kommersant.ru/doc.aspx?DocsID=680490

AP-15: *Парк рубят – студенты летят* (When they chop a park, students will fly).
Persecution of students who were protesting against cutting trees in the city park of Kharkov.
New lexical content.
http://mediaua.com.ua/detail/72777

AP-16: *Лес рубят – зубы летят* (When they chop wood, teeth will fly).
Fights between residents of Yaltinskaya street in Kaliningrad and a contractor who decided to build an apartment building in the place of the old park.
New lexical content.
http://www.klops.ru/news/24745.html

AP-17: *Лес рубят — иски летят* (When they chop wood, law-suits will fly).
Court disputes about illegal auctions where forest plots in Mos-cow oblast were sold for less than fair value.
New lexical content.
http://www.kommersant.ru/doc.aspx?DocsID=896441

AP-18: *Лес рубят — протесты летят* (When they chop wood, protests will fly).
The legislature of Novosibirsk oblast found cases of illegal forest harvesting.
New lexical content.
http://newsib.net/index.php?newsid=3135

AP-19: *Лес рубят — головы летят* (When they chop wood, heads will fly).
Minister of Forestry of Primorsky Kray is suspended for the time of investigation of alleged illegal forest harvesting in his region.
New lexical content.
http://www.expert.ru/news/2010/05/28/primorie?esr=19

AP-20: *Лес рубят – подати летят* (When they chop wood, forestry tax will fly).
Should tax payers pay forestry taxes.

New lexical content.
http://www.lawmix.ru/comm/5147/

AP-21: *Калий рубят – крошки летят* (When they chop potassium, crumbs will fly).
State monopoly for exporting potassium salt in Belorussia.
New lexical content.
http://www.belgazeta.by/20060828.34/040260421/

AP-22: *Капусту рубят – кочерыжки летят?* (When they chop cabbage, cabbage stalks will fly?)
Bankruptcy procedure for "Alyans-Bank" and the consequences for minority shareholders in Kazakhstan.
Metaphor; polysemy.
http://www.respublika-kaz.info/news/finance/7813/

AP-23: *Кабель рубят – жалобы летят* (When they chop cable, complaints will fly).
Thefts of phone cable in Donetsk; as a result, phones of residents do not work.
New lexical content.
http://old.donbass.ua/get-news/id/5408/article.html

AP-24: *Лес рубят – дрова в Европу летят* (When they chop wood, firewood will fly to Europe).
Export of firewood from Belorussia to Europe.
New lexical content.
http://lida.in/news/a-504.html

AP-25: *Лес рубят – искры летят* (When they chop wood, sparks will fly).
Illegal harvesting of forest often leads to disruption of electricity, when trees fall on power lines.
New lexical content.
http://www.ust-kazan.ru/les-rubyat-iskri-letyat-262970.php

AP-26: *НДС рубят – щепки летят* (When they chop VAT, woodchips will fly).

Russian government plans to lower value added tax and at the same time to eliminate industries that are exempt from the tax; thus, it is expected that the amount of tax collected will increase.
New lexical content.
http://dlib.eastview.com/browse/doc/3664584

AP-27: *Лес рубят, спутники летят* (They chop wood, satellites fly.)
Photographs from space found stolen timber worth nearly five billion rubles; 2005.
New lexical content.
http://www.mnr.gov.ru/part/?act=print&id=862&pid=431

AP-28: *Лёд рубят – искры летят!* (When they chop ice, sparks will fly!)
Festival of ice sculptures in Novosibirsk.
New lexical content.
http://novosibirsk.rfn.ru/rnews.html?id=94873

AP-29: *"Кедр" рубят — щепки летят* (When they chop "Kedr," woodchips will fly).
Hockey club "Kedr" lost a game to another club, "Barys."
Polysemy.
http://www.info-tses.kz/red/article.php?article=13313&print=Y

AP-30: *Лес рубят, чешуя летит* (When they chop wood, scale will fly).
Ministry of agriculture of RF now includes all renewable resources, including fish industry and forest industry.
New lexical content.
http://www.agroru.com/news/151628.htm?print=Y

Comments: This is the largest group of anti-proverbs based on one traditional proverb. This can partly be explained by the fact that both key words that are preserved in all new coinages (both verbs) can have multiple meanings. Thus, the first verb – *рубят* besides its meaning "to chop, cut," which is realized in the original phrase, can also mean "speak bluntly, to criticize or persecute somebody"; the second verb – *летят* – again, besides the usual meaning "to fly" used in the traditional proverb can mean "disappear, be demoted," etc. Thus, we have more or less two basic groups here: one does talk about wood, whether it be illegal wood harvesting (#12, 19, 25, 27), or a wood processing plant going bankrupt (#1), or paying forestry tax (#20). The other group, using the traditional structure, talks about something completely different: criminal charges against former ministers in Ukraine (#10), reforming the Ministry of the Interior of Russia (#9), ice sculptures (#28), students and environmentalists protecting parks and forests (#5, 15). Thus, the word *щепки* (woodchips) can be used to mean people (#5); in another example, *кочерыжки* (cabbage stalk) has the same meaning, as in the context it refers to minority shareholders (#22). Linguistically, several examples are of interest: in #5, there is a metaphor (woodchips=people; both of no importance); another metaphor in #22, where cabbage stalk once again refers to people who are not important; in the same proverb, we have polysemy: *капуста* (cabbage) in slang means "money", and since the article describes bancrutpcy procedure, it is clear that money is the key problem for share-holders. In #9, there is an example of metonymy (*shoulder straps* mean military people); and in #29, the name of the hockey team is *Kedr*, which means "cedar" in Russian; this creates a play on two meanings of the word: one can chop wood (including cedar), and the team lost the game, so it was "chopped" in a sense.

Чем дальше в лес, тем больше дров (The farther into the forest, the more wood).
The further one is involved into some undertaking, the more problems or unexpected circumstances appear which are not easy to deal with.

AP-1: *Чем дальше в лес, тем больше стресс* (The farther into the forest, the more stress).
Confrontation of environmentalists, builders, and thugs in the Khimki forest near Moscow, where a new highway is being built.
Internal rhyme.
http://www.kp.ru/daily/24529/674915/

AP-2: *Чем дальше в лес, тем больше срок* (The farther into the forest, the longer the term).
Initiatives of Russian politicians to extend the presidential term in Russia.
New lexical content.
http://articles.gazeta.kz/art.asp?aid=108448

AP-3: *Чем дальше в Таможенный союз, тем больше вопросов* (The farther into the Customs Union, the more questions).
Problems of the customs union of Russia, Belorussia, and Kazakhstan.
New lexical content.
http://www.ej.by/economy/2010-01-27/chem_dalshe_v_tamojenniy_soyuz_tem_bolshe_voprosov.html

AP-4: *Чем дальше в тундру, тем больше кочек...* (The farther into tundra, the more knolls…)
Disputes about creating an agency representing all saami of Murmansk oblast.
http://www.mvestnik.ru/shwpgn.asp?pid=20090203197

AP-5: *Чем дальше в лес, тем больше SMS* (The farther into the forest, the more text messages).
More and more people in Latvia are getting anonymous fraudulent text messages or messages with threats.
New lexical content; internal rhyme.
http://www.chas-daily.com/win/2010/03/11/lk059.html?r=2&

AP-6: *Чем дальше в лес – тем больше штрафы* (The farther into the forest, the bigger the fines).
Fines for violating environmental laws in Belorussia.
New lexical content.
http://abw.by/number/see_note/7104/

AP-7: *Чем дальше в лес, тем больше... хлама!* (The farther into the forest, the more… garbage!)
The problem of garbage left by people in the forests.
New lexical content.

http://www.stapravda.ru/20050129/Chem_dalshe_v_les_tem_bol
she_hlama_16196.html

AP-8: *Чем дальше в лес, тем больше скинхедов* (The farther into the forest, the more skinheads).
A fight between young people of different nationalities in Stravropol; May 2007.
New lexical content.
http://www.gazeta.ru/2007/05/25/oa_240114.shtml

AP-9: *Чем дальше в рекламу, тем больше партизан* (The farther into advertisement, the more guerillas).
"Guerilla" PR and marketing.
Polysemy.
http://articles.gazeta.kz/art.asp?aid=145426

AP-10: *Чем дальше в лес, тем меньше мебели* (The farther into the forest, the less furniture).
Production of furniture in Latvia: though export of furniture increased, import of furniture in 2006 increased much more: 4.6% and 40.2%.
Antonym.
http://www.gorod.lv/novosti/33634-chem_dalshe_v_les_tem_
menshe_mebeli

AP-11: *Чем дальше в лес — тем больше ущерб* (The farther into the forest, the more the damage).
Damages from illegal forest harvesting in Grodno oblast in Belorussia.
New lexical content.
http://respublika.info/4952/crime/article37638/

Comments: We have two different groups of anti-proverbs here: in the first one, the reference to forest is used in the same way as it is used in the traditional proverb, that is, metaphorically: the deeper one is involved in some undertaking, the more problems appear. Consequently, proverbs in this group talk about problems of the customs union (#3), or anonymous text messages (#5), or a suggestion to extend the presidential term in Russia (#2). The other group uses the phrase about the forest literally, and hence talks about garbage left by campers (#7), or fines for illegal harvesting (#6), or fights between environmentalists and builders for Khimki forest near Moscow (#1). From the point of view of the form, some new coinages have more features of the traditional proverbs than the real one; thus, some of them boast internal rhyme (the traditional proverb in question does not have it) – #1 and 5; another interesting coinage is #9, about guerilla PR. Obviously, guerillas, in the true sense of the word, are associated with forests, thus, even though this particular anti-proverb has no forest in its structure, this association seems to be enough to substitute for that.

Лбом стену не прошибешь (You can't break a wall by beating your head against it).
It makes no sense and is useless to resist a force, or those in power; you will achieve nothing.

AP-1: *Чиновничью стену ларьком не прошибешь* (You can't break bureaucratic wall by a kiosk).
Small businesses against the government of Saint-Petersburg; 2006.
Metonymy.
http://www.kadis.ru/daily/dayjust.phtml?id=26581

AP-2: *Бюрократическую стену НАНУ и ВАК лбом не прошибешь* (You cannot break the bureaucratic wall of National Academy of Science of Ukraine and of Higher Attestation Commission [organ approving academic degrees and titles] by beating your head against it).
The situation in Ukraine with fundamental research and grants for it; real scientists cannot work and have to leave; the author – Vasily Tkach (originally from Ukraine), University of North Dakota, USA.
New lexical content.
http://www.zn.ua/3000/3100/56374/

Comments: Both new coinages preserve the message of the traditional proverb: it is useless to resist those in power, both for small businesses (represented, by way of metonymy, by a kiosk in the phrase) and for scientists.

На ловца и зверь бежит (Wild animals run into hunters).
Said with satisfaction when one unexpectedly meets someone whom one wanted to see.

AP-1: *На истца и зверь бежит* (Wild animals run into plaintiffs).
Swiss citizens go to a referendum to answer the question if animals who suffered from human abuse need defense attorneys in courts.
Hidden rhyme.
http://www.runewsweek.ru/globus/32884/

AP-2: *На пловца и зверь бежит* (Wild animals run into swimmers).
Different types of swimming techniques.
Hidden rhyme.
http://www.top4man.ru/telo/dvizhenie/kak-nauchitsya-plavat/

AP-3: *На бойца и зверь бежит* (Wild animals run into fighters).
A review of the movie "The Men Who Stare at Goats."
Hidden rhyme.
http://www.kommersant.ru/doc.aspx?DocsID=1289300

AP-4: *На иностранца и зверь бежит* (Wild animals run into foreigners).
Hunting tourism for foreigners in Latvia.
New lexical content.
http://www.telegraf.lv/tags/turizm/news/na-inostranca-i-zvery-bezhit

AP-5: *На кредитного ловца и зверь бежит* (Wild animals run into credit hunters).
Swindlers offer loans without security deposits or processing documents.
New lexical content.

http://fin.zakon.kz/kazakhstan/72108-na-kreditnogo-lovca-i-zver-bezhit.html

AP-6: *На Кэмерон Диаз и зверь бежит* (Wild animals run into Cameron Diaz).
The name of Cameron Diaz is often used by phishers to attract users to malicious websites.
New lexical content.
http://ins.tut.ua/news/view/61798/

Comments: None of the new coinages retain the original message of the proverb, and use it simply as the literal expression; thus, discussing animal rights in courts (#1), or hunting tourism for foreigners (#4), or people's obsession with Cameron Diaz used by hackers (#6). The first three anti-proverbs use hidden rhyme as another means to create a stronger association with the traditional proverb; all three substitutions: *истца, пловца, бойца* (plaintiff, swimmer, fighter) rhyme with the original word *ловца* (hunter).

Дорога ложка к обеду (A spoon is valuable at dinner time).
Precious is that which appears when it is necessary.

AP-1: *Дорога ложка не к обеду* (A spoon is valuable not at dinner time).
A band of spoon players from Amur oblast, Chigirinskaya high school.
Antonym.
http://www.ampravda.ru/2009/06/09/021836.html

AP-2: *Дорога ложка к обеду, а ланч-боксы к завтраку* (A spoon is valuable at dinner time, and lunch boxes – at breakfast).
Advertisement of lunch boxes and other disposable tableware.
Syntactic extension.
http://www.centrpak.ru/lanch_boksi.html

AP-3: *Дорога ложка к обеду, а сеялка – к посевной* (A spoon is valuable at dinner time, and a seed planter – at sowing time).

Because of lack of money, peasant in Kazakhstan cannot purchase the necessary machinery for spring field work.
Syntactic extension.
http://agrozharshy.kz/index.php?option=com_content&view=article&id=52:2010-02-08-05-57-31&catid=11:2010-01-30-05-54-38&Itemid=13

AP-4: *Дорога ложка к обеду, а льнотеребилки – к уборке* (A spoon is valuable at dinner time, and flex pullers – at the harvest time).
In Belorussia.
Syntactic extension.
http://news.21.by/economics/2010/02/23/468870.html

AP-5: *Ложки не к обеду дороги* (Spoons are valuable not at dinner time).
An artisan carving unique wooden spoons.
Antonym.
http://www.msn.kg/ru/news/27833/

AP-6: *Дорога ложка к обеду, а дача – к лету, или Выбираем дачу!* (A spoon is valuable at dinner time, and dacha[summer cottage] – in summer!)
How to find a dacha for summer; Uzbekistan.
Syntactic extension.
http://www.stroyka.uz/publish/doc/text55053_doroga_lojka_k_obedu_a_dacha_-_k_letu_ili_vybiraem_dachu

AP-7: *Дорога дыня к обеду* (A melon is valuable at dinner time).
What dishes can be prepared from melons.
New lexical content.
http://newspaper.moe-online.ru/view/221448.html

AP-8: *Юрий Луценко: дорога рюмка к обеду* (Yury Lutsenko: a wineglass is valuable at dinner time).
International alcohol scandal with the chief policeman of Ukraine.
New lexical content.

http://noviny.narod.ru/smi-00000851.html

AP-9: *Дорога но-шпа к обеду* (No-spa [a popular medicine] is expensive at dinner time).
Citizens of the city of Omsk prefer cash to reduced-price medicine.
New lexical content.
http://www.rg.ru/2007/12/11/reg-irtysh/dlo.html

AP-10: *Дорога картошка к обеду...* (Potato is expensive at dinner time…)
High potato prices in Belorussia.
New lexical content.
http://www.perspektiva-info.com/-mainmenu-7/7/3776-2010-07-16-15-23-17

AP-11: *Дорога рыбка к обеду* (Fish is expensive at dinner time).
Should fish hatcheries in Irkutsk oblast be restored?
New lexical content.
http://pressa.irk.ru/friday/2008/06/008001.html

Comments: These anti-proverbs use various meanings of the polysemic word *дорогой* (valuable, important, precious, expensive, dear). Thus, some of them claim that something is valuable at a certain time – in the same way that a spoon is at dinner time (#2, 3, 6, 7); others state that something is too expensive (#9, 10. 11). Besides, using an antonymous structure, some new proverbs claim that a spoon is important at some other time – and they do mean spoon (#1, 2). As for #8, which describes a scandal with the chief policeman of Ukraine, it looks like here the reference to the traditional proverb is used simply to attract readers' attention, and has little to do with its message.

Близок локоть, да не укусишь (Your elbow is close, but you can't bite it).
It seems that something is easy to achieve, but it turns out there is no possibility to do it.

AP-1: *Близок трактор, да не укусишь...* (A tractor is close, but you cannot bite it…)
Cash for old tractors program; why it is not effective: discounts are only 250,000-600,000 rubles, while a new combine costs four million rubles.
New lexical content.
http://1kmv.ru/blog/event/376.html

AP-2: *Близок бонус, да не укусишь* (A bonus is near, but you can't bite it).
European parliament limited bonuses for bankers.
New lexical content.
http://www.tribuna.ru/news/2010/07/29/news4321/

AP-3: *Близок "Локо", да не укусишь* ("Loko" is close, but you can't bite it).
Soccer championship in Kazakhstan; "Lokomotiv" is one of the best teams.
Paronymy; hidden rhyme.
http://www.vecher.kz/?S=19-200909240540

AP-4: *Близок газ, да не укусишь* (Gas is near, but you can't bite it).
Problems with gasification of villages in the republic of Chuvashiya.
New lexical content.
http://gov.cap.ru/hierarhy.asp?page=./22/20106/20109/40498/40539

AP-5: *Близок овощ, да не укусишь* (Vegetables are near, but you cannot bite them).
Problems with growing vegetables in Krasnoyarsky krai.
New lexical content.
http://www.regnum.ru/news/1044676.html

Comments: All anti-proverbs in this group preserve the meaning of the traditional proverb: it is impossible to achieve/get something even though it seems to be so close or near. Linguistically, the best coinage is #3, where the shortened name of the soccer team *Локо* (Loko) sounds very similar to the original word *локоть* (elbow).

Против лома нет приема (There is no way to fight/nothing you can do against a crowbar).
It is impossible and useless to confront force, power.
English equivalent: Might makes right.

AP-1: *Государство — это тот самый лом, против которого нет приёма* (Government is that very crowbar against which you can do nothing).
The role of government in volatility of the stock market in Russia.
Syntactic extension.
http://superinvestor.ru/archives/4417

AP-2: *Против лома нет пункта приема* (There is no collection station against scrap metal).
How much money one can make for scrap metal; Saint-Petersburg.
Homonymy.
http://www.kadis.ru/daily/?id=15302

AP-3: *Против лома нет приема, если в доме нет домкома* (There is nothing you can do against a crowbar if the house has no house committee).
How to effectively control the work of the house managing company.
Syntactic extension, internal rhyme.
http://gorgaz.tomsk.ru/2010/06/10/protiv-loma-net-priema-esli-v-dome-net-domkoma/

AP-4: *Против разлома нет приема* (There is nothing you can do against a seismic fault).
What will happen to Almaty (Kazakhstan) in case of an earthquake.
Hidden rhyme; internal rhyme.
http://www.nomad.su/?a=20-200806180808

AP-5: *Против лома нет приема, коль на рынке мало лома* (There is nothing you can do against a crowbar if there is little scrap metal on the market).
High prices for scrap metal in Middle East led to increase in prices for long products.
Syntactic extension, internal rhyme.
http://www.metaldaily.ru/news/news28639.html

AP-6: *Физика рукопашного боя. Против лома нет приема – против лома есть рычаг* (Physics of the hand-to-hand combat. There is nothing you can do against a crowbar – but there is a lever against a crowbar).
Syntactic extension.
http://www.russtil.ru/info/massmedia/43-2010-06-26-13-34-22

AP-7: *Против ЛОМа нет приема* (There is nothing you can do against LOM [abbreviation for "railway transport police unit"]).
Safety of cargo transported by railway.
Homonymy.
http://www.uzmetronom.com/2008/03/03/protiv_loma_net_prie ma.html

AP-8: *Против взлома нет приема* (There is nothing you can do against hacking).
National bank of Ukraine warned about vulnerability of internet-banking.
Hidden rhyme; internal rhyme.
http://proit.com.ua/digest/telecom/2010/05/17/091447.html

AP-9: *Против слома нет приема* (There is nothing you can do against demolition).
Court executive continue demolishing houses in Rechnik settlement [allegedly built illegally].
Hidden rhyme; internal rhyme.
http://www.zagolovki.ru/article/27Jan2010/snos

AP-10: *Против иены нет приема* (There is nothing you can do against yen).
Investors are buying Japanese securities, protecting their savings

against a possible growth of interest rates in the USA and Europe.
New lexical content.
http://www.kommersant.ru/doc.aspx?DocsID=1485088

AP-11: *Против комы нет приема* (There is nothing you can do against coma).
Measures taken by the US government to stop recession and their effectiveness.
Hidden rhyme; internal rhyme.
http://dlib.eastview.com/browse/doc/19376829

AP-12: *Против Месси нет приема* (There is nothing you can do against Messi).
Lionelle Messi scored four goals in the match Barcelona – Arsenal, 4:1.
New lexical content.
http://fanat.ua/news/uefa/2010/04/07/lch_protiv_mess_72592.html

AP-13: *Против "грома" нет приема* (There is nothing you can do against "Thunder").
NBA match between Boston Celtics and Oklahoma Thunder.
Hidden rhyme; internal rhyme.
http://pressball.by/news.php?&id=66770

Comments: Some of the new coinages use the play on words, based on homonymy of two Russian words: *лом* (crowbar) and *лом* (scrap metal) – namely, #2 and 5. One more anti-proverb uses the same device, but this time we have a homonymous abbreviation – *ЛОМ* (in this case, it is "railway transport police unit"; #7). Also, there is another group that follows the pattern of the original proverb and preserves internal rhyme by choosing a new word which rhymes with the original word *лома* ("crow-bar" in the genitive case), and by preserving the basic message – there is nothing you can do against something (#4, 7, 8, 9, 11, 13). The most interesting in this group is the last one where the proverb substitutes the original word *лома* by the Russian word *грома* (thunder), which is a perfect fit, as it both rhymes with the word it replaces and with the remaining part of the original proverb; besides, rhythmically this substitution is perfect, as both words (*грома – лома*) are two-syllable words with the stress on the second syllable. Obviously, the proverbs where the internal rhyme is lost look much less attractive (#10, 11, 12).

Поспешишь – людей насмешишь (If you do something in haste, you will only make people laugh).
If you do something in a hurry, you will do it badly. Said as advice not to be in a hurry, or as a reproach when something done in haste led to poor results.
English equivalent: Haste makes waste.

AP-1: *Поспешишь — людей испугаешь* (If you do something in haste, you will scare people).
Too quick enforcing the official language in Kyrgyzstan.
New lexical content.
http://www.msn.kg/ru/news/14061/

AP-2: *Поспешишь – людей... восхитишь!* (If you do something in haste, you will be admired by people!)
A quick goal, on the first minute of the game, in a soccer match in the championship of Russia.
New lexical content; hidden rhyme, internal rhyme.
http://sport.rambler.ru/news/football/582274728.html

Comments: Between these two proverbs, the second one preserves the internal rhyme and thus also has hidden rhyme with the original wording; the first one does not have that, and as a result, looks and sounds much worse. It is still, no doubt, associated with the traditional proverb, as it preserves two key parts: *Поспешишь – людей* ______ (If you do something in a hurry, _____people).

Свои люди – сочтемся (We are close relatives, so we will pay back what we owe each other).
Close relatives will always pay back what they owe to each other.

AP-1: *Свои люди – сочтёмся: нам – газ, им – флот* (We are close relatives, so we will pay back what we owe each other: we get gas, they get fleet).
Agreement between Russia and Ukraine about the Russian Black Sea fleet to stay in Ukraine for 25 years after 2017.
Syntactic extension.
http://www.from-ua.com/politics/fb65aa760c409.html

Comments: Syntactic extension narrows down the meaning of the proverb, as it talks about a specific deal between Russia and Ukraine – who are close relatives: Kiev, the capital of Ukraine, was originally the capital of Kievan Rus, medieval state of Eastern Slavs (late 9th – middle of 13th century). During soviet times, Ukraine was one of the republics of the Soviet Union, together with Russia and 13 others.

M

Мавр сделал свое дело, мавр может уходить (The Moor has done his duty; he can leave).
A person who has fulfilled his or her mission becomes unnecessary, and can leave.

AP-1: *Хиддинк сделал свое дело, Хиддинк может уходить* (Hiddink has done his duty; Hiddink can leave).
Gus Hiddink quits work as head coach of the Russian national soccer team.
New lexical content.
http://www.utro.ru/articles/2010/02/13/872692.shtml

AP-2: *Пауль сделал свое дело, Пауль может уходить* (Paul has done his duty; Paul can leave).
Octopus Paul forecasted the results of eight matches in a row during World Soccer Cup-2010.
ew lexical content.
http://www.ntv.ru/novosti/198583/

AP-3: *Жара сделала свое дело, жара может уходить* (Heat has done its duty; heat can leave).

Abnormal heat in Russia in July 2010 came to an end.
New lexical content.
http://www.dp.ru/a/2010/07/29/ZHara_sdelala_svoe_delo_zh

AP-4: *Инвестор сделал свое дело, инвестор может уходить?* (Investors have done their duty; investors can leave?)
Corporate raiding in Belorussia against foreign investors.
New lexical content.
http://naviny.by/rubrics/economic/2009/12/24/ic_articles_113_165996/

AP-5: *Кризис сделал свое дело, кризис может уходить* (Crisis has done its duty; crisis can leave).Real estate market in Kazakhstan during economic crisis.
New lexical content.
http://profinance.kz/2008/10/31/krizis-sdelal-svoe-delo-krizis-mozhet-uxodit.html

AP-6: *Познер сделал своё дело, но уходить не собирается* (Pozner has done his duty, but he is not going to leave).
Rumors about Vladimir Pozner [TV host of a popular program] leaving Russia turned out to be not true.
Antonym.
http://www.newsland.ru/News/Detail/id/407484/

AP-7: *Маврин сделал свое дело, Маврин должен уходить* (Mavrin has done its duty; Mavrin can leave).
A concert of the rock-band “Mavrin” in Volgograd.
Paronymy.
http://www.molodoi-gazeta.ru/article-6768.html

AP-8: *Мавроди сделал свое дело – Мавроди может уходить* (Mavrody has done his duty; Mavrody can leave)
Financial pyramids in modern Russia [Sergey Mavrodi was the founder of the first pyramid].
Paronymy.
http://www.profile.ru/items/?item=2562

AP-9: *Савалайнен сделал свое дело. Финн может уходить?*

(Saavolainen has done his duty. The Finn can leave?)
Representative of International Monetary Fond Tapio Savolainen finished his three-year term of work in Kyrgyzstan.
New lexical content.
http://www.msn.kg/ru/news/11229/

AP-10: *Рынок сделал своё дело. Рынок может уходить* (The market has done its duty. The market can leave).
Russian stock market has fulfilled its mission – attracting people's saving and investing them in economy.
New lexical content.
http://www.rus-obr.ru/ru-web/877

Comments: All new proverbs continue the message of the traditional saying: someone (or something) that has done their job, can leave (though #6 claims that the person in question is not leaving), be it a soccer coach (#1) or octopus Paul (#4), or investors in Belorussian economy (#4). Linguistically, the two proverbs where the new lexical content is a paronym to the original word *Мавр* (Moor) are the best: *Маврин* (Mavrin is the name of the rock band; #7), and *Мавроди* (Mavrodi is the last name of the founder of one of the biggest ponzi schemes in Russia; #8).

Два медведя в одной берлоге не уживутся (Two bears will not live in the same den).
There cannot be two masters in the same house, or two bosses in one place.

AP-1: *Два москвича в одной берлоге* (Two Muscovites in the same den).
Two Muscovites, members of United Russia party, elected to the general council of the party.
Note: Bear is the symbol of United Russia party.
New lexical content.
http://www.apn-nn.ru/539011.html

Comments: Though I have only one example, it is a good one, as it very cleverly uses a play on the word *den* (which is associated with bears, though the word *bear* is not used in the anti-proverb) and the well-known fact that the symbol of United Russia party is a bear. Thus, *two Muscovites in the same den* in this context means *two bears in the same den*, or *two members of the United Russia party in the same place*.

О мертвых – или хорошо, или ничего (About the dead – either good, or nothing).
One should not speak badly about deceased persons. Often said as an explanation, why only praise is said about the dead.
The proverb is often quoted in *Latin*: De mortibus aut bene, aut nihil.

AP-1: *О выборах или хорошо, или ничего* (About the elections, either good or nothing).
Presidential elections in Poland after the tragic death of president Kachinsky.
New lexical content.
http://www.kommersant.ru/doc.aspx?DocsID=1354461

AP-2: *О Селигере-2010: хорошо или ничего* (About Seliger, either good or nothing).
A journalist for a Saint-Petersburg newspaper was evicted from the Seliger camp for criticizing it.
Note: Seliger is an annual youth camp organized by the ruling United Russia party.
New lexical content.
http://www.newsland.ru/News/Detail/id/534185/

AP-3: *Об МВД — или хорошо, или ничего* (About the Ministry of Interior, either good or nothing).
Police officers will be prohibited to criticize their bosses, according to the amendment to the law “On Militia.”
New lexical content.
http://www.mk.ru/social/article/2010/06/30/513412-ob-mvd-ili-horosho-ili-nichego.html

AP-4: *О союзнике либо хорошо, либо ничего* (About an ally, either good or nothing).

Vladimir Putin, prime-minister of Russia at the time, did not mention Alexander Lukashenko's [president of Belorussia] name during his meeting with prime-minister of Belorussia.
New lexical content.
http://www.kommersant.ua/doc-rss.html?docId=1251405&issueId=7000247

AP-5: *О Казахстане либо хорошо, либо ничего* (About Kazakhstan, either good or nothing).
A summit of foreign minister of countries – members of OSCE [Organization for Security and Cooperation in Europe]; they did not criticize Kazakhstan government there, though behind the scenes it was obvious that there were reason for criticism: Kazakhstan did not meet its obligation in the area of human rights, freedoms, elections, etc.
New lexical content.
http://www.respublika-kaz.biz/news/polit_process/3341/

AP-6: *Про Юлию Тимошенко теперь либо хорошо, либо ничего* (About Yulia Timoshenko, either good or nothing).
New lexical content.
media.rin.ru/news/215456/

Comments: All new proverbs continue the message of the original phrase, with one important difference: the traditional proverb explains and approves of not talking badly about deceased person, while the new proverbs criticize some entity or people for not allowing any criticisms, be it elections in Poland (#1), a youth camp (#2), or an ally (#4).

Не место красит человека, а человек место (It isn't the place that graces the man, but the man the place).
The qualities of people are important, not their position or status. Often said to acknowledge the accomplishments of a person who occupies a very modest position, or of a person who deserves a higher status.

AP-1: *Не одежда красит человека, а человек одежду* (It is not the clothes that grace the man, but the man the clothes).

New lexical content.
http://www.woman.ru/psycho/personality/thread/3979597/

AP-2: *Не имя человека красит, а человек имя* (It is not the name that graces the man, but the man the name).
An article about Kazakh personal names.
New lexical content.
http://diapazon.kz/aktobe/aktobe-news/29625-ne-imja-cheloveka-krasit-a-chelovek-imja.html

AP-3: *Не фамилия красит человека, а человек фамилию* (It is not the family name that graces the man, but the man the family name).
The genealogical tree of the Bezobrazov family.
Note: Bezobrazov means "ugly" in Russian, hence the message of the title and of the article.
New lexical content.
http://www.sbras.ru/HBC/hbc.phtml?32+173+1

Comments: The new coinages use the message of the traditional proverb, but specify it, and make it less general and probably less important, more adjusted to a concrete situation; the best example is the last anti-proverb (#3) that basically says that even if your last name sounds awful (its literal meaning is "ugly") it does not mean anything, because what you do as a person (or what other people in your family, with the same last name, do) is much more important.

Свято место пусто не бывает (The holy place is never empty).
A position which is lucrative or has great prospects will never be empty – there will always be people who would like to take it.

AP-1: *Пусто место свято не бывает…* (An empty place is never holy…)
Traffic police fabricating traffic accidents to avoid investigation.
Chiasmus.
http://www.mk.ru/auto/article/2010/01/13/411558-pusto-mesto-svyato-ne-byivaet.html

AP-2: *Свято место уже не пусто* (A holy place is not empty any more).
A Moscow company wants its share of the oil market in Stavropolsky krai.
Antonym.
http://www.stapravda.ru/20050303/Svyato_mesto_uzhe_ne_pusto_16665.html

AP-3: *Свято ГИУ пусто не бывает* (A holy Ukrainian State Agency is never empty).
Staff problems in Ukrainian State Mortgage Agency have negative effect on its work.
New lexical content.
http://www.oligarh.net/?/themeofday/10217/

AP-4: *И свято место бывает пусто* (A holy place can be empty, too).
Review of the movie *The Boondock Saints II: All Saints Day*.
Antonym.
http://art.gazeta.kz/news/?id=1660

AP-5: *"Свято" здание пусто не бывает* (A "holy" [sacred] building is never empty).
French association for the right to housing occupied an empty building in Paris next to Arc de Triumph to protest current housing situation in France; 2003.
New lexical content.
http://www.rian.ru/world/20030105/294382.html

Comments: Only one new proverb continues the message of the original phrase – #2. All the rest have little to do with it. Thus, #1 reverses the syntax of the original statement and talks about police fabricating traffic accidents; #4 uses an allusion to the title of the movie (and that is the only connection between the proverb and the movie), while #5 uses the word *holy* simply to emphasize that desperate people will occupy any empty building, even if it is next to one of the most famous monuments in Paris.

Насильно мил не будешь (You can't win love by force).

Said with disappointment when a person, in spite of all the efforts, is not sympathetic to someone else, and has to put up with it.

AP-1: *Насильно Милош не будешь* (You can't be Milosh by force).
Russian soccer Central Army Club sold Milosh Krasich to Uventus for 15 million euros.
Paronymy.
http://www.rusfootball.info/rss/1146126836-nasilno-milosh-ne-budesh.html

AP-2: *Насильно трезв не будешь* (You can't be sober by force).
Members of the Public Chamber [advisory body to President of Russia] demanded to close all sobering-up stations [a medical facility in which intoxicated people can spend one night to become sober under medical control] as de facto illegal jails.
New lexical content.
http://news.vtomske.ru/news/20398.html

AP-3: *Насильно чист не будешь* (You can't be tidy by force).
How to teach children to keep their country tidy.
New lexical content.
http://www.ng.by/ru/issues?art_id=46502

AP-4: *Насильно привит не будешь* (You can't get vaccinated by force).
Immunization of children and whether it is obligatory or not in Russia.
New lexical content.
http://www.stapravda.ru/20061115/Nasilno_privit_ne_budesh_6769.html

AP-5: *Насильно здоров не будешь* (You can't be healthy by force).
Treating drug addicts – should it be obligatory.
New lexical content.
http://info.sibnet.ru/?id=276122

AP-6: *Насильно беден будешь* (You can be poor by force).
Kazakh national currency tenge fell sharply because of the economic crisis.
New lexical content.
http://www.zakon.kz/135032-nasilno-beden-budesh.-vnezapnoe-padenie.html

AP-7: *Шон Пенн. Насильно Милк не будешь* (Sean Penn. You can't be Milk by force).
Sean Penn's interview to *Rolling Stone* magazine.
Paronymy.
http://www.rollingstone.ru/articles/7667

Comments: All new coinages retain a part of the original message – you can't do something by force, but change what this something is. The most interesting coinages are #1 and #7, where there is paronymy between the original *мил* (loved) and the last name of the soccer player *Милош* (Milosh) or the name of the main character Harvey Milk, an American gay rights activist, played by Sean Penn in the movie with the same title.

Худой мир лучше доброй ссоры (Better a bad peace than a good quarrel).
Tense but peaceful relations are better than open hostility or conflict.
English equivalent: A bad compromise is better than a good lawsuit.

AP-1: *Худой Кабмин лучше доброй ссоры* (Bad cabinet of ministers is better than a good quarrel).
Two members of Ukrainian government made up their dispute.
New lexical content.
http://obkom.net.ua/articles/2010-03/24.1703.shtml

AP-2: *Добрая ссора лучше худой "Дружбы"?* (A good quarrel is better than a bad "Friendship"?)
Relations between Russia and Belorussia.
Chiasmus.
http://www.izvestia.ru/debate/article3100044/

AP-3: *Худой мир или добрая ссора?* (A bad peace or a good quarrel?)
Should one keep negative emotions inside?
Syntactic restructuring.
http://www.aif.ru/health/article/36477

Comments: If the first anti-proverb reaffirms the message of the original proverb, the other two question it, and both do this by changing the syntax: in #2, good quarrel becomes the subject of the Russian sentence (it was an object in the traditional proverb), while in #3 we have an alternative question, which is not something the traditional proverb meant. Besides, there is a wordplay in #2: the Russian word *дружба* (friendship) in quotation marks is the name of the oil and gas pipeline built in the soviet times and going through the territory of the former soviet republics – Ukraine and Belorussia (now independent countries).

Горбатого могила исправит (Only grave will cure the hunchback). A person's habits or drawbacks cannot be changed. Usually said when people witness another situation when those drawbacks or habits are revealed.
English equivalent: Can the leopard change its spots?

AP-1: *Милицию могила исправит?* (Only grave will cure police?).
Reform of the Ministry of the Interior of Russia.
New lexical content.
http://www.kommersant.ru/doc.aspx?DocsID=1484396

AP-2: *"Горбатую гору" могила исправит* (Only grave will cure the "Brokeback Mountain").
The death of Heath Ledger.
Homonymy (cognate words)
http://www.kommersant.ru/doc.aspx?DocsID=844910

AP-3: *Маньяков только могила исправит* (Only grave will cure maniacs).
Pedophiles in Saint-Petersburg.

New lexical content.
http://www.rosbalt.ru/2010/06/08/743714.html

AP-4: *Чарли Шина могила исправит* (Only grave will cure Charlie Sheen).
The famous actor is accused of domestic violence towards his wife, Brook Muller.
New lexical content.
http://eg.dev.kp.ru/daily/worldstars/16462/

AP-5: *Горбатую оппозицию могила не исправит* (Only grave will cure the hunchbacked opposition).
Opposition and government in today's Ukraine; 2010.
New lexical content.
http://lb.ua/news/2010/05/18/44971_Gorbatuyu_oppozitsiyu_mogila_ne_isp.html

AP-6: *Горбатый "Запорожец" могила не исправит* (Only grave will not cure hunchbacked "Zaporozhets").
Note: *Zaporozhets* was a popular model of a small car in the Soviet Union; because of its shape, it got the nick-name "hunchback."
Old broken cars take all the parking spots in the yards of apartment homes.
New lexical content.
http://yuzle.com/cars/1027.html

AP-7: *Вора могила исправит?* (Only grave will cure the thief?)
Chinese police caught an 83-year old thief with 52 years of criminal record.
Syntactic restructuring; new lexical content.
http://www.zabinfo.ru/modules.php?op=modload&name=News&file=article&sid=52016&mode=thread&order=0&thold=0

AP-8: *Российский суд могила исправит* (Only grave will cure the Russian judicial system).
Court reform in Russia failed.
New lexical content.
http://svpressa.ru/society/article/27983/?from=10

AP-9: *Унылого могила исправит* (Only grave will cure a depressed person).
Advice of psychologists: in order to fight depression – dig yourself in a grave for three hours.
Defeated expectancy.
http://www.liveinternet.ru/journalshowcomments.php?jpostid=133330057&journalid=3826733&go=prev&categ=0

AP-10: *МакКартни могила исправит* (Only grave will cure McCartney).
Paul McCartney is getting married, again, soon after his divorce from Heather Mills.
New lexical content.
http://mp3ex.net/news/read.php?lid=20062

AP-11: *Windows могила исправит* (Only grave will cure Windows).
Old interface Window Mobile in new smartphones.
New lexical content.
http://news-mobil.org.ua/archives/773

AP-12: *Горбушу могила исправит* (Only grave will cure humpback salmon).
Problems of fishing industry in Russia and how to solve them and make fish cheaper and of better quality.
Paronymy.
http://www.rosinvest.com/news/592772/

Comments: The majority of anti-proverbs preserve the central message of the traditional one: you cannot change someone's habits or behavior, or you cannot change some institution. At the same time, two anti-proverbs differ substantially in their meaning: #2 and #9. In the former, the phrase is based on the fact that both the title of the movie (*Brokeback Mountain*) and the original proverb use the same word in Russian, *горбатый* (hunchback). Thus, the article, with some black humor, narrates about the death of the leading actor in the movie, Heath Ledger. In the latter, we have a very interesting example of defeated expectancy. When one reads the title, the first interpretation is that it is another case when nothing can be done (in this case – to fight depression). But after reading the article itself, it becomes clear that the message is quite the opposite, and partly because the world *могила* (grave) is used here literally, not metaphorically (as it is used in the traditional proverb and in the majority of anti-proverbs). It does talk about a recommendation of psychologists for depressed people to spend some time in the grave – and their depression will be cured.

Москва слезам не верит (Moscow does not believe in tears). Tears cannot justify someone's fault or wrongdoing. Said when someone's tears or crying does not bring compassion.

AP-1: *Украина слезам не верит* (Ukraine does not believe in tears).
TV show in Ukraine.
New lexical content.
http://ukrainaslezamneverit.com/

AP-2: *Лондон слезам не верит* (London doesn't believe in tears).
Review of the film "Bigga than Ben."
New lexical content.
http://www.kommersant.ru/doc-rss.aspx?DocsID=915314

AP-3: *Константин Меладзе слезам не верит* (Konstantin Meladze [famous Russian producer] does not believe in tears).
Casting for the new TV show in Belorussia.
New lexical content.
http://news.tut.by/177215.html

AP-4: *Россия слезам не верит* (Russia does not believe in tears).
Romanian journalists about a soccer match between Russia and Romania.
New lexical content.
http://news.sportbox.ru/Vidy_sporta/Futbol/Liga_Chempionov/spbnews_Rossiya-slezam-ne-verit

AP-5: *Прогресс слезам не верит* (Progress does not believe in tears).
Treatment of dry eyes syndrome.
New lexical content.
http://www.mosmedclinic.ru/articles/oftalmologia/310

AP-6: *Моссад слезам не верит* (Mossad does not believe in tears).
Review of the film "Munich" by Steven Spielberg.
New lexical content.
http://www.stengazeta.net/article.html?article=1130

Comments: The traditional proverb, *Москва слезам не верит* (Moscow does not believe in tears) is very popular in modern Russian, mostly because it was used as the title for the famous movie (1980), which won an Academy Award for Best Foreign Language Film in 1980. So it is little surprise that it is referenced in many modern versions, but at the same time, most of them have nothing to do with the original message, with the exception of the last proverb; it is also one of the best coinages, as *Моссад* and *Москва* (unlike Mossad and Moscow) not only sound quite similar, but also have the same rhythm and stress patterns.

Муж и жена – одна сатана (Husband and wife live the same life; *literally*: Husband and wife are the same devil).
Husband and wife are similar in their actions, wishes, aspirations. Said when a couple is perceived as a unit, connected by common interests, way of life, etc.

AP-1: *Путин, Абрамович – одна сатана* (Putin, Abramovich are the same devil).
Relationships between Putin and Abramovich [one of the richest man in Russia]; 2005.
New lexical content.
http://www.ej.ru/?a=note&id=1970

AP-2: *Муж и жена — не одна сатана* (Husband and wife are not the same devil).
Carla Bruni denies that she influences the political decisions of

her husband, French president Nikolas Sarcozy.
Antonym.
http://www.rbcdaily.ru/2009/11/16/world/441964

AP-3: *Муж и жена – не одна сатана* (Husband and wife are not the same devil).
A Vatican priest found out that men and women sin differently.
Polysemy.
http://www.newizv.ru/news/2009-08-12/113136/

Comments: All three new coinages are interesting for different reasons: while #1 claims that there is no difference between Vladimir Putin and one of the Russian oligarchs, thus effectively confirming the message of the traditional proverb (although describing a different type of relationships), #2, going back to literally husband and wife, denies the moral of the traditional proverb, at least, for that particular couple. Finally, #3 is the most interesting case. While in the traditional proverb (and other anti-proverbs), the word *сатана* (devil) is used metaphorically, in the meaning, "of the same breed" and have nothing to do with the enemy of mankind, in this case, the word *сатана* is used literally, as the sinful nature of humanity, and thus, the proverb is not simply denying that husband and wife are very much alike, but specifically says that men and women sin in a different way.

Русский мужик задним умом крепок (The Russian is wise after the event).
The best ideas or best solutions for a problem come when they are no longer needed.
English equivalent: Wise after the event.

AP-1: *Москва крепка задним умом – после "Курска"* (Moscow is wise after the event – after "Kursk").
Polish media about the different reactions of the Russian government to the catastrophe with the *Kursk* submarine (2000) and to forest fires around Moscow (2010).
New lexical content.
http://www.inosmi.ru/poland/20100810/162004725.html

AP-2: *Российский автомобилист задним умом крепок* (Russian motorists are wise after the event).
An article about problems with electric wiring in modern cars.
New lexical content.
http://www.auto99.ru/?page=373

AP-3: *Рязанский рыбак задним умом крепок* (A fisherman from Ryazan is wise after the event).
A person tried to fish illegally using the electric current from a high-voltage line; he was killed on the spot.
New lexical content.
http://www.fresher.ru/2008/05/14/ryazanskij-rybak-zadnim-umom-krepok/

Comments: All three anti-proverbs reaffirm the message of the traditional proverb: someone is being wise after the event, be it the Russian government (it was trying to hide the truth about the catastrophe on the *Kursk* submarine for a long time), or a fisherman who was killed because he did not think well before doing what he did.

Кто платит, тот и заказывает музыку (He who pays orders the music).
Those who pay the bills have the right to do as they please.
*English equiva*lent: He who pays the piper calls the tune.

AP-1: *Кто платит налоги, тот и систему заказывает* (He who pays taxes orders the system [of taxation]).
Different types of taxation for businesses in Russia.
http://lawmix.ru/comm/6303

AP-2: *Кто не платит – тот заказывает музыку* (He who does not pay orders the music).
Political, economic, language, cultural differences between various regions of Ukraine; regions who produce more do not have influence on political decisions.
Antonym.
http://www.ruska-pravda.com/index.php/200902271509/stat-i/monitoring-smi/2009-02-27-09-02-38/pechat.html

AP-3: *Кто находится при власти, тот и заказывает решение КС* (He who is in power orders the decision of the Constitutional Court).
Criticism of the work of the Constitutional Court of Ukraine.
New lexical content.
http://ubr.ua/ukraine-and-world/power/konstitucionnyi-sud-uzakonivaet-bezzakonie-52804

Comments: Two of the three anti-proverbs confirm the message of the original phrase: those who have the power (because of money or position) decide how things will be done. Anti-proverb #2 differs in the sense that it describes a reversed situation: those regions of Ukraine that produce most of the goods (eastern Ukraine where most industries are situated) have no say in political decisions.

H

Благими намерениями вымощена дорога в ад (The road to hell is paved with good intentions).
Good intentions may not guarantee good results of some actions, and may, on the contrary, lead to negative consequences.
English equivalent: Hell is paved with good intentions.

AP-1: *Благими намерениями вымощена дорога к аварии?* (The road to accidents is paved with good intentions?)
Police in Czech Republic conducted an experiment that failed: they placed cardboard figures of female police officers in min-skirts at crossroads with heavy traffic. As a result, these figures distracted drivers.
New lexical content.
http://pikabu.ru/view/blagimi_namereniyami_vyimoshchena_doroga_k_avarii_111263

AP-2: *Благими намерениями вымощена траектория полета* (The trajectory of the flight is paved with good intentions).
Decision of the US senate to authorize a new series of tests of anti-ballistic missiles after it became know that North Korea

developed and tested a new rocket that could reach the west coast of the US.
New lexical content.
http://www.apn.ru/publications/article977.htm

AP-3: *Благими намерениями вымощена... дорога в детскую поликлинику* (A road to an outpatient hospital for children is paved with good intentions).
Obligatory medical examinations of all school children in Ukraine; it is not easy for parents to comply because of long lines.
New lexical content.
http://martime.com.ua/news/104/1835/

AP-4: *Дорога в суд вымощена благими намерениями* (The road to court is paved with good intentions).
Religious sects in Russia and how difficult it is to interfere into their activities even if they mistreat children.
New lexical content.
http://blog.aif.ru/users/844254/post138521750/

AP-5: *Благими намерениями вымощена дорога в бюджетный ад...* (The road to budget hell is paved with good intentions…)
Reform of secondary education faces financial problems in Russia.
New lexical content.
http://www.ivgorod.ru/news/29139

Comments: All new proverbs, except #2, continue the message of the traditional proverb: good intentions may lead to negative consequences, be it long lines in the hospital, #3 (who would argue that regular medical exams are good), or lack of money in order to implement education reform, #5, or placing female figures on busy crossroads (#1). An unusual (and interesting) example is the phrase about trajectory of flight: in a way, it is also a kind of road, and it was authorized with really good intentions – protecting the west coast of the USA from a nuclear attack by North Korea. Thus, this new proverb clearly has a different message, and does not confirm the traditional wisdom.

Что русскому здорово, то немцу смерть (What is good for a Russian is death for a German).
What is good for one person may be bad or even dangerous for another.

AP-1: *Что русскому рублю здорово, то доллару – смерть* (What is good for the Russian ruble is death for the dollar).
Weakening of the US dollar.
New lexical content.
http://www.kp.ru/daily/23192/25820/

AP-2: *Что Америке здорово, то Евросоюзу смерть* (What is good for America is death for the European Union).
Economic recovery measures used in the US cannot be used in Europe, according to EU.
New lexical content.
http://www.inopressa.ru/article/30Mar2009/times/topolanek.html

AP-3: *Что человеку здорово, то кролику — смерть* (What is good for a human being is death for a rabbit).
Experiments using animals for testing new drugs.
New lexical content.
http://gazeta.aif.ru/online/health/428/06_01

AP-4: *То, что для "Автодора" – смерть, для Chrysler – здорово* (What is death for "Avtoдor" [Russian automakers] is good for Chrysler).
Chrysler talks with Chinese carmakers to create a joint venture; something that Russian automakers do not want to do.
New lexical content.
http://times.ua/story/21822/

AP-5: *Что корове здорово, то человеку смерть* (What is good for cows is death for people).
Some people looking for alcohol by mistake drank some medicine for cows, and got sick.

New lexical content.
http://www.ng.by/ru/issues?art_id=13128&is_pril=1

Comments: The word "death" in the traditional proverb is used metaphorically, as a symbol of something bad; three of the anti-proverbs do the same (#1, 2, 4), while the other two read the traditional phrase literally and really talk about death: in #3, it is about animals dying in order to have new drugs tested, while #5 describes a ridiculous, though tragic episode when people looking for a drink got cow's medicine by mistake and got sick.

В ногах правды нет (There is no truth in the legs).
There is no need to be standing; an invitation to sit down, usually after the words, "Please be seated."

AP-1: *В ТВ правды нет* (There is no truth on TV).
TV documentary about Sergey Esenin [a famous Russian poet of the 20th century].
New lexical content.
http://www.izvestia.ru/petrovskaya/article3019595/

AP-2: *В Химках "Правды" нет* (There is no "Truth" in Khimki).
Absence of opposition newspaper in the city of Khimki, Moscow oblast.
New lexical content; polysemy.
http://www.polit.ru/event/2010/11/11/himki.html

AP-3: *В мужиках правды нет!* (There is no truth in males!)
Video advertisement of female taxis – all drivers are women.
New lexical content.
http://rutube.ru/tracks/3423655.html?v=a9f5e7104c6ded9d7708ae99ff95ecd1

AP-4: *В деньгах правды нет* (There is no truth in money).
Inflation in Russia in 2007, and forecast for 2008.
New lexical content.
http://www.kommersant.ru/doc.aspx?DocsID=814403

Comments: None of the new proverbs has anything to do with the original saying, as they all use the word *правда* (truth) literally (etymologically, the traditional proverb did use "truth" as part of the message, but this idea is lost now). Hence, they use new lexical content to claim that there is no truth in something, be it money (because of high inflation, #4), or in TV shows (#1), or even in male taxi drivers (#3).

Своя ноша не тянет (A burden of one's own choice is not felt).
What you do for yourself does not seem to be difficult or hard.

AP-1: *Когда своя ноша тянет, или поймать грыжу в... "сети"* (When a burden of one's own choice is felt, or how to catch a hernia in the "net").
Treating a hernia by means of a special "net."
Syntactic extension.
http://donbass.ua/news/health/2009/11/19/kogda-svoja-nosha-tjanet-ili-poimat-gryzhu-v-seti.html

AP-2: *Своя ноша тянет* (A burden of one's own choice is felt).
Romanian tennis player Simona Halel underwent plastic surgery on her breasts, as their size made it difficult for her to play tennis.
Antonym.
http://www.rusrep.ru/2009/26/news_tennisistka/

AP-3: *Своя ноша* (A burden of one's own choice).
New trends in design of women's purses.
Ellipsis.
http://my-madonna.ru/index.php?option=com_content&task=view&id=551&Itemid=7

AP-4: *Интернет-магазин "Своя Ноша"* (Internet store "A Burden of One's Own Choice").
Online store selling backpacks, slings, etc. for mothers, as well as clothes for pregnant women.
New lexical content.
http://www.xn----etbobmnzoaj.xn--p1ai/

AP-5: *Если своя ноша тянет или боли в спине* (If a burden of one's own choice is felt, or back pain).
Back pain of pregnant women.
Syntactic extension.
http://www.mamochka.kz/article.php?article_id=341

Comments: Once again, all new coinages interpret the word *ноша* (burden) literally, and talk about physical weight or discomfort of something, be it a hernia (#1), female breasts (#2), or a baby (#4 and 5). The only exception is anti-proverb #3: it is about purses for women that can hardly be interpreted as a burden.

У семи нянек дитя без глазу (Seven nannies have a child without an eye).
When several people are all responsible for the same thing, the result is bad.
English equivalent: Too many cooks spoil the broth.

AP-1: *У семи нянек цены без глазу* (Seven nannies have prices without an eye).
Cost of living in Moldova is getting higher and higher, as well as inflation, while salaries are the same; 2010.
New lexical content.
http://aif.md/index.php/2010/11/17/u-semi-nyanek-ceny-bez-glazu/

AP-2: *У семи нянек МЧС без глаза* (Seven nannies have the Ministry of Emergency Situations without an eye).
Violations in the Ministry of Emergency Situations in one of the republics – subjects of RF.
New lexical content.
http://www.sknews.ru/main/38766-u-semi-nyanek-mchs-bez-glaza.html

AP-3: *У семи нянек – весь город в пробках* (Seven nannies have the whole town in traffic jams).
Government officials of five agencies responsible for transportations and roads tried to explain to journalists the reasons for

traffic jams in Saint-Petersburg.
New lexical content.
http://www.spbvoditel.ru/2010/09/10/028/

AP-4: *У семи нянек дитя без... отдыха?* (Seven nannies have children without… rest?)
Problems of organizing summer camps for children; 2010.
New lexical content.
http://chelyabinsk.ru/news/260682.html

AP-5: *У семи нянек пешеход без ноги* (Seven nannies have pedestrians without legs).
Ice on the streets of Yaroslavl leads to people breaking arms and legs; too many agencies responsible, and too little pay for those who shovel the snow and ice.
New lexical content.
http://www.sevkray.ru/news/5/10784/

AP-6: *У семи нянек дитя без газу* (Seven nannies have a child without gas).
Problems with heating houses in winter in Kyrgyzstan; 2009.
Hidden rhyme.
http://www.msn.kg/ru/news/29348/

AP-7: *У семи нянек дворник в дефиците* (Seven nannies have too few street sweepers).
Lack of street sweepers in Saint-Petersburg, and too many agencies responsible for that.
New lexical content.
http://www.baltinfo.ru/2010/02/24/U-semi-nyanek-dvornik-v-defitcite-131510

Comments: For a change, all new proverbs reaffirm the message of the traditional saying: when too many people are responsible for something, the result is poor. Thus, too many agencies responsible for transportation lead to traffic jams (#3); too many agencies responsible for cleaning the streets lead to lack of street sweepers (#5 and 7), or problems with summer camps for children (#4), etc. Linguistically, the best coinage is #6, as the new phrase *без газу* (without gas) rhymes with the original phrase *без глазу* (without an eye).

О

Всякому овощу свое время (Every vegetable has its season).
All in good time. Said when someone is in a hurry to do something.
English equivalent: Everything is good in its season.

AP-1: *Всякому оружию – свое время* (Every weapon has its season).
The title of a book, describing the history of the Sten machine gun.
New lexical content.
http://vse-knigi.su/book/53530

AP-2: *Всякому извещению свое время* (Every notifications has its season).
Procedure of excluding someone from the share-holders of a limited company.
New lexical content.
http://www.neg.by/publication/2009_09_15_12007.html

AP-3: *Всякому овощу свой пятновыводитель, или чем вывести пятна* (Every vegetable has its stain remover, or how to remove stains).
Syntactic extension.
http://www.familynews.ru/dom/3078-vivoditel.html

Comments: Though few in number, these proverbs are quite diverse. While the first two more or less continue the idea of the traditional proverb (all things are good in their own time), the third one, though formally it follows the traditional proverb much more closely, having changed only one word, interprets it in a completely different way: the word *vegetable* here means literally what it says, and thus, we are told about different stain removers for different vegetables.

С паршивой овцы хоть шерсти клок (Even a bad sheep can give a bit of wool).
If something or someone is not very useful, one has to be content with little use from it.

AP-1: *С «сочинской овцы» хоть шерсти клок* (Even a bad Sochi sheep can give a bit of wool).
Scandals during elections of the mayor of the city of Sochi in 2009.
New lexical content.
http://www.moscow-post.ru/politics/000012390801158/

AP-2: *С государства хоть шерсти клок* (Even the government can give a bit of wool).
Tax benefits when one buys an apartment in Russia.
New lexical content.
http://www.7ya.ru/article/S-gosudarstva-hot-shersti-klok/

AP-3: *С Мэла Гибсона, хоть шерсти клок* (Even Mel Gibson can give a bit of wool).
Court dispute between Mel Gibson and Oksana Grigorieva.
New lexical content.
http://www.newsland.ru/news/detail/id/556841/cat/100/

AP-4: *С Lehman Brothers хоть шерсти клок* (Even Lehman Brothers can give a bit of wool).
Lehman Brothers debt payments.
New lexical content.
http://www.rbcdaily.ru/2010/06/17/world/487052

Comments: All new coinages continue the message of the traditional proverb: if you cannot get much from somebody or something, be content with getting a little, be it getting back a part of your money from a bankrupt company (#4), scoring some political points during elections (#1), or suing Mel Gibson (#3).

Овчинка выделки не стоит (The sheepskin is not worth tanning).
The matter is not worth the money and trouble.

English equivalent: The game is not worth the candle.

AP-1: *Плотина выделки не стоит?* (The dam is not worth the tanning?)
Raising the level of water in Cheboksary dam on the Volga river may have negative consequences for the city.
Hidden rhyme.
http://www.mpr-nn.ru/index.php/2010-04-27-04-09-51/28-2010-04-26-19-15-10/369-q---q-q-q-80--28072010-

AP-2: *Починка выделки не стоит* (Repairing is not worth tanning).
Repairs services market in Russia has difficult times.
Hidden rhyme.
http://www.kommersant.ru/doc-rss.aspx?DocsID=1152419

AP-3: *«Нефтяная овчинка» выделки не стоит?* ("Oil sheepskin" is not worth tanning?)
It is more profitable to sell crude oil to other countries than processed oil.
New lexical content; metaphor.
http://fintimes.km.ru/ekonomika-rossii/neft/8787

AP-4: *Почему Косово не стоит выделки* (Why Kosovo is not worth tanning).
An article from *Newsweek*, "Why Kosovo was not worth it" 09/2008, about Kosovo precedent.
New lexical content.
http://www.inosmi.ru/world/20080901/243686.html

AP-5: *Машина выделки не СТОит* (A car is not worth tanning/ repairing).
Car thefts in car service centers in Kazakhstan, Almaty.
Homonym.
http://ust-kamenogorsk.autostan.kz/news/753

Comments: All new coinages have the same message as the original proverb: some undertaking is not worth the trouble, be it building a new dam (#1) or processing crude oil (# 3). Linguistically, we have three interesting cases: in #1 and 2, there is a hidden rhyme, as the word replacing the original word *овчинка*, rhymes with it: *плотина* (dam, #1) and *починка* (repairs, #2). A very interesting case is the last new proverb, where there is a play on words based on the coincidence between the root of the Russian word *стоит* (worth) and the abbreviation *СТО* (car servicing center); thus the proverb says: it makes no sense to have your car repaired at service centers, as chances are it will be stolen.

По одежке встречают, по уму провожают (One is greeted according to one's clothes; one is seen off according to what one knows).
Clothes count for the first impression only; a person's character, knowledge, abilities are much more important.
English equivalent: Never judge a book by its cover. Handsome is as handsome does.

AP-1: *Встречают по упаковке. Лучших провожают в музей* (One is greeted according to the packaging. The best are seen off to the museum).
Museum of the history of world packaging opened in Moscow.
Hidden rhyme. Defeated expectancy.
http://www.kp.ru/daily/24566/739409/

AP-2: *На «Оскаре» встречают по одёжке. Провожают тоже* (At Oscar ceremony, one is greeted according to one's clothes. One is seen off according to one's clothes, too).
Discussion of clothes of celebrities during Oscar ceremony.
Defeated expectancy.
http://www.lady.ru/celebs

AP-3: *Встречают по рекламе, провожают по рейтингу* (One is greeted according to the advertisements; one is seen off according to ratings).
Low quality of many MBA programs in Russia.
New lexical content.
http://www.ng.ru/education/2005-08-26/11_reklama.html

AP-4: *Встречают по выплатам, провожают по тарифу* (One is greeted according to premiums, one is seen off according to tariffs).
Tendency of development of insurance market in Ukraine in 2010.
New lexical content.
http://banki.ua/theme/?news_id=281

AP-5: *Провожают по результатам, встречают по одежке* (One is seen off according to the results; one is greeted according to one's clothes).
Sport uniforms designed for Olympic team of Ukraine for Vancouver winter Olympics in 2010.
New lexical content.
http://other.sport.ua/news/82868

AP-6: *По этикетке встречают ... а по качеству провожают* (One is greeted according to the label, one is seen off according to the quality).
Quality of food products in grocery stores in Belorussia.
New lexical content.
http://www.ng.by/ru/issues?art_id=41173

AP-7: *По одёжке встречают, по IQ провожают* (One is greeted according to one's clothes, one is seen off according to one's IQ).
Educational programs for schoolchildren in secondary school in Belorussia.
New lexical content.
http://www.zorika.by/?p=3903

AP-8: *Встречают по автомобилю, а провожают по уму* (One is greeted according to one's car; one is seen off according to one's brain).
Car tuning in Voronezh.
New lexical content.
http://www.automag.vrn.ru/10_22/0.html

AP-9: *Встречают по прописке – провожают по счетам*

(One is greeted according to one's registration; one is seen off according to one's bills).
Kazakhstan students' families whose children get education in other countries continue to pay for services where the students are registered (water, gas).
New lexical content.
http://www.zakon.kz/69943-vstrechajut-po-propiske-provozhajut-po.html

AP-10: *Встречают по фасаду и провожают — тоже* (One is greeted according to one's front of the building, and one is seen off according to it, too).
An article about plasters for the front of the buildings.
Defeated expectancy.
http://www.domlv.lv/index.php?n=624&a=7426

AP-11: *Встречают по упаковке, провожают по подарку!* (One is greeted according to the wrapping; one is seen off according to the gift!)
How to wrap your gift nicely.
New lexical content.
http://www.davanu-amins.lv/index.php?option=com_content&view=article&id=18:2010-01-11-12-11-26&catid=8:2010-01-11-11-21-28&Itemid=53

Comments: We have three groups of anti-proverbs here. One continues the message of the traditional proverb, saying that the content of something or the inner world of somebody is much more important than appearances (#3, 4, 5, 6, 7, 11). At the same time, there is a group of proverbs that, using the popularity of the traditional phrase, creates an effect of defeated expectancy, as the second part usually contradicts the traditional wisdom. Thus, #1 is about a museum of packaging, and thus, packaging (that is, appearance) is the center of attention. AP #2 criticizes an Oscar ceremony that pays much more attention to the dresses than the content (movies); #10 is an advertisement for plaster, and of course maintains that the front of your house is the most important thing. Finally, we have a small fraction of examples, where, as we have already seen, the association with the tra-

ditional proverb is strictly formal, and in fact, they have nothing to do with the original message (and do not create a new one); #8 and 9 are examples of these: they do not either confirm or contradict the traditional proverb; their messages – if they have one – are in a completely different area. The first one is an advertisement for car tuning, while the second one simply describes the red tape created by bureaucrats responsible for collecting payments: as long as students are registered at home, their families have to pay for them, as well, even though they do not use water or heat.
Note: Traditionally, the payments for water and heat are based on the number of people living in a house or apartment, not on the amount of water or gas consumed. This is slowly changing, as more and more apartments are metered.

Видит око, да зуб неймет (Eyes see but teeth cannot reach).
Something that is very close and seems reachable, but in reality is not.
This is a line from the poem by Ivan Krylov "Fox and Grapes" (1808); it became a proverb soon after the poem was published. The plot of the poem goes back to a fable by Aesop (620-564 B.C.), a Greek writer credited with a number of popular fables.

AP-1: *Око у российских покупателей видит, да кошелек неймет* (Eyes of Russian consumers see but their purses cannot reach).
Inflation in Russia in 2008; translation of the article from *Financial Times,* UK, "Russia's shoppers can look but cannot afford to buy."
New lexical content.
http://www.inosmi.ru/inrussia/20080717/242642.html

AP-2: *Видит око, да статист неймёт?* (Eyes see, but statistics cannot reach?)
Official statistics in Russia "does not notice" the increase in the cost of living; 2010.
New lexical content.
http://www.beriki.ru/2010/10/27/vidit-oko-da-statist-neimet

AP-3: *Акционер банкрота видит, да суд неймет* (A shareholder sees the bankrupt, but the court cannot reach).
A shareholder in Ukraine was denied court protection in a bankruptcy case; 2006.
New lexical content.
http://www.bankruptcyukraine.com/index.php?option=com_content&task=view&id=1379&Itemid=110

AP-4: *Видит Интерпол, да зуб неймет* (Interpol sees, but teeth cannot reach).
The international arrest warrant for Pavel Borodin, Secretary of the Union of Russia and Belorussia; January 2000.
New lexical content.
http://www.mk.ru/editions/daily/article/2000/01/29/128548-vidit-interpol-da-zub-neymet.html

AP-5: *Видит глаз, да рубль неймет* (Eyes see but ruble cannot reach).
A protest of private businessmen against the decision of the city hall of Minsk, Belorussia, to ban selling groceries from trucks in one of the city markets.
New lexical content.
http://www.newsvm.com/news/30/14682/

Comments: All five anti-proverbs, building on the traditional message, create their own content; thus, they all continue, in different ways, the idea of something close but unreachable, be it court protection (#3) or buying cheap groceries in the market (#5). The most interesting example is #1: this is the title of an article about inflation in Russia. It is a Russian translation of an article originally published in the British newspaper *Financial Times* under the title "Russia's Shoppers Can Look but Cannot Afford to Buy." Using a modern version of the traditional proverb as the title of the Russian translation was a great idea: it both preserved the message of the original title and made the title interesting.

В тихом омуте черти водятся (Devils live in a quiet waterhole).

A quiet, reserved person may be capable of unexpected actions, even bad actions.
English equivalent: Still waters run deep.

AP-1: *В тихом омуте Лены водятся* (Elenas live in a quiet water-hole).
Russian tennis player Elena Dementyeva announced that she is quitting her sports career, November 2010.
New lexical content.
http://www.mk.ru/sport/article/2010/10/31/540799-v-tihom-omute-lenyi-vodyatsya.html

AP-2: *В "тихом омуте" наркотики водятся* (Drugs live in a "quiet water-hole").
A quite man of 36 years old turned out to be a drug-addict; Konstatinovka, Ukraine.
New lexical content.
http://www.vp.donetsk.ua/statya.php?vstat=5889

AP-3: *В тихом омуте красноперки водятся* (Redfin fish lives in a quiet water-hole).
An article about this fish and how to catch it.
New lexical content.
http://www.lpr.lv/texnika-i-taktika-lovli/v-tixom-omute-krasnoperki-vodjatsja.html

AP-4: *В тихом омуте стоки водятся?* (Waste lives in a quiet water-hole?)
Control over waste water by the Ministry of Ecology in Belorussia.
New lexical content.
http://www.ng.by/ru/issues?art_id=43396

AP-5: *В тихом дворике Mercedes'ы водятся...* (Mercedes cars live in a quiet yard…)
Traffic police of the city of Lvov in Ukraine found stolen Mercedes cars in the backyard of a 24-year citizen of Ukraine.
New lexical content; an English word with Russian morphological ending.

http://news.avtoprom.ua

AP-6: *В тихом озере проблемы водятся...* (Problems live in a quiet lake…)
Preservation of the natural lake in the center of Murmansk.
New lexical content.
http://www.mvestnik.ru/shwpgn.asp?pid=20090122106

AP-7: *В тихом округе черти водятся* (Devils live in a quiet district).
Scandals around municipal elections in one of the districts of Saint-Petersburg; 2005.
New lexical content.
http://www.kadis.ru/daily/?id=19357

AP-8: *В тихом городе черти водятся* (Devils live in a quiet town).
A museum of Russian myths and superstitions opened in Uglich (2003).
New lexical content.
http://www.cargobay.ru/news/trud/2003/1/4/id_175163.html

AP-9: *В тихом банке инсайдеры водятся* (Insiders live in a quiet bank).
Economic crimes based on inside information.
New lexical content.
http://www.bos.dn.ua/view_article.php?id_article=86

AP-10: *В тихом омуте стрессы водятся* (Stress lives in a quiet water-hole).
The work of accountants, the majority of whom are women in Latvia, involves a lot of stress, even though many people consider this job an easy one.
New lexical content.
http://www.ves.lv/article/7779

AP-11: *Кто водится в тихом омуте российской науки?* (Who lives in the quiet water-hole of Russian science?)
Lack of financing for research and absence of the government

policy about innovations in Russia; April 2009.
Syntactic restructuring; new lexical content.
http://nauka21vek.ru/archives/3292

AP-12: *Швеция. В тихом обществе убийцы водятся* (Sweden. Killers live in a quiet society).
Assassination of Foreign Minister of Sweden Anna Lind, and others; September 2003.
New lexical content.
http://dlib.eastview.com/browse/doc/5305008

Comments: The majority of new coinages continue the message of the traditional proverb: quiet appearance (of a person or some object) can hide unexpected things or actions, be it a decision to quit a sports career (#1), finding expensive foreign cars in a modest backyard (#5), or discussing political assassinations in an exemplary European country (#12). A small number of anti-proverbs, though, interpret the message literally, and do talk about water-holes. Thus, #3 talks about fishing, and #6 about the preservation of a natural lake in the city of Murmansk. In the same way, another proverb does talk about devils, or to be more exact, about the museum of Russian myths and superstitions that was opened in the quiet Russian city of Uglich on the Volga river (#8).

Охота пуще неволи (Desire is more powerful than coercion).
Said when someone voluntarily decided to do something difficult, something which another person will not do unless he or she is forced to.

AP-1: *Свобода пуще неволи* (Freedom is more powerful than coercion).
Russia acknowledged sovereignty of South Ossetia and Abkhazia in 2008; what the citizens of these republics think about it in 2010.
New lexical content.
http://www.kommersant.ru/doc.aspx?DocsID=1489082

AP-2: *Дакота пуще неволи* (Dakota is more powerful than coercion).
Photographer John Willis published a book about two late elders of Pine Ridge reservation who became his friends: Grandfather Eugene Reddest and Uncle Tommy Crow. He was taking pictures of the reservation since 1992.
Hidden rhyme.
http://esquire.ru/photo/rezervation

AP-3: *Охта пуще неволи* (Ohta is more powerful than coercion).
Plans to build a Gasprom skyscraper in Ohta district in Saint-Petersburg; the city governor does not listen to the opinion of experts and citizens.
Paronymy.
http://www.sunhome.ru/journal/120804

AP-4: *Фотоохота пуще неволи* (Photo hunting is more powerful than coercion/captivity).
Human rights activists were arrested in Chechnya for taking pictures of a building where they believe people are unlawfully detained and kept.
Hidden rhyme; polysemy.
http://www.gazeta.ru/politics/2008/06/18_a_2757632.shtml

AP-5: *Тихая охота пуще неволи* (Quiet hunting is more powerful than coercion).
Travel agencies offer special "mushroom tours" for citizens of Saint-Petersburg; but they are not responsible for those who get lost in the forest.
Homonymy.
http://www.izvestia.ru/russia/article38424/

AP-6: *Соседство пуще неволи* (Neighborhood is more powerful than coercion/captivity).
The article argues to move the jail from the center of Almaty.
New lexical content.
http://www.vecher.kz/?S=7-201008140840

AP-7: *Свобода пуще неволи* (Freedom is more powerful than coercion/captivity).
Every third person who was in prison in Russia returns to prison during the first five years after getting out of it.
Polysemy.
http://www.mk.ru/incident/article/2010/12/12/551454-svoboda-pusche-nevoli.html

AP-8: *Наручник пуще неволи* (Bracelets are more powerful than coercion/ imprisonment).
Introducing electronic monitoring bracelets in Russia.
Polysemy.
http://www.rg.ru/2007/08/24/naruchnik.html

AP-9: *Off-road пуще неволи* (Off-road is more powerful than coercion).
Accessories for off-road vehicles in Russia.
New lexical content.
http://www.automania.ru/articles/autoshop/0004271/

AP-10: *Пехота пуще неволи* (Infantry is more powerful than coercion/captivity).
Israel army attack on Gaza strip in order to free the captured caporal Gilad Shalit.
Hidden rhyme.
http://www.newsru.co.il/press/29jun2006/k_pehota.html

AP-11: *Пуща неволи* (Forest preserve of coercion).
Presidential elections in Belorussia; newsreel of Russian TV.
Paronymy; syntactic restructuring.
http://www.casttv.com/video/ht1c5g7/19-12-2010-video

AP-12: *Забота пуще неволи* (Attention is more powerful than coercion).
Interference of the government into private businesses; only those whom government supports will survive; February 2009.
Hidden rhyme.
http://dlib.eastview.com/browse/doc/19573747

Comments: This is a very interesting and a very diverse selection of anti-proverbs; thus, there are at least three different groups here. The first group (the smallest) is represented by those proverbs that are more or less in line with the original message: something is more powerful than coercion. Thus, #9 is about off-road driving (there are people who love it, and there are other who would never do it unless they were forced to); # 3 is about citizens of Saint-Petersburg protesting against constructing an ugly skyscraper that would violate the image of the historic part of the city; their opinion was more powerful than that of city officials and managers of the largest Russian company. The second group is represented by anti-proverbs that are built around other meanings of the polysemic word *неволя* (which can mean, as it does in the original proverb, *coercion*, or it can also mean *captivity, imprisonment*). Thus, #4 is about a human rights activist literally arrested for taking pictures of detention center; #6 is about neighborhood protesting against a jail next to them; #8 is about electronic monitoring being more efficient than incarcerating; #10 is about Israel infantry fighting to save their comrade from captivity. Now, the third group is a strange group which semantically has nothing to do with the original proverb. It may mean that the original meaning becomes more and more vague for modern Russian speakers, and they often use the phrase simply to catch readers' attention. Thus, #2 has nothing to do with coercion or captivity; it is simply a catchy title (and it does tell an interesting story); in the same way, #5 is about mushroom tours for citizens of Saint-Petersburg (again, no connection with coercion); #7, in fact, contradicts the message of the article itself (it says, literally, that freedom is more powerful than the imprisonment, while the article says exactly the opposite). Finally, the most interesting case is #11. It is built around two linguistic mechanisms: the word *пуща* (forest reserve) is a paronym to the word from the original proverb – *пуще* (more powerful); on top of that, the anti-proverb has a different syntax. In the original phrase, the word *пуще* is an adjective in a comparative form, part of predicate; in the anti-proverb, *пуща* is a noun in a nominative sentence. Now, the second part, *неволи* (coercion) in the original proverb is an object, while in the anti-proverb, *неволи* is a modifier to the noun, acting as an adjective. Thus, the meaning of the anti-proverb is that Belorussia remains that last reserve of dictatorship in Europe. It is very well coined, and serves as a great title.

П

Написано пером – не вырубишь топором (If something is written by pen, it cannot be cut out by an axe).
Something that has been written down and become known cannot be changed; one has to live with that; what is done cannot be undone.
English equivalent: The pen is mightier than the sword.

AP-1: *Не написано пером — руби топором* (If it is not written by a pen, cut by an axe).
Red tape around the decision to protect national forest in Moscow oblast; February 2010.
Antonym.
http://www.kvadroom.ru/journal/news_33047.html

AP-2: *Перо зарубили топором* (A pen was cut by an axe).
Attempt to murder, using a metal axe, a prominent journalist Vadim Rogozhin in Saratov, March 2009.
Metonymy.
http://www.kommersant.ru/doc-y.aspx?DocsID=1133789

AP-3: *Госдума пытается вырубить топором, что написано пером* (Russian parliament is trying to cut out with an axe what has been written by a pen).
A member of Russian parliament contradicts himself.
New lexical content.
http://stringer.ru/publication.mhtml?Part=48&PubID=13813

Comments: All new proverbs have a message connected with the meaning of the traditional proverb. Thus, #1 claims that while government officials are in no hurry to make a decision (write with a pen) the construction of the highway will continue and the national forest will continue to be cut by an axe. Linguistically, the most interesting coinage is #2, where we have metonymy (*pars pro toto*): *pen* means *the journalist,* and *axe* means the *killer.* Lastly, in #3, axe represents an awkward attempt to renounce a previous statement.

Из песни слова не выкинешь (One cannot drop a word out of a song).
One has to tell the whole truth, with all the details, no matter how unpleasant they might be.

AP-1: *С вывески слова не выкинешь?* (One cannot drop a word from a shop-sign?)
Photos of silly or stupid slogans and advertisements; August 2007, Latvia.
New lexical content.
http://www.chas-daily.com/win/2007/08/24/v_015.html?r=3&

AP-2: *Из «фанеры» слова не выкинешь, или чем добросовестные гастроли отличаются от так называемого чёса* (One cannot drop a word from "ply-wood" [mute singing], or what is the difference between bona fide road tour and mala fide road tour).
The difference between real artists who sing live during tours and those who sing using phonograms and who travel only to get money.
New lexical content; syntactic extension.
http://www.gazeta-nedeli.ru/article.php?id=1741

AP-3: *Из документа слова не выкинешь* (One cannot drop a word from a document).
Publication of the collection of archive documents about old parks in Almaty; March 2009.
New lexical content.
http://www.vecher.kz/?S=15-200903260510

AP-4: *Из опроса слова не выкинешь* (One cannot drop a word from an opinion poll).
An opinion poll in Russia; June 2008: 58% of respondents are in favor of censorship in Russian mass media; 24% against, and

18% had no opinion.
New lexical content.
http://old.wciom.ru/novosti/publikacii-v-smi/nas-kritikujut/publikacija/single/10322.html?cHash=7ccc888836&print=1&no_cache=1

AP-5: *Из истории, как из песни, слова не выкинешь* (One cannot drop a word from history, in the same way one cannot drop a word from a song).
A book about museums in Moldova; February 2006.
New lexical content.
http://www.allmoldova.com/int/interview/tatiana-niculaescu-230206.html

AP-6: *Из сказки крови не выкинешь* (One cannot drop blood from a fairy-tale).
By changing folk fairy tales, writers destroy them and bring harm to children, creating happy ends instead of original stories.
New lexical content.
http://www.ogoniok.com/archive/2001/4708/33-31-33/

AP-7: *Из налоговой песни слов не выкинешь!* (One cannot drop words from tax song!)
Printing house "Kometa-S" filed a law suit against tax inspection of Almaty.
New lexical content.
http://www.respublika-kz.info/news/politics/10296/

AP-8: *Из гимна слова не выкинешь* (One cannot drop a word from the anthem).
A bill to include in the Criminal Code of RF a provision about criminal responsibility for desecration of the Russian anthem; January 2002.
New lexical content.
http://dlib.eastview.com/browse/doc/3032367

Comments: All new coinages, except #7, build on the meaning of the traditional proverb: one has to tell the whole truth, be it all the results of an opinion poll ($3), or the authentic version of a

fairy-tale (#6), or publications of archive documents (#3). In #7 we have another example when the association with the traditional proverb is used only to create a catchy title, while #8 interprets the original proverb literally and talks about criminal responsibility for desecration of the Russian national anthem.
Note: The current national anthem of Russia was adopted in 2000, but is in fact the old national anthem of the Soviet Union, with new lyrics. Its adoption was met with numerous protests, as many people believed it is wrong to use the old soviet anthem for a new democratic Russia. What makes the situation especially bizarre is the fact that the lyrics of this anthem have been changed several times: the first version was written in 1944; the second in 1977 (since 1956 till 1977 the anthem was used without any lyrics); in 2000, the third version was adopted, and all three versions were written by the same poet – Sergey Mikhalkov (1913-2009).

Береги платье снову, а честь смолоду (Look after your clothes since they are new; and after your honor since you are young).
Take care of your good name, honor, and dignity since early age.

AP-1: *Береги платье снову, а кредитную историю смолоду* (Look after your clothes since they are new, and after your credit history since you are young).
The law on credit history took effect in Russia; June 2005.
New lexical content.
http://news.samaratoday.ru/news/59779/

AP-2: *Береги пенсию смолоду* (Look after your pension since you are young).
Pension reform in Russia.
Ellipsis.
http://www.pfrf.ru/ot_vologda_iviews/7490.html

AP-3: *Береги платье снову, а кожу смолоду* (Look after your clothes since they are new, and your skin since you are young).
How to take care of your skin.
New lexical content.

http://www.gay.ru/style/health/looking/mack2005.html

Comments: All new proverbs have the same message: look after something important in your life since young age, be it your retirement money (#2), or credit history (#1), or your skin (#3). In a sense, all three adjust the traditional message to a new era, where one's credit history is as important as one's good name. In fact, one's credit history is a part of one's good name now.

Плетью обуха не перешибешь (One can't break a head of an axe with a whip).
It is useless to try to stand against those in power – you will achieve nothing.

AP-1: *Нефтегазовый транзит: тарифом Москву не перешибешь* (Oil and gas transit: One can't break Moscow by tariffs).
Fees for transit of Russian gas and oil through Belorussia to Europe.
Metonymy.
http://naviny.by/rubrics/economic/2010/08/16/ic_articles_113_170073/

AP-2: *Обухова дротиком не перешибешь* (One cannot break Obukhov by a dart).
Roman Obukhov from Penza got the silver medal at the Russian championship in darts.
Paronymy.
http://pravda-news.ru/node/3751

AP-3: *Биржей бартера не перешибешь* (One cannot break barter by the stock exchange).
The nature of barter transactions in Russia; November 1997.
New lexical content.
http://www.kommersant.ru/doc.aspx?DocsID=20953

AP-4: *Гриппом кризиса не перешибешь* (One cannot break cri-sis by flu).
Swine flu epidemic in 2009 and its influence on world economy.

New lexical content.
http://www.dp.ru/a/2009/04/29/Grippom_krizisa_ne_pereshi

AP-5: *Обухова с битой – не перешибешь?* (One cannot break Obukhov with a club?)
A traffic accident with hockey player Dmitry Obukhov.
Paronymy.
http://www.evening-kazan.ru/article.asp?from=number&num_dt=11.08.2007&id=26441

AP-6: *Еврами доллар не перешибешь* (One cannot break dollar by euros).
Euro to dollar ratio in 2002.
New lexical content.
http://www.ural.ru/news/business/news-18800.html

AP-7: *Червонцем доллар не перешибешь* (One cannot break dollar by chervonets [10 ruble coin made from pure gold]).
A project to issue "gold coin" to be used instead of dollars in Russia; 1999.
http://www.kommersant.ru/doc.aspx?DocsID=22920

Comments: Once again, the majority of new proverbs preserve the core message of the traditional proverb: it is useless to stand against some powerful force, be it Russian government dictating price for oil and gas (#1), or barter transactions in the 1990s in Russia that were much more popular (powerful) than transactions in stock exchange (#3), or the status of the US currency (#6). At the same time, we have a couple of anti-proverbs that use a play on words and have much less to do with the original moral (#2 and 5). Both used the coincidence of the last name of two athletes – Roman Obukhov and Dmitry Obykhov – and the Russian word *обух* (back of the axe); thus, saying that no one can beat Roman in darts and that Dmitry was ok after his car accident.

Один в поле не воин (One man in the field is no worrier).
It is difficult for one person to persevere, achieve something, to win in a fight.

AP-1: *Один Хренов в поле не воин* (One Hrenov in the field is no warrior).
Physician Hrenov told Putin during his live TV address about violations in Ivanovo hospital, but the special commission found no violations.
New lexical content.
http://sobesednik.ru/incident/odin-khrenov-v-pole-ne-voin?from=qip

AP-2: *И один в поле воин* (One man in the field is a warrior).
Nikolay Syrotinin alone stopped a tank division of Guderian during the Second World War.
Antonym.
http://www.fire-of-war.ru/p1270.htm

AP-3: *Один в поле не Голем* (One in the field is not Golem).
Review of the movie *Der Golem* by Paul Wegener.
New lexical content.
http://www.zvuki.ru/R/P/13533

AP-4: *Один в поле не рыбак* (One in the field is not a fisherman).
Iceland wants to join the EU; July 2009.
New lexical content.
http://www.newizv.ru/news/2009-07-27/112369/

AP-5: *Один в поле не апельсин* (One in the field is not an orange).
President Yushchenko's low ratings and situation in Ukraine; September 2005.
Note: Yushchenko came to power as a result of the so-called "orange revolution" in Ukraine; to identify themselves, his followers used orange color.
Metonymy.
HTTP://WWW.ANTI-ORANGE-UA.COM.RU/CONTENT/VIEW/1212/54/

AP-6: *Один в поле воин. Москвичка намерена засудить власти из-за дыма* (One in the field is a warrior. A muscovite is

suing city hall because of the smoke).
A muscovite lawyer Svetlana Dobronravova wants to sue the city government for damages from smog; August 2010.
Antonym. Syntactic extension.
http://www.aif.ru/politic/article/37232

AP-7: *Один в поле не партиец* (One in the field is not a party member).
Social democratic party of Sweden did not agree with its member Morgan Johansson on the question of censoring electronic information; December 2010.
New lexical content.
http://www.sweden4rus.nu/rus/info/radio/news.asp?id=9857

AP-8: *Один в поле не мэр* (One in the field is not a mayor).
The new mayor of Moscow, Sergey Sobyanin; 2010.
New lexical content.
http://slovodnya.ru/2010/11/odin-v-pole-ne-mer-i-nemnogo-iz-istorii-cerkvi/

AP-9: *Один в поле не батька* (One in the field is not a bat'ka [*bat'ka* means "father" in Belorussian]).
International situation of Belorussia in 2005.
Note: This term – *bat'ka* –refers to the president of Belorussia, Alexander Lukashenko.
New lexical content.
http://www.belgazeta.by/20050425.16/010060142/

AP-10: *Восемьдесят один в поле воин* (Eighty-one in the field is a warrior).
NBA match between *Los Angeles Lakers* and *Toronto Raptors*; a player from Californian team scored 81 points in the game, which his team won 122-104.
New lexical content.
http://www.kommersant.ru/doc.aspx?DocsID=642937

AP-11: *Один в поле не понял* (One in the field did not get it).
Governor of Vyatka Nikolay Shaklein and financial machinations during his time in office; December 2008.

Syntactic restructuring.
http://www.osobaya.net/607

Comments: Most of the new proverbs repeat the message of the traditional phrase: it is difficult for one person to achieve something, to oppose the majority, stand against those in power, etc. Most interesting are examples that violate this rule; thus, #2 and 6 describe situations when even one person, alone, can achieve something, while #10, even though it technically says "eighty-one" in fact means the same: one player decided the result of the game. The last anti-proverb, #11, has very little to do with the original phrase, both semantically and syntactically: it has the structure *subject – action verb*, while in the traditional proverb the structure is *subject – subject complement* (with omitted link verb).

Каков поп, таков и приход (Like priest, like flock).
The leaders define what the employees will be like. Usually said as a criticism (lack of discipline, orderliness, and other necessary qualities).

AP-1: *Каков топ, таков и приход* (Like top [managers], like the flock).
Top managers of companies and marketing.
Hidden rhyme.
http://www.marketing.spb.ru/lib-mm/tactics/top_marketing.htm

AP-2: *Каков «Поп», таков и приход* (Like "Priest," like flock).
A new film by Vladimir Hotinenko, *Priest*, about the Russian orthodox church during the Second World War on the occupied territory of the Soviet Union; April 2010.
Polysemy.
http://www.baltinfo.ru/2010/04/06/Kakov-Pop-takov-i-prikhod-137952

AP-3: *Каков приход, таков и поп* (Like flock, like priest).
About the Church of Sofia the Wise in the center of Moscow; the business of its priest Vladimir Volgin and his elite congregation.
Chiasmus.

http://www.sobesednik.ru/incident/sobes_21_10_pop

AP-4: *Каков «Поп», таков и Тамбов?* (Like "Priest," like [the city of] Tambov?)
The assassination of the deputy of Tambov oblast duma Leonid Novopavlovsky, organized by Andrey Popov who controls Tambov city market; his nickname is "Pop" ["priest" in Russian].
Homonymy.
http://www.flb.ru/infoprint/47465.html

AP-5: *Итоги-2009: каков год — таков и приход* (The results of 2009: like the year, like the flock).
Major arts events of 2009.
Internal rhyme.
http://artinvestment.ru/invest/analytics/20091223_top_2009_itogi.html

AP-6: *"Какой тост, такой и напиток", — отозвался Путин* ("Like toast, like drink," replied Putin).
This is a famous quote of Vladimir Putin. He said that at his meeting with the participants of the charity concert for the benefit of sick children. A popular rock musician Yury Shevchuk proposed a toast, on behalf of our children. He said, "What type of country they will live in – dark, corrupted, totalitarian, with one party, one hymn, one thought – or in a bright, democratic, where everyone is really equal before the law. Nothing else is needed. I would very much like that our children live and restore their health in such a country. This is my toast." To this, Putin replied: "Like toast, like drink." Later, the press secretary of Putin, Dmitry Peskov, said that all the guests had water in their wine glasses. May 31, 2010.
New lexical content.
http://www.forbes.ru/ekonomika/vlast/50459-vpechatlenie-chto-shevchuk-vyvel-iz-sebya-putina

AP-7: *Каков поп, таков и приход. Какой Путин, такой и Тулеев* (Like priest, like flock. Like Putin, like Tuleyev [gover-

nor of Kemerovo oblast]).
Russian opposition members promised help to miners in Kemerovo oblast, whose meeting was brutally dispersed by police in the town of Mezhdurechensk; May 2010.
Syntactic extension.
http://www.nr2.ru/moskow/283520.html

AP-8: *Каков мастер, такова и бригада* (Like foreman, like workers).
A team of electricians under the leadership of Alexander Muratov shows excellent results. Tambov, December 2008.
New lexical content.
http://smi.lanta-net.ru/pressa/vestnik/10618-kakov-master-takova-i-brigada.html

AP-9: *Каков поп, таков и рок* (Like priest, like rock).
A rock concert in Kiev dedicated to Christianization of Russia anniversary.
New lexical content.
http://www.kommersant.ua/doc.html?docId=795234

AP-10: *Поп таков, каков приход* (Like flock, like priest).
Elections of the new patriarch of Russia in 2009; among electors many government officials and businessmen, which shows that church and government are not separate in Russia.
Chiasmus.
http://news.babr.ru/?IDE=49872

Comments: We have at least three groups of proverbs here. First, several new coinages repeat the message of the traditional proverb, only adjusting it to their situations (#1, 4, 7, 8). Secondly, we have two proverbs that reverse the traditional wisdom and claim the opposite: it's the flock who defines the priest; these are #3, and 10. Interestingly, these two proverbs literally talk about priests. Thirdly, we have – as usual – proverbs that have little to do with the original message; a typical example is #9, which talks about a rock concert dedicated to an anniversary of Christianization of Russia. There is no connection between it and the concert, except for the fact that it was dedicated to that event. The same is true for anti-proverbs #2 and 5: the first one is a review of the movie that happens to have the title *Priest*; the second is the title of an article about major arts events of 2009 (incidentally, it has the internal rhyme *год – приход* (year – flock) that is absent in the traditional proverb). Finally, the most interesting case is #6, where Vladimir Putin coined a new proverb using the structure and the message of the traditional phrase. In other words, he meant to say that the content of the toast defines the content of their glasses. Since we know that there was water in the glasses, we can deduct from this fact that he did not like the toast proposed by Yury Shevchuk.

Привычка – вторая натура (Habit is a second nature).
It is difficult to change one's way of thinking or actions that became customary.
The proverb is often quoted in *Latin*: Consuetudo est altera natura.

AP-1: *Еда — вторая натура* (Food is a second nature).
Types of food determine the types of persons depending on their attitude to food.
New lexical content.
http://www.kiz.ru/content/body/eda__vtoraja_natura.html

AP-2: *Вредные привычки – вторая натура?* (Bad habits are a second nature?)
Why people knowingly keep their bad habits.
New lexical content.
http://www.womenhealthnet.ru/psychotherapy/86.html

AP-3: *Вторая натура* (A second nature).
A list of bad habits of Russians; 2008.
Ellipsis.
http://www.newizv.ru/news/2008-04-22/88983/

AP-4: *Nokia — «вторая натура»* (Nokia is a "second nature").
A new commercial about Finnish cell phones.
New lexical content.

http://www.adme.ru/nokia/nokia-vtoraya-natura-novaya-reklamnaya-kampaniya-finskogo-proizvoditelya-ot-grey-london-academy-films-london-16729/

AP-5: *Стиль – вторая натура* (Style is a second nature).
New HSE trim of the car Land Rover Freelander 2 HSE; 2007.
New lexical content.
http://www.5koleso.ru/news/990

AP-6: *Улыбка вторая натура* (A smile is a second nature).
The importance of smile in human relations.
New lexical content.
http://tolstiki.ru/2010/03/13/ulybka-vtoraya-natura.html

AP-7: *Инстинкт – вторая натура* (Instincts are a second nature).
The role of instincts in human beings.
New lexical content.
http://www.gazeta.bg/news/view/342

AP-8: *Психологи: аватар – вторая натура* (Psychologists: avatar is a second nature).
An avatar can tell a lot about its owner.
New lexical content.
http://www.altairegion.ru/news/139379/

AP-9: *Духи вторая натура!* (Perfume is a second nature!)
Each person has her own perfume.
New lexical content.
http://kate.li/blog/152-perfumes-the-second-nature.html

Comments: Most new proverbs shift the message from the traditional "it is difficult to change something that became a custom with a person" to "something (food in #1, cell phones in #4, smiles in #6, instincts in #7, etc.) is important in the life of a person." The most interesting example is #3, which has an elliptical form of the original proverb; this proves that the traditional proverb is alive and well among modern Russian speakers, and its elliptical form – *second nature* – is enough for it to be recognized.

Дурной пример заразителен (A bad example is contagious). Bad habits, actions or opinions of one person can influence another person. Said when someone copies bad features of somebody else.

AP-1: *Дурной развод заразителен* (A bad divorce is contagious).
Friends and relatives of divorced couples often follow their example.
New lexical content.
http://www.pravda.ru/society/04-08-2010/1039498-divorce-0/

AP-2: *Дурной пример авиакампаний заразителен* (A bad example of an airline is contagious).
Lithuanian energy company *E-energija* sued the Latvian government following the example of Latvian airline *FlyLAL*; October 2008.
New lexical content.
http://www.runet.lt/news-lt/5900-durnojj-primer-aviakompanijj-zarazitelen.html

AP-3: *Косовский пример заразителен?* (Kosovo example is contagious?)
Independence of Kosovo and reaction to it from different countries.
New lexical content.
http://podrobnosti.ua/analytics/2010/07/23/703223.html

AP-4: *Премьер заразителен* (Prime-minister is contagious).
Putin took part in international bikers rally in Crimea; July 2010.
Paronymy; hidden rhyme.
http://www.mk.ru/politics/article/2010/07/26/519010-premer-zarazitelen.html

AP-5: *Пример Германии не заразителен* (German example is not contagious).
Germany could not persuade other countries to ban short sales;

2010.
New lexical content.
http://www.finmarket.ru/z/nws/hotnews.asp?id=1502011

AP-6: *Хороший пример тоже заразителен* (A good example is contagious, too).
Bruce Springsteen reissues his classic 1978 album *Darkness on the Edge of Town;* it looks like he follows the example of the Rolling Stones, who reissued their *Exile on Main St.*
Antonym.
http://www.zvuki.ru/R/P/23125/

AP-7: *Солидный вес заразителен* (Heavy weight is contagious).
If your friends are overweight, you can become overweight, too.
New lexical content.
www.gzt.ru/health/2007/07/26/210032.html

AP-8: *Хороший пример не заразителен* (A good example is not contagious).
Lowering interest rate by Sberbank is not followed by other Russian banks.
Antonym.
http://www.tv100.ru/news/Horoshij-primer-ne-zarazitelen-25917/

AP-9: *Чужой пример заразителен* (A stranger's example is contagious).
A British citizen threw a shoe at the Chinese prime-minister during his visit to Cambridge University; February 2009 (following the example of Muntadar al-Zaidi, an Iraqi journalist who through a shoe at President George W. Bush).
Hidden rhyme.
http://www.ntv.ru/novosti/149570/

Comments: Once again, we have several distinct groups of anti-proverbs. In the first one, there are proverbs that repeat the original message: bad habits of one person tend to be repeated by other people (#1, 2, 7). At the same time, we have a group of proverbs that claim that good habits are contagious, as well (#3, 6). Then, there are proverbs that deny that good habits are contagious (and thus, in a way, confirm the original message) – #5 and 8. Finally, we have a proverb that uses the association with the traditional phrase to create wordplay, but has nothing to do with it – it is #4; it uses paronymy between the Russian words *пример* (example) in the traditional proverb and *премьер* (prime-minister) in the anti-proverb.

Нет пророка в своем отечестве (There is no prophet in his own country).
We do not appreciate great persons who live next to us.
The proverb comes from the *Bible*: A prophet is not without honor, save in his own country, and in his own house (Matthew 13:57).

AP-1: *Нет Рублева в своем отечестве* (There is no Rublev in his own country).
There are no icons by Andrey Rublev left in Russia.
Note: Andrey Rublev (1375-1428) was the most famous and respected icon painter of the Moscow school.
New lexical content.
http://www.izvestia.ru/culture/article3138988/

AP-2: *Нет стандарта в своём отечестве* (There are no standards in our own country).
Russian products do not meet international standards.
New lexical content.
http://www.strf.ru/material.aspx?CatalogId=223&d_no=28679

AP-3: *Нет тренера в своем отечестве...* (There is no coach in his own country…)
The national soccer team of Belorussia hired a foreign coach.
New lexical content.
http://triumfy.ru/?p=834

AP-4: *Нет режиссера в своем отечестве* (There are no producers in our country).
Alexander Kalyagin [famous Russian actor] about many talented

producers who died during 2009, and lack of new ones.
New lexical content.
http://www.stdrf.ru/node/1296

AP-5: *Нет ипотеки в своем отечестве* (There are no mortgage loans in our country).
The governor of Omsk oblast lied to the president of Russia about mortgage programs for state employees with zero interest rate, etc.; December 2010.
New lexical content.
http://www.novayagazeta.ru/data/2010/139/11.html

AP-6: *Нет онколога в своем отечестве?* (There are no oncologists in our country?)
Why parents take their children to treat cancers abroad.
New lexical content.
http://www.ng.ru/health/2003-05-16/8_rak.html

AP-7: *Нет Рыбака в своем отечестве* (There is no Rybak in his own country).
Few in Belorussia believed that Alexander Rybak, a Belorussian residing in Norway, would win Eurovision in 2009.
New lexical content.
http://svetlahorsk.belarda.org/index.php?mod=news&id=59#

AP-8: *Иноземцы в своем отечестве* (Foreigners in their own country).
People coming to Moscow from other regions of Russia, and attitudes of Muscovites to them.
New lexical content.
http://rest.kuda.ua/3913

AP-9: *Фантаст в своем отечестве* (A science fiction writer in his own country).
Interview with Boris Strugaztky, a famous Russian science fiction writer (he wrote together with his (now late) brother, Arkady).
New lexical content.

http://korrespondent.net/showbiz/651956-fantast-v-svoem-otechestve-intervyu-s-borisom-strugackim

AP-10: *Не стало в своем отечестве* (There is no more in his own country).
The death of Alexander Solzhenitsyn; August 2008.
New lexical content.
http://www.gazeta.ru/politics/2008/08/05_a_2801652.shtml

Comments: There are two groups of anti-proverbs here. One continues the message of the traditional proverb: we do not appreciate great people who live among us, and often this appreciation comes too late (#7, 9, 10). The majority of new coinages, however, belong to the other group and interpret the traditional phrase in a different way, as the literal absence of someone (or something) in our own country (#1, 2, 3, 4, 5, 6), be it absence of icons by Andrey Rublev, or absence of mortgage loans, or soccer coaches. The most interesting case is #10: it uses ellipsis (there is no object in the sentence, so we do not know who is no more in his own country), which shows that the remaining part of the original proverb (*in his own country*) is enough for readers to recognize it.

Простота хуже воровства (Simplicity is worse than stealing).
Too naïve people bring a lot of troubles.

AP-1: *Пустота хуже воровства* (Emptiness is worse than stealing).
Most information on the web is rewriting of old content.
Hidden rhyme; internal rhyme.
http://www.kommersant.ru/doc.aspx?DocsID=1333615

AP-2: *Когда аренда хуже воровства* (When leasing is worse than stealing).
A company leasing a mine refused to pay wages and maintain equipment.
New lexical content.

http://www.ukrrudprom.com/analytics/Kogda_arenda_huge_vorovstva.html

AP-3: *Кремлёвская простота хуже воровства...* (Kremlin simplicity is worse than stealing…)
President Medvedev uses the Internet to speak to the citizens of Russia, while most Russians do not have Internet access.
New lexical content.
http://www.newsland.ru/news/detail/id/437474/cat/42/

AP-4: *Правота хуже воровства?* (Being right is worse than stealing?)
Red tape in the court system in Russia and how impossible it is to prove you are right in court; September 2010
Hidden rhyme; internal rhyme.
http://www.beriki.ru/2010/09/20/pravota-khuzhe-vorovstva

AP-5: *ЖКХ хуже воровства* (Housing maintenance and public utilities services are worse than stealing).
Cost increase for utilities services; March 2010.
New lexical content.
http://www.progkh.ru/interesting/2264/

AP-6: *Фальш хуже воровства* (Sounding off-key is worse than stealing).
Copyright violations by ring-tones for cell phones.
New lexical content.
http://izvestia.ru/internet/article10991/

AP-7: *Красота хуже воровства* (Beauty is worse than stealing).
Female beauty that brings evil.
Hidden rhyme; internal rhyme.
http://www.ves.lv/article/32340

AP-8: *Быстрота хуже воровства* (Speed is worse than stealing).
Quick loans are dangerous; one needs to read small print attentively.

Hidden rhyme; internal rhyme.
http://www.offtop.ru/credit/v20_238049__.php?of7683=8a9fcccdee1c29dc47f8a070540b1825

AP-9: *Хвастовство хуже воровства* (Boasting is worse than stealing).
A person stealing money from others' credit cards and bank accounts made a picture of his son on the background of numerous bills; that started police investigation.
New lexical content.
http://www.expert.ru/russian_reporter/2008/29/hvastovstvo/

Comments: Surprisingly, all new proverbs confirm the original wisdom: some other quality is worse than stealing. However, there is a difference between the anti-proverbs and the traditional proverb (besides the obvious fact that the new proverbs compare other qualities to stealing): most of them (except #3 and 7) treat the comparison with stealing literally, be it stealing from other people's bank accounts (#9) or prohibitively high rates for services (#5), or violating copyright for music (#6), or trying to prove something in Russian courts (#4). Between the two exceptions, #3 and 7, the first anti-proverb is the closest to the original message, only instead of simplicity in general it talks about *Kremlin simplicity*: naïve belief of the president of Russia that he can reach out to his citizens via Internet.

Р

Работа дураков любит (The work likes fools).
Said, usually jokingly, about someone who does unnecessary or useless work.

AP-1: *Работа любит гендиректора* (The work likes CEOs).
The workload of CEOs.
New lexical content.
http://www.penza-job.ru/view/786.html

AP-2: *Работа любит инициативных* (The work likes those with initiative).

Small businesses development in Kazakhstan.
New lexical content.
http://www.spk-ontustik.kz/news/detail.php?ID=151

AP-3: *Работа в России китайцев любит* (The work in Russia likes the Chinese).
Building of a cement plant in North-West Russia by a Chinese company; April 2008.
New lexical content.
http://www.internovosti.ru/text/?id=2246

AP-4: *Работа пермяков любит* (The work likes the citizens of Perm).
Unemployment in the city of Perm.
Hidden rhyme.
http://chitaitext.ru/novosti/index.php?nomer=8949

AP-5: *Работа немца любит – решили в российском правительстве и утвердили федеральную программу* (The work likes Germans – the Russian government decided, and approved the federal program).
The federal program of socio-economic and cultural development of Russian Germans. for 2008-2012.
Syntactic extension.
http://rulit.org/read/386/

Comments: All new proverbs are similar in one aspect: they have nothing to do with the original message of useless or unnecessary work, and thus use the association with the traditional proverb simply to create a catchy title. It may mean that the original meaning is being lost.

Кто не работает, тот не ест (He who does not work, shall not eat).
Used as an explanation to a lazy person, why he or she earned nothing.
The proverb comes from the *Bible*: He who does not work, neither shall he eat. (2 Thessalonians 3:10)

AP-1: *Кто не работает, тот ест* (He who does not work, shall eat).
Disputes about unemployment benefits in Germany.
Antonym.
http://eastwest-review.com/rus/article/kto-ne-rabotaet-tot-est-spory-o-sotsialnoi-politike-frg

AP-2: *Кто не работает, тот болеет* (He who does not work, is sick).
Unemployed young people at the age of 18-25 show decrease in cognitive and physical abilities.
New lexical content.
http://iscience.ru/2009/02/12/kto-ne-rabotaet-tot-boleet/

AP-3: *Кто не работает, тот читает anpe.fr* (He who does not work, reads anpe.fr).
Website publishing job vacancies.
New lexical content.
http://www.sostav.ru/news/2008/08/29/zar7/

AP-4: *Кто не работает – тот не устает* (He who does not work, does not get tired).
About accidents with MI-8, the most mass produced Russian helicopter, and their reasons.
New lexical content.
http://army.lv/ru/mi-8/830/2482

AP-5: *Кто не матерится – тот не работает* (He who does not swear, does not work).
Commentary to the law on the Russian language enacted by the Russian parliament in 2003.
New lexical content.
http://news.tut.by/society/21408.html

AP-6: *Кто не работает, тот отдыхает* (He who does not work, have a rest).
It is not enough to have a job; one should get satisfaction from one's job to maintain psychological health and avoid depression.
New lexical content.

http://www.studyaustralia.ru/cgi-bin/issue.cgi?action=article&
ar_id=629

AP-7: *Кто не работает, а главное, не учится, тот ест* (He who does not work, and more importantly, does not study, does eat).
Criticism of the new pension reform law in Russia; 2009.
Syntactic extension.
http://www.spravedlivo.ru/news/smi/659.php

Comments: Each of the new proverbs has its own message, often having little to do with the original one. In fact, #1, discussing unemployment benefits, and #7, criticizing new Russian pension law (according to which the years of studying are not included into the overall length of work), directly contradict it. Among others, anti-proverb #5 needs some explanation. The law in question prohibits swearing, and some commentators said that if enforced the law would cause a decrease in the productivity, because swearing is a huge part of many manual jobs. The members of the Russian parliament replied that the law is obligatory only for legal persons, not individuals and will not influence “interpersonal relationships.”

Семь раз примерь – один отрежь (Measure seven times, cut once).
Think well before you make a decision.

AP-1: *Семь раз подумай, один раз уволь* (Think seven times, fire once).
The cost of firing an employee and finding another one.
New lexical content.
http://www.tv100.ru/news/Sem-raz-podumaj-odin-raz-uvol-30585/

AP-2: *Выбираем дубленку: Семь раз проверь, один – плати* (Choosing a fur coat: check seven times, pay once).
How to choose a quality fur coat.
New lexical content.
http://www.kp.ru/daily/24567.4/739782/

AP-3: *Семь раз узнай, один – припаркуй* (Find out seven times, park once).
Complicated parking regulations in downtown Tallinn.
New lexical content.
http://www.dzd.ee/?id=254467

AP-4: *Семь раз подумай, один — установи* (Think seven times, install once).
Using alternative energy source – wind turbines – in Belorussia.
New lexical content.
http://www.ng.by/ru/issues?art_id=47212

AP-5: *Семь раз подумай, один – поешь* (Think seven times, eat once).
How to diet and not do harm to your health.
New lexical content.
http://minus5.ru/articles/17

AP-6: *Семь раз подумай, один наколи* (Think seven times, make a tattoo once).
An exhibition of tattoo pictures.
New lexical content.
http://www.ntv.ru/novosti/184656/

AP-7: *Семь раз подумай, один раз отдохни* (Think seven times, have a rest once).
Bankruptcies among travel agencies in Ukraine.
New lexical content.
http://www.ukrrudprom.com/digest/Sem_raz_podumay_odin_raz_otdohni.html

AP-8: *Молодежное жилье: один раз возьми, семь раз верни?* (Housing for the young people: take once, return seven times?)
Problems with house loans for young families: the government refuses to pay its part of the interest.
New lexical content.
http://censor.net.ua/ru/resonance/view/4213/molodejnoe_jile_odin_raz_vozmi_sem_raz_verni_viktoriya_vladina_dlya_quottsenzornetquot

AP-9: *Семь раз сравни, один раз купи* (Seven times compare, once buy).
Site offering prices for goods from different retailers.
New lexical content.
http://sravnim.ru/

AP-10: *Green Card: семь раз отмерь, один отправь* (Green card: measure seven times, send once).
Fraud around Green Card lottery in Ukraine.
New lexical content.
http://www.zagran.kiev.ua/article.php?new=300&idart=3006

AP-11: *Семь раз продлить и один – отменить* (To extend seven times, and to cancel once).
Extension of the time period of privatization in Belorussia.
New lexical content.
http://www.belmarket.by/ru/74/60/5766/

AP-12: *Семь раз отмерь, чтобы не отрезали* (Measure seen times lest you be cut).
How to invest wisely.
New lexical content.
http://algoritmus.ru/?p=3645

Comments: With two exceptions (#8 and 11), all the new variants confirm the traditional wisdom: think twice before making a decision, be it installing new equipment (#4), investing your money (#12), buying a new fur coat (#2), or choosing a travel agency (#7). Anti-proverb #8 reverses the numbers (instead of *seven – one* it has *one – seven*), to emphasize the problems with mortgage loans for young people, while #11 describes the situation in Belorussia: citizens are in no hurry to receive their privatization vouchers; hence the deadline for privatization was moved several times, and now there is a talk to establish the final deadline, and to announce all unused vouchers cancelled. Thus, it has nothing in common with the message of the traditional proverb.

С милым рай и в шалаше (With your loved one, even a hut is

heaven).
When you are with your loved one, material or other problems are not important.

AP-1: *С милым рай не в шалаше* (With your loved one, heaven is not in the hut).
A review of the movie *Slumdog Millionaire*.
Antonym.
http://cn.com.ua/N546/culture/cinema/2.html

AP-2: *С милым рай и в шалаше, но в квартире лучше* (With your loved one, even a hut is heaven, but an apartment is better).
About a special mortgage program for young families in Tver.
Syntactic extension.
http://www.tverlife.ru/news/36136.html

AP-3: *С Мелом рай и в шалаше* (With Mel, even a hut is heaven).
Description of the house that Mel Gibson and Oksana Grigorieva bought before they split.
Paronymy.
http://heat.ru/articles/1009

AP-4: *С финном рай и в шалаше?* (With a Finn, even a hut is heaven?)
Marriages between Finnish men and Russian women, and their problems.
New lexical content.
http://www.smena.ru/news/2007/06/18/11239/

AP-5: *С Миллой рай и в шалаше* (With Milla, even a hut is heaven).
About a new movie *Vykrutasy* (English title: *Lucky Trouble*; 2011) where actress Milla Jovovich chooses between two men.
Paronymy.
http://tden.ru/articles/show/2225

AP-6: *С "айфоном" рай в шалаше* (With iPhone, even a hut is heaven).

Opinions polls about the modernization of economy in Russia; October 2010.
New lexical content.
http://www.interfax.ru/business/txt.asp?id=161072

AP-7: *Москвичи согласились на рай в шалаше* (Moscovites agreed to heaven in a hut).
Moscovites are buying more cheap apartments; 2010.
Syntactic restructuring; metaphor.
http://www.finmarket.ru/z/nws/hotnews.asp?id=1248269&hot=1327593

Comments: The majority of new coinages confirm the message of the traditional proverb: with someone dear (or something dear – #6) one can survive material problems. Anti-proverb #1 rejects that idea and claims that heaven is not in a hut (though the main characters of the movie did live in awful conditions), while #7 metaphorically claims that Muscovites are ready to live in modest conditions (small apartments built during the soviet period). The most interesting variants are based on paronymy: #3 uses this type of relationships between the phrase *с Мелом* (with Mel) and the original *с милым* (with your loved one); while #5 substitutes the original phrase by another paronym, *с Миллой* (with Milla).

Где тонко, там и рвется (It will break where it is thin).
Problems occur where something is not reliable, insecure.
English equivalent: The chain is no stronger than its weakest link.

AP-1: *Где топка, там и рвется* (It will break where the furnace is).
A review of the movie *Kochegar* (Furnace Fireman) by Aleksey Balabanov.
Hidden rhyme.
http://www.kommersant.ru/doc.aspx?DocsID=1517309

AP-2: *Где танки, там и рвётся* (It will break where tanks are).
Four tanks burnt at a military base; October 2010.

Paronymy.
http://www.time.kz/index.php?newsid=19509

AP-3: *Где толсто, там и рвется* (It will break where it is thick/fat).
Obesity in the US.
Antonym.
http://www.aif.ru/health/article/36479

AP-4: *Где сыро, там и рвется* (It will break where it is damp).
Moisture that invades most vulnerable places in the car, and how to fight it.
New lexical content.
http://www.mashins.ru/articles/tuning/gde_syro_tam_i_rvetsya.html

AP-5: *Где специалисты узкие, там и "рвется"* (Where the physicians are specialized, it will "break").
Lack of physicians specializing in specific areas is a problem for outpatient clinics.
Polysemy; metaphor.
http://www.grani21.ru/pub/gde-specialisty-uzkie-tam-i-rvetsja

AP-6: *Где топка, там и рвется* (It will break where the furnace is). (cf. #1)
Bad heating in Moscow apartments in winter; December 2010.
Paronymy.
http://www.mk.ru/editions/daily/article/2008/12/10/8550-gde-topka-tam-i-rvetsya.html

AP-7: *Где много, там и рвется* (It will break/explode where there are many).
Explosions at the ammunition warehouses in Ulyanovsk; November 2009.
Polysemy.
http://www.kommersant.ru/doc-rss.aspx?DocsID=1276968

AP-8: *Где пропитано – там не рвётся* (It will not break where it is saturated).

Protective finish for floors in industrial facilities.
New lexical content.
http://www.stroypuls.ru/vipusk/detail.php?article_id=30617

AP-9: *Где тоньше, там не рвётся* (It will not break where it is thin).
New thin materials with unique characteristics.
Antonym.
http://gazeta.aif.ru/_/online/moskva/712/28_01

AP-10: *Где скользко, там и рвется* (It will break where it is slippery).
A critical review of the play *Artist Descending a Staircase* (by the British playwright Tom Stoppard), staged in the Moscow theatre MXAT.
Hidden rhyme.
http://www.mxat.ru/press/texts/4888/

Comments: This is a very diverse group of anti-proverbs. In fact, hardly any of them have any direct semantic connection with the traditional proverb (with the possible exception of #4). Some of them do describe various problems, though: obesity in the US (#3), explosion of ammunition warehouses (#7), bad staging of a play by a famous British playwright (#10), or absence of physicians specializing in certain areas (#5). Interestingly, two articles use the same anti-proverb: #1 and #6, though their content is vastly different: the first is a review of a movie, the second one discusses problems with heating Moscow apartments in winter. Linguistically, quite a few of the anti-proverbs are very well coined, as they use paronymy (#1, 2, 6): *тонко* (thin, in the original proverb) and *топка* (furnace) or *танки* (tanks); polysemy (#7): *рвется* can mean (as it does in the traditional proverb) *break*, but it can also mean *explode*; antonymous expression (#8), and hidden rhyme in #10: *скользко – тонко* (slippery – thin).

Риск – благородное дело (Risk is a noble deed).
Said as justification of risky undertakings; often jokingly.
English equivalent: Nothing venture, nothing have.

AP-1: *Иск – благородное дело* (A lawsuit is a noble deed).
Investors filed a lawsuit against the company that was supposed to build apartment houses, but did nothing.
Hidden rhyme.
http://www.zakon.kz/136079-isk-blagorodnoe-delo.-dolshhiki.html

AP-2: *Риск – дело благородное и прибыльное!* (Risk is a noble and lucrative deed!)
Starting your own business is risky but profitable.
Syntactic extension.
http://www.ivanovo.ws/business/risk_delo_blagorodnoe.php

AP-3: *Рис – благородное дело* (Rice is a noble deed).
Asian countries that have reserves of rice, united similarly to OPEK.
Paronymy.
http://dlib.eastview.com/browse/doc/14787976

AP-4: *Свист – благородное дело* (Whistling is a noble deed).
Exposition of the works of Valery Kurtmulayev from Uglich who makes ceramic whistles.
New lexical content.
http://www.sevkray.ru/news/3/14019/

AP-5: *Риск на льду – не благородное дело* (Risk on the ice is not a noble deed).
It is dangerous to be on ice during spring time when ice on the river starts to melt; Severodvinsk.
Antonym.
http://www.vdvsn.ru/papers/vs/2010/11/25/83513/

AP-6: *Риск — дело не благородное* (Risk is not a noble deed).
Only 16% of all CRM (customer relationship management) projects in the US and Europe gave profit; 2008.
Antonym.
http://offline.cio-world.ru/2008/72/359687/

Comments: Only one new proverb continues the message of the traditional saying (#2), adding that risk may also be profitable. All others use the familiar structure to send their own message which has nothing to do with risks (rice reserve, #3; filing a law suit, #1; or making ceramic whistles, #4). Two anti-proverbs are antonymous to the original message, and warn the readers about the dangers of going on ice in spring (#5), or participating in CRM projects (#6). Linguistically, #1 and #3 are the best, as the new words differ from original in one letter only: *риск* (risk) in the original proverb, and *иск* (lawsuit) and *рис* (rice) in the new coinages.

Где родился, там и пригодился (Where one was born, there one was useful).
It is easier for people to find their place in life where they were born, in their home country.

AP-1: *Леон Нганкам: где учился, там и пригодился* (Leon Hgankam: where one studied, there one was useful).
A physician, who is originally from Cameroon, is a neurosurgeon in Tver oblast hospital.
Hidden rhyme, internal rhyme.
http://www.tverinfo.ru/interview/leon_ngankam_gde_uchilsya_tam_i_prigodilsya.html

AP-2: *Где родился — там не пригодился* (Where one was born, there one was not useful).
There are many job vacancies in North-West Russia, but people go to other parts of the country because of low wages.
Antonym.
http://www.eg-online.ru/article/53582/

AP-3: *Где находился, там и пригодился* (Where one was situated, there one was useful).
The soviet lunar vehicle, Lunokhod-14, 1970, is used today by US researchers to reflect light beams; April 2010.
Hidden rhyme, internal rhyme.
http://nauka.izvestia.ru/space/article100950/print.html

AP-4: *Где родился – там и оздоровился!* (Where one was born, there one got healthy!)

Resorts and spas in Pskov oblast.
Hidden rhyme, internal rhyme.
http://www.informpskov.ru/servis/59393.html

AP-5: *Где родился, там и усыновился* (Where one was born, there one was adopted).
Adoption by Russian families as compared to adoption of Russian kids by foreigners; November 2004.
Hidden rhyme, internal rhyme.
http://www.edu.ru/mon-site/press/smi/726/

Comments: The traditional proverb has internal rhyme: *родился – пригодился* (was born – was useful), and all the anti-proverbs preserve this important feature, thus creating also a hidden rhyme – which makes the association with the original phrase much stronger. An interesting case is #2, which denies the traditional message by using antonymous (negative) construction. Anti-proverbs #1 and 3 adjust the original message and claim that one can be useful not only where one was born, but also where one studied (#1) or happened to be (#3). The remaining two proverbs leave the first part intact and tell that one can get healthy or be adopted where one was born (#4 and 5).

Своя рубашка ближе к телу (One's own shirt is closer to the body).
Our own well-being is more important for us than the well-being of other people.
English equivalent: Charity begins at home.

AP-1: *Воронеж: своя газета ближе к телу?* (Voronezh: one's own newspaper is closer to the body?)
What people read and watch in the city of Voronezh.
New lexical content.
http://www.bbc.co.uk/russian/multimedia/2010/03/100311_voronezh_mediavox.shtml

AP-2: *Своя краюха ближе к телу* (One's own loaf is closer to the body).

Ukraine, following Russia's example, decided to limit export of grain; August 2010.
New lexical content.
http://www.lenta.ru/articles/2010/08/18/zerno/

AP-3: *Своя татушка ближе к телу* (One's own tattoo is closer to the body).
About tattoos and why people do that.
Hidden rhyme.
http://www.sobesednik.ru/showbiz/svoya-tatushka-blizhe-k-telu

AP-4: *Своя карьера ближе к телу* (One's own career is closer to the body).
Your boss, who left for another company, asks you to join him: think before you leave.
New lexical content.
http://www.hr-portal.ru/article/svoya-karera-blizhe-k-telu

AP-5: *Своя живопись – ближе к телу* (One's own painting is closer to the body).
World body painting festival in Austria.
New lexical content.
http://www.newizv.ru/fotoreport/foto/6647/

AP-6: *Своя ванна ближе к телу* (One's own bathtub is closer to the body).
Bathroom remodeling.
New lexical content.
http://www.djournal.com.ua/?p=2218

AP-7: *Своя мансарда ближе к телу* (One's own mansard is closer to the body).
How to get permission to use attics in apartment buildings for people living in the upper floor; Kiev.
New lexical content.
http://www.first-realty.com.ua/art/19/1112.html

AP-8: *Своя решетка ближе к телу* (One's own bars are closer to the body).

Russian ombudsman Vladimir Lukin wrote a book of advice for persons in prison.
New lexical content.
http://www.izvestia.ru/russia/article538754/

AP-9: *Своя больница ближе к телу?!* (One's own hospital is closer to the body?)
Patients in UK prefer the nearest hospital even though a hospital next block can be better.
New lexical content.
http://medportal.by/novosti/svoya-bolnitsa-blizhe-k-telu.html

AP-10: *Своя розница ближе к телу* (One's own retail is closer to the body).
Megafon (a Russian cell phone company) keeps creating its own retail store chain in Russia; November 2010.
New lexical content.
http://www.sotovik.ru/news/svoya-roznica-blije-k-telu.html

AP-11: *Своя рубашка ближе к телу или полевое испытание термобелья* (One's own shirt is closer to the body, or field trials of thermal underwear).
Comparison of warm underwear for snowboarders produced by five companies.
Syntactic extension; defeated expectancy.
http://www.risk.ru/users/homohomeni/3033/

AP-12: *Своя таблетка ближе к телу* (One's own pill is closer to the body).
How to start production of Russian prescription drugs in Russia; November 2009.
New lexical content.
http://www.kadis.ru/daily/?id=72811

AP-13: *Своя стипендия ближе к телу* (One's own scholarship is closer to the body).
College students in Russia demand that the scholarships be comparable with the cost of living; October 2007.
New lexical content.

http://www.ng.ru/education/2005-10-07/8_stipendia.html

AP-14: *Своя Сеть ближе к телу?* (One's own net is closer to the body?)
Russian government plans to create an independent Russian internet by 2015; 07.2007.
New lexical content.
http://www.vmdaily.ru/article/37098.html

AP-15: *Сборка ПК: своя отвертка ближе к телу* (Assembling PC: one's own screw-driver is closer to the body).
Building your own PC from components; pros and cons; February 2004.
New lexical content.
http://www.morepc.ru/motherboard/moth190220041.html

Comments: The majority of new proverbs build their message on the basis of the traditional proverb, claiming that something is more important for us, be it you own career (#4) or your own retail chain (#10), or even your own Internet (#14). At the same time, the most interesting coinages are those that interpret the message of the traditional proverb literally, thus creating the effect of defeated expectancy. The best example is #11, which does talk about underwear: repeating the traditional proverb verbatim, it creates a false expectation on the part of the reader that it is another example of a figurative meaning – but it is not. Similarly, though not so dramatically, the same device is used in #3 and 5, where the word *тело* (body) is used in its literal meaning, as both talk about tattoos. On top of that, #3 has a hidden rhyme: *рубашка – татушка* (shirt – tattoo).

Не имей сто рублей, а имей сто друзей (Don't have a hundred rubles, rather have a hundred friends).
It's good to have many friends; friendship is more important than money. Said when friends help someone who is in trouble.

AP-1: *Не имей сто друзей, а имей Windows NT* (Do not have a hundred friends, rather have Windows NT).
A review of the new – 1996 – version of Windows targeted at

corporate servers.
Syntactic extension.
http://citforum.ru/database/articles/art_4.shtml

AP-2: *Не имей сто рублей, не имей сто друзей, а имей портрет Алисы Порет* (Do not have a hundred rubles, do not have a hundred friends, but rather have a portrait by Alisa Poret).
About the Russian painter Alisa Poret; Art museum in Petrozavodsk has nine paintings of hers.
Syntactic extension.
http://www.gov.karelia.ru/Karelia/887/29.html

AP-3: *Не имей 100 рублей, а имей свой IMEI* (Do not have a hundred rubles, rather have your own IMEI [International Mobile Equipment Identifier]).
Thefts of cell-phones in Voronezh.
Internal rhyme; hidden rhyme; homonymy.
http://imei.lipetsk.ru/index.php?option=com_content&task=view&id=25&Itemid=31

Comments: Two things are of interest about this group of anti-proverbs. First, it is surprisingly small, taking into account the popularity of the traditional proverb among jokesters who post dozens of their versions on the Web. Secondly, neither of the three has anything to do with the idea of friendship; all of them use the association with the traditional proverb simply to catch readers' attention and send their own message – a new Windows shell, a famous painter, or cell phone thefts. Linguistically, the last one is the best, as it preserves the internal rhyme of the traditional proverb (and thus creates a hidden rhyme, too): *друзей – IMEI* (friends – IMEI). As one can see, the Russian word *друзей* (friends) rhymes with the English abbreviation IMEI; besides, this abbreviation is a homonym to the Russian word *имей* (have).

Своя рука владыка (One's own hand is the master).
Said when someone who has money, resources, food, etc. can do with them whatever one wants.

AP-1: *Своя мука — владыка* (One's own flour is the master).
Price for flour and bread keep rising. Bishkek [capital of Kyrgyzstan]; August 2010.
Hidden rhyme.
http://gazeta.kg/news/2010/08/21/svoya-muka-vladyka-cena-na-hleb-i-muku-prodolzhaet-rasti-vlasti-goroda-opasayutsya

AP-2: *Своя Noga владыка* (One's own Noga is the master).
Swiss firm *Noga* sued the Russian Federation for unpaid contracts concluded with the Russian government, and the court in Paris ruled in its favor: bank accounts of Russian consulates and embassies in Marseilles and Strasburg were blocked; July 2000.
Homonymy.
http://www.kommersant.ru/doc.aspx?DocsID=152853

AP-3: *Своя голова — владыка* (One's own head is the master).
DVD-manual how to start consulting business.
New lexical content.
http://www.msn.kg/ru/news/29680/

AP-4: *Своя мечта владыка* (One's own dream is the master).
Hiking in Perm oblast.
New lexical content.
http://gps.yapl.ru/splav-description.php?id_description=12

AP-5: *Своя игра владыка* (One's own game is the master).
A review of recent soccer games; May 2010.
New lexical content.
http://sb.by/print/post/100689/

AP-6: *Своя река владыка* (One's own river is the master).
Water cruise as the best type of vacation.
Paronymy; hidden rhyme.
http://dlib.eastview.com/browse/doc/9540583

Comments: This is a rather diverse, though small, group of anti-proverbs, claiming the importance of various things, so that most of the proverbs have little to do with the original message. The striking exception (and a brilliant linguistic example) is #2.

There are several layers of wordplay here. First of all, the name of the Swiss firm – *Noga* – happens to coincide with the Russian word *нога* (leg or foot), which in itself creates an association with the traditional proverb that uses the word *рука* (hand or arm) because both words belongs to the same thematic group (limbs). Thus, the first reading of the phrase for Russian speakers will be, "One's own leg is the master" – this is unusual enough to make the people keep on reading and find out that *Noga* is the name of the firm. Thus, this anti-proverb does confirm the original message, only adjusted to a modern-day situation.

Рыба тухнет с головы (Fish begins to stink at the head).
Corruption or other problems in any group of people start with the leaders.

AP-1: *Россия тухнет с головы* (Russia begins to stink at the head).
Tobacco and alcohol lobbies block bills in the Russian parliament that would decrease consumption of alcohol and smoking; November 2010.
New lexical content.
http://www.oodvrs.ru/article/index.php?id_page=18&id_article=2088

AP-2: *Yahoo! тухнет с головы* (Yahoo! begins to stink at the head).
Conflicts among the major shareholders of the company; July 2008.
New lexical content.
http://www.sfors.ru/news/Yahoo-tuhnet-s-golovy/

Comments: Both anti-proverbs preserve the original message: problems or corruption start at the very top, be it the Russian parliament or the major share-holders of a famous Internet company.

Рыба ищет, где глубже, а человек – где лучше (Fish seek where it is deeper, and people where it is better).
Said about people who decide to change their lives hoping for

better.

AP-1: *Рыба ищет, где глубже, а бизнес, где лучше* (Fish seek where it is deeper, and business where it is better).
Meeting of presidents of Finland and Tatarstan.
New lexical content.
http://karim-yaushev.ru/2010/11/10/930/

AP-2: *Рыба ищет, где глубже, а футболист – где лучше* (Fish seek where it is deeper, and soccer players – where it is better).
Two famous soccer players from Chelsea – Joe Cole and Michael Ballack – left the club because they did not like the new contracts; 06.2010.
New lexical content.
http://novostimira.com/novosti_mira_1907.html

AP-3: *Рыба ищет, где глубже, а капитал, где лучше* (Fish seek where it is deeper, and capital where it is better).
Foreign investments in Russia after the new law "On Foreign Currency" was enacted (2005).
New lexical content.
http://www.spekulant.ru/archive/2005/63/2005_01_st3.html

AP-4: *Рыба ищет где глубже, а микроб – где лучше* (Fish seek where it is deeper, and microbes where it is better).
Infectious diseases in summer time when it is hot and microbes spread easily.
New lexical content.
http://www.leonon.ru/healt/Zdorove_goroda_ryba_iset.html

Comments: This is a surprisingly homogeneous group: all new proverbs replace the word *человек* (people) from the original phrase and substitute it with something else, thus leaving the internal rhyme *глубже – лучше* (deeper – better) intact. The message is equally intact: all new proverbs claim that someone or something seeks a better place, be it soccer players (#2), investors (#1, 3), or even microbes (#4).

Рыбак рыбака видит издалека (A fisherman sees another fisherman from afar). People who have similar interests quickly bond and start doing things together.
English equivalent: Birds of a feather flock together.

AP-1: *Рыбак голубка видит издалека?* (Rybak/fisherman sees a gay person from afar?)
Homosexuality as an allegedly decisive factor in the Eurovision song competition.
Hidden rhyme; internal rhyme; homonym.
http://www.kp.ru/daily/24497.3/651121/

AP-2: *Литвак литвака видит издалека* (A Lithuanian sees another Lithuanian from afar).
Economic cooperation between Lithuania and Israel (where many have Lithuanian roots).
Hidden rhyme; internal rhyme; neologism.
http://news.rambler.ru/8551122/

AP-3: *Маньяк маньяка видит издалека* (A maniac sees another maniac from afar).
A review of the movie *Dexter*.
http://www.kinokopilka.tv/reviews/4046

AP-4: *Врач врача видит издалека* (A doctors sees another doctor from afar).
An interview with two actors playing two friends-physicians in a Russian TV series.
New lexical content.
http://teleweek.ru/12737

AP-5: *Инспектор рыбака видит издалека* (Inspector sees a fisherman from afar).
Meetings of the Estonian and Russian fish protection agencies.
New lexical content; internal rhyme.
http://pravdapskov.ru/rubric/3/6708

AP-6: *Учёный учёного видит издалека...* (A scientist sees another scientist from afar…)

Video conferences between researchers from Novosibirsk Akademgorodok [Russian research center in Siberia] and the National Research Council of Taiwan; during these conferences, joint projects are discussed.
New lexical content.
http://www.portalnano.ru/news/read/420

AP-7: *Казак казака видит издалека* (A Cossack sees another Cossack from afar).
Revival of Cossacks in Ukraine.
Hidden rhyme; internal rhyme.
http://kp.ua/daily/270208/35764/

AP-8: *Рыбак простака видит издалека* (Rybak/fisherman sees a simpleton from afar).
A critical review of the concert of Alexander Rybak, winner of Eurovision competition of 2010.
Homonymy; hidden rhyme; internal rhyme.
http://www.jamsession.ru/?page=news&type=15&id=1334

AP-9: *Бандюк бандюка видит издалека* (A bandit sees another bandit from afar).
Presidents of two republics, South Ossetia and Abkhazia, will leave with official visits to Nicaragua and Venezuela – the only countries that acknowledged their independence; July 2010.
Hidden rhyme; internal rhyme.
http://www.ua-today.com/modules/myarticles/article_storyid_34584.html

AP-10: Грибник грибника видит издалека (A mush-roomer sees another mushroomer from afar).
A person went to pick mushrooms in the forest and got lost; another one helped him come out of the forest safely.
Hidden rhyme; internal rhyme.
http://www.stavropolye.tv/sfdnews/view/13512

Comments: The traditional proverb has internal rhyme, and interestingly, the majority of new proverbs (except #4 and 6) preserve this feature (and as a result, have hidden rhyme). In order to do that, anti-proverbs often have to use morphologically strange or colloquial forms of words. Thus, in #2, we have the word *литвак* (Lithuanian). This form is as far from the literary standard as it can be (the standard form will be *литовец*), but it is done to preserve the rhyme. The same is true for #9 – *бандюк* (bandit) is a low colloquial form of the word *бандит*. Besides, most of them preserve the message of the traditional proverb, too, claiming that people who have something in common (be it bandits or Lithuanians) stick together. On this background, we have a very interesting example in #1 (and partly in #8). It is based on the homonymous relations between the word *рыбак* (fisherman) in the original proverb, and the last name of the singer – *Рыбак* (Rybak), who won Eurovision competition in 2010. The author of the article alleges that gay artists have more chances to win at this competition, and Alexander Rybak won because he was gay. To understand this hint, one has to keep in mind that in Russian slang, gay is *голубой*, (literally: blue), and to preserve the internal rhyme the author of the article has to use this word in a strange, though contextually understandable, form: *голубка.* The same homonymy is used in #8, which claims that Rybak does a bad job during his concerts, and only naïve people can like it: because *Rybak* is the first word of the sentence, it can be interpreted both as the last name of the singer and also as the word for "fisherman," which is enough to establish an association with the traditional proverb. The second word, *fisherman* (from the traditional proverb), is replaced by the Russian word *простака* (simpleton), which rhymes with *рыбака* and thus preserves the internal rhyme of the original phrase. Another interesting case, though for completely different reasons, is #6. Here, the phrase "sees from afar" is used literally, as the article describes video-conferences between Russian and Taiwanese scientists who literally see each other via video conferencing.

C

Не в свои сани не садись (Do not sit in somebody else's sledge).
Do not try to do something that you cannot cope with.

AP-1: *Не в свой Saab не садись* (Do not sit in somebody else's Saab).
General Motors sold Saab.
New lexical content.
www.izvestia.ru/auto/article3137827/

AP-2: *Не в свою систему не садись* (Do not sit in somebody else's system).
Comparison of sound amplifiers used with different acoustic systems.
New lexical content.
http://hi-fi.ru/review/detail/698964

Comments: The proverb with Saab is very good, as it preserves the rhythm of the traditional phrase; besides, Saab, though not a paronym to the Russian word *сани* (sledge) still sounds quite similar, because the first syllable (the stressed one) is the same: *са-* and *Sa-*. The second anti-proverb is less interesting, as it ruins the rhythm of the original phrase (the new word has three syllables, and the stress is on the second one); besides, it has little to do both with the traditional proverb and with the content of the article; thus, used mostly to catch attention with little or no concern about the meaning.

Всяк сверчок знай свой шесток (Every cricket should know its place).
Know your place, status; usually said to someone who interferes with others' business or behaves contrary to his or her status.
English equivalent: The cobbler should stick to his last.

AP-1: *Каждый судья – знай свой шесток!* (Every judge should know his place!)
Judge Tatyana Shevlyakova was dismissed after she tried to interfere into violations in the construction firm in Khabarovsk.
New lexical content.
http://www.debri-dv.com/article/3136

AP-2: *Знай свой шесток* (Know your place).
The governor of the Republic of Karelia publicly reprimanded

the mayor of Petrozavodsk [capital of Karelia] city council for the lack of day care centers in the city.
Ellipsis.
http://politika-karelia.ru/?p=4554

AP-3: *Бюрократия. Знай, Европа, свой шесток* (Bureaucracy. Europe, know your place).
Problems for Russians and Europeans trying to obtain a US visa or get into the US.
New lexical content.
http://dlib.eastview.com/browse/doc/5170154

AP-4: *Каждый танцор знай свой шесток* (Each dancer, know your pole/place).
A journalist worked for a week in strip club.
Polysemy.
http://www.nomad.su/?a=8-200404130004

AP-5: *Казахстан: Русский сверчок, знай свой шесток?* (Kazakhstan: Russian cricket, know your place?)
Treating Russians in Kazakhstan as second-rate citizens.
New lexical content.
http://www.zonakz.net/blogs/user/kazakaza/10073.html?mode=reply

Comments: Except #4, all new proverbs continue the message of the traditional phrase: know your place, status, be it a judge (#1), a mayor (#2), or Russians in Kazakhstan (#5). The most interesting example, however, is #4, where the word *шесток* (literally: little pole) is used in two meanings simultaneously, thus creating a wordplay: one is the meaning used in the original proverb: place, status; but in this context, it is also used in its literal meaning – a pole, since dancers in strip clubs dance around poles, and so they should know the correct movements – "their poles."

Свет клином не сошелся (The earth is not only limited to this small plot of land).
One can live without something desirable, and find something

similar.
Note: *Клин* in this context means a narrow land plot.
English equivalent: There are plenty more fish in the sea.

AP-1: *Лукашенко: на России свет клином не сошелся* (Lukashenko: The earth is not limited only to Russia).
Belorussia should search for other markets, as Russia does not fulfill its promises; March 2010.
New lexical content.
http://actualcomment.ru/news/11080/

AP-2: *На лампочках свет клином не сошелся* (The earth is not limited only to bulbs).
Ministry of economic development of Russia, to save energy, plans to ban bulbs more than 100 watt; Russia does not produce energy-saving bulbs, and has to import them.
New lexical content.
http://www.kadis.ru/daily/?id=73562

AP-3: *На Европе и США свет клином не сошелся* (The earth is not limited to only Europe and USA).
Relations between Russia and US and Europe; 10.2008.
New lexical content.
http://news.km.ru/na_evrope_i_ssha_svet_klinom_ne_

AP-4: *На Renault свет клином не сошелся* (The earth is not limited to only Renault).
If Renault does not want to invest in Russian auto industry, Avtovaz [one of the largest car manufacturers in Russia] will look for other investors.
New lexical content.
http://www.interfax.ru/business/txt.asp?id=110147

AP-5: *На Джобсе свет клином не сошелся!* (The earth is not limited to only Jobs!)
Investors and specialists overestimate the role of Steve Jobs in Apple; 12.2008.
New lexical content.
http://www.sotovik.ru/news/svet-klinom-na-jobse.html

AP-6: *Транспорт будущего: на нефти свет клином не сошелся* (The transport of the future: the earth is not limited only to oil).
05.2004.
New lexical content.
http://www.pravda.ru/science/eureka/inventions/06-05-2004/47177-autofuture-0/

AP-7: *На Chrome и Firefox свет клином не сошелся* (The earth is not limited to only Chrome and Firefox).
Choosing web browser; May 2010.
New lexical content.
http://debback.blogspot.com/2010/05/chrome-firefox.html

AP-8: *На ICQ свет клином не сошелся* (The earth is not limited only to ICQ).
Other IM programs; 09.2010.
New lexical content.
http://frash.od.ua/na-icq-svet-klinom-ne-soshelsya/

AP-9: *На золоте свет клином не сошелся* (The earth is not limited only to gold).
What other metals are good for investing money besides gold.
New lexical content.
http://www.extra-n.ru/text/koshelek/dragotcennie_vi_nashi_na_zolote_svet_klinom_ne_soshelsya/

AP-10: *На МГУ свет клином не сошелся* (The earth is not limited to MGU [Moscow State University]).
Most prestigious and expensive colleges and universities – 2008.
New lexical content.
http://www.faito.ru/archnews/1214505732,1225812544/

AP-11: *Если на школе свет сошелся клином* (If the earth is limited to school).
Difficulties for 6-7 years old kids when they start school, especially during the first 2-3 months.
Antonym.
http://www.happymagazin.ru/articles/id/762

Comments: All anti-proverbs in this group are very similar, as they all have the same message as that of the traditional proverb: there are plenty more fish in the sea, be it finding new markets (#1), alternatives to oil (#6), choosing a web browser (#7), or new ways to invest money besides buying gold (#9). The only exception is #11, which treats the original proverb literally, that is, describes a situation when there is no choice, and what parents should do to help kids to adjust to their school environment.

Седина в бороду, бес в ребро (Grey hair in the beard, devil into the rib).
Said about an elderly person who starts paying attention to women.

AP-1: *Джеб в бороду, хук в ребро* (Jab into the beard, hook into the rib).
A review of several professional boxing matches; July 2007.
New lexical content.
http://www.sports.ru/boxing/3147781.html

AP-2: *Коса в бороду, тату в ребро* (Braid in the beard, tattoo in the rib).
Fashionable hair-dos and tattoos in Moscow, for summer holidays.
New lexical content.
http://7days.ucoz.ru/publ/8-1-0-5

Comments: Both anti-proverbs are prime examples of a situation when the new versions have nothing to do with the traditional phrase, and the association with it is needed for the writers simply to catch readers' attention.

В семье не без урода (The family is not without a freak).
Said about a person who differs from others (in the family, or company) by bad habits, character, behavior, etc.
English equivalent: Accidents will happen in the best regulated families.

AP-1: *В армии не без урода* (Army is not without a freak).
Drafting in the Russian army people with medical problems, as well as former convicts.
New lexical content.
http://www.gazeta.ru/social/2009/10/01/3268409.shtml

Comments: This lonely example both continues the message of the traditional proverb and adjusts it to the new context, talking not so much about bad habits or character but about people with medical problems or former convicts.

Сила есть – ума не надо (If one has muscles, one does not need brains).
Physical force used without thinking is useless and harmful. Said as a negative opinion of some action or its results based only on using force.

AP-1: *Деньги есть — ума не надо* (If one has money, one does not need brains).
Low professionalism and irresponsibility of Russian traders lead to losses for the clients; 02.2009.
New lexical content.
http://www.banki.ru/news/daytheme/?id=836901

AP-2: *Пиво есть — ума не надо?* (If one has beer, one does not need brains?)
Parents of schoolchildren are concerned that beer is sold in places near secondary schools; November 2010.
New lexical content.
http://www.ozersk74.ru/news/city/6357.php

AP-3: *Деньги есть – ума не надо?* (If one has money, one does not need brains?)
DUI accidents in Switzerland with sons of Russian billionaires; 11.2009.
New lexical content. Cf. #1
http://corrupcia.net/news/price/fact-483.html

AP-4: *Тариф есть – ума не надо* (If one has tariff, one does not

need brains).
Increase of the cost of electricity, water, gas; 12.2010.
New lexical content.
http://karavanros.ru/arhive.php?c=74&pc=1248&m=1478

AP-5: *Поиск есть – ума не надо* (If one has search, one does not need brains).
The lack of knowledge in young people, due to modern technology.
New lexical content.
http://www.charodey.ru/modules.php?op=modload&name=News&file=article&sid=118

AP-6: *Крылья есть. Ума не надо?* (One has wings. One does not need brains?)
After a TU-154 plane crashed near Donetsk, an inspection of all airports and airlines started in Russia.
New lexical content.
http://gazeta.aif.ru/online/aif/1350/07_04

AP-7: *У нас пока действует принцип "свобода есть – ума не надо"* (We still use the principle, "If one has freedom, one does not need brains.")
An interview with Yasen Zasurskiy [Dean of journalism department of Moscow University] about journalism today, and how many young reporters understand freedom as a license to write about anything; October 2004.
New lexical content.
http://www.rg.ru/2004/10/29/zasurskij-dz.html

AP-8: *Викинг Викки: ум есть, силы не надо* (Viking Vikki: if one has brains, one does not need muscles).
A popular character of the book for children *Vicky the Viking* written by Swedish writer Runer Yonsson (1963).
Chiasmus.
http://www.dw-world.de/dw/article/0,,4658338,00.html

AP-9: *Ксива есть – ума не надо?* (If one has an ID, one does not need brains?)

A person with a fake ID pretending to be a policeman.
New lexical content.
http://www.izvestia.kz/news.php?date=27-08-09&number=7

AP-10: *Google есть, ума не надо* (If one has Google, one does not need brains).
Laura Rosenberg, a California native, accessed Google Maps on her Blackberry while in Utah to get walking directions. Google directed her toward a rural highway with no sidewalk. The woman walked down the highway and was struck by a vehicle. She turned around and sued Google for $100,000 plus punitive damages. May 2010.
New lexical content.
http://www.paranoiac.ru/2010/06/google-est-uma-ne-nado/

Comments: An interesting common feature of all new proverbs (except #8, see below) is that all of them replace only one word in the traditional proverb – *сила* (muscles) and leave everything else intact. This, of course, helps to establish clear association with the original phrase. Moreover, all of the proverbs confirm (even if they question it) the original message, as well: if you have something (money – #1, 3, fake ID – #9, search engine – #5, wings – #6) you do not have to think. The only exception is #8, which is an example of chiasmus to the original proverb, as it claims that if one has brains one does not need physical force. This is the message of Runer Yonsson's book (1963) that was later made into cartoons and a movie. The most striking example – not linguistically, but from the point of view of the situation that is being described by the proverb – is the last one, #10: on the one hand, it is ridiculous, but on the other, it shows the extent to which people today rely on their gadgets, and this is not funny at all.

Лучше синица в руке, чем журавль в небе (It is better to have a chickadee in the hand than a crane in the sky).
It is better to really possess something little than try to get something bigger or better but hardly achievable.
English equivalent: A bird in the hand is worth two in the bush.

AP-1: *Лучше депутатство в руке, чем губернаторство в небе* (Better a position of a lawmaker in hand than governorship in the sky).
Elections of the mayor of Saint-Petersburg: one of the candidates decided not to take part in the elections, having been promised a seat in the Russian parliament; 07.2003.
New lexical content.
http://www.flb.ru/info/19165.html

AP-2: *Лучше голубь в руке, чем ракета «земля - воздух» в небе!* (Better a dove in the sky than a ground-to-air missile in the sky!)
On March 8, 2003 (International Women's Day) people in Moscow let doves into the air with their wishes attached to the doves' legs.
New lexical content.
http://www.kp.md/daily/22983/2068/

AP-3: *Лучше яблоко в руке, чем апельсин в небе...* (Better an apple in hand than an orange in the sky).
The caption to a photo: a girl sits with an apple core in hand and looks at the falling orange.
New lexical content.
http://www.photosight.ru/photos/1718506/

Comments: Only the first anti-proverb continues the message of the traditional proverb; the other two use the association simply as a catchy title (#2) or caption (#3).

Скупой платит дважды (A miser pays twice).
It does not pay to be a miser; saving on something now one will have to pay more in the future.
English equivalent: Penny wise and pound foolish.

AP-1: *Водитель платит дважды* (Drivers pay twice).
New taxes in 2011 for gasoline, on top of the old "transport tax."
New lexical content.

http://www.pravda.ru/economics/rules/lobbyists/20-07-2010/1041483-news-0/

AP-2: *Толстяк платит дважды* (A fatty pays twice).
Finland introduced a new tax on sweets: candy, ice-cream, etc. 12.2010.
New lexical content.
http://slon.ru/blogs/kranks/post/496422/

AP-3: *Любой платит дважды* (Anyone pays twice).
The first paid highway was opened in Russia, 50 km long; only 18% of citizens agreed to pay for the roads; over 40% said under no circumstances they will use paid roads; 12.2010.
Hidden rhyme.
http://digest.subscribe.ru/auto/roads/n428993284.html

AP-4: *Толстый платит дважды* (A fat person pays twice).
Air companies in different countries make obese passengers buy a second seat.
New lexical content.
http://www.ntv.ru/novosti/184995/

AP-5: *Город платит дважды* (The city pays twice).
Rates for public transport in Saint-Petersburg increased in January 2011.
New lexical content.
http://www.novayagazeta.spb.ru/2010/93/8

AP-6: *Бедный платит дважды* (The poor pay twice).
Russian taxpayers twice paid for the film by Nikita Mikhalkov [famous Russian producer] “Sibirsky Tsirulnik”: once, when he got money from the federal budget, and the second time, when state TV paid for showing the movie.
New lexical content.
http://www.compromat.ru/page_10483.htm

AP-7: *Курильщик платит дважды* (Smokers pay twice).
Damage to health from smoking.
New lexical content.

http://www.likar.info/coolhealth/35380/

AP-8: *В Смоленске экономный платит дважды* (In Smolensk, thrifty people pay twice).
Why water meters are not saving money; September 2010.
New lexical content.
http://www.rabochy-put.ru/tocustomer/10721-v-smolenske-jekonomnyjj-platit-dvazhdy.html

AP-9: *Нарушитель платит дважды* (Violators pay twice).
Traffic fines payment: drivers have to notify traffic police that they did pay the fine; if they do not, court executives will start enforcement procedure and double the fine.
New lexical content.
http://www.novayagazeta.ru/data/2007/driver12/01.html

AP-10: *Парковки Киева: рассеянный платит дважды* (Parking in Kiev: absent-minded pay twice).
If drivers misplace their ticket, they pay a fine.
New lexical content.
http://www.smart-parking.com.ua/pressa/100211/

AP-11: *Скупой не платит дважды* (A miser does not pay twice).
Drip irrigation is saving money in greenhouses and small land plots.
Antonym.
http://www.agro-technika.ru/issue/14/873/

Comments: With the exception of the last anti-proverb, no new coinage has any semantic connection to the original message – don't be penny wise and pound foolish. Instead, they all tell their own stories, either connected with paying too much for something that is not worth it (#1, 3, 8) or they treat the phrase literally and tell about paying two times for the same thing (#4, 6, 9, 10). The last proverb, #11, denies the traditional wisdom and claims that being thrifty – in the context of irrigation equipment – is paying off. Linguistically, the best coinage is #3, as it has hidden rhyme: *скупой* (miser) – *любой* (anyone). All other proverbs not only have no hidden rhyme, but many of them also replace the original two-syllable word *скупой* (miser) with three-four syllable words.

Слезами горю не поможешь (Tears will not alleviate the grief).
Crying will not help change the situation.
English equivalent: It's no use crying over spilt milk.

AP-1: *Судами горю не поможешь...* (Courts will not alleviate the grief).
Constitutionality of President Yushchenko dismissing Ukrainian parliament in 2008.
Hidden rhyme.
http://www.zn.ua/1000/1550/64492/

AP-2: *Деньгами горю не поможешь* (Money will not alleviate the grief).
Money handouts to the victims of the catastrophe at Sayano-Shushenskaya hydro electric station; August 2009.
Hidden rhyme.
http://smi.liga.net/articles/IT094982.html

AP-3: *Словами горю не поможешь* (Words will not alleviate the grief).
British Petroleum bought from Google and Yahoo! key words concerning the oil spill in the Gulf of Mexico; 06.2010.
Hidden rhyme.
http://www.ko.ru/articles/22179

AP-4: *Штрафом горю не поможешь* (Fines will not alleviate the grief).
Fines do not stop people from illegally buying and selling various scrap metal; 11.2000.
New lexical content.
http://www.kazpravda.kz/c/1006111550/2000-11-15

AP-5: *Рублём горю не поможешь, нужны миллионы* (A ruble will not alleviate the grief; millions are needed).

The article traces the lives of people who were injured during a fire in the night club in the city of Perm.
Syntactic extension. Defeated expectancy.
http://www.mediamonitor.perm.ru/?go=1344702&pass=0538fda68076b654cb7f31c0a7f2b4d9

Comments: The only proverb that keeps the traditional message is #2: money handouts will not help the families that lost their loved ones during the catastrophe. All other new proverbs use the association with the traditional proverb simply to catch readers' attention. At the same time, they are coined very well: three proverbs have hidden rhyme (#1, 2, and 3), and #5 uses defeated expectancy: the first part (A ruble will not alleviate the grief) seems to mean, as usual, that money will not solve some problem; but when one reads further, it becomes clear that the word *ruble* is used here not in the general sense (money) but in its literal sense – one ruble, that is, very little money. Thus, much more is needed – this is the message.

Слово не воробей, вылетит – не поймаешь (A word is not a sparrow; once it flies out, you won't catch it).
One cannot take back or deny what one has already said. Used as advice to think carefully before saying something.
English equivalent: A word spoken is past recalling.

AP-1: *Джек Воробей: вылетит – не поймаешь* (Jack Sparrow: once he flies out, you won't catch him).
A review of the film *Pirates of the Caribbean*.
Polysemy.
http://depp-site.narod.ru/Review/pirates_total_film.htm

AP-2: *Пуля не воробей! вылетит – не поймаешь* (A bullet is not a sparrow! once it flies out you won't catch it).
A person accidently shot himself in the eye playing with his gun.
New lexical content.
http://0-50.ru/news/incident/2010-01-05/id_6553.html

AP-3: *Сумка не воробей, вылетит не поймаешь* (Luggage is not a sparrow, if it flies out you won't catch it).

European association of air carriers published data on lost luggage; 02.2006.
New lexical content.
http://www.transport.ru/1/5/i31_1612p1.htm

AP-4: *Авто — не воробей, улетит — не поймаешь* (Automobile is not a sparrow, once it flies out you won't catch it).
Car thefts in Latvia and a company specializing in car security.
New lexical content.
http://www.autoavize.lv/index.php?n=571&a=3335

Comments: None of the new coinages has any semantic relation with the traditional proverb; thus, they all use the association simply to catch readers' attention. Linguistically, the best coinage is #1, where the wordplay is based on the fact that the last name of the pirate is *воробей* (Sparrow) (the same play on words is preserved in Russian).

Слухом земля полнится (The earth gets filled with rumor).
Said as an explanation for why one knows something, without telling the source of information; similar to the English phrase, *A little bird told me.*

AP-1: *«Мирянами» земля полнится* (The earth gets filled with "Miryane").
Dating service for people with disabilities, named "Miryane," opened in the city of Yekaterinburg.
New lexical content.
http://ekaterinburg.bezformata.ru/listnews/miryanami-zemlya-polnitsya/89284/

AP-2: *Земля трупами полнится* (The earth gets filled with corpses).
A review of the thriller movie "Yulenka."
New lexical content.
http://www.kinonews.ru/article_1911/

AP-3: *Тезками земля полнится* (The earth gets filled with namesakes).

Famous soccer players who share the same name – Ronaldo.
New lexical content.
http://www.soccer.ru/articles/118167.shtml

Comments: Once again, the anti-proverbs have no connection to the message of the traditional phrase, which they use at its face value, describing the increase in the number of people – disabled (#1), dead (#2), or soccer players (#3).

Перед смертью не надышишься (You can't breathe enough before death).
There is no sense trying to do something at the last moment.

AP-1: *Перед отставкой не надышишься* (You can't breathe enough before stepping down).
President of Bashkiria Murtaza Rakhimov tries to use all his resources to stay in power; 10.2009.
New lexical content.
http://www.moscow-post.ru/politics/001256538313853/

AP-2: *Перед 1 сентября... не надышишься* (You can't breathe enough before the 1st of September).
Advice to parents whose kids go to school for the first time.
New lexical content.
http://www.shans.com.ua/?m=nr&id=10440&in=100

Comments: The first proverb continues the message of the traditional phrase, only using resignation, not death, as a benchmark, though for a political figure, and especially president of the country, stepping down is a political death. The second proverb advises parents to stay calm and do their best to prepare kids for school, and thus has little to do with the original proverb.

Двум смертям не бывать (а одной не миновать) (There cannot be two deaths (but you cannot avoid one).
Said when one decided to try some risky action. Usually only the first part of the proverb is used.

AP-1: *Двум не бывать, а одного не миновать* (There cannot be two, but you cannot avoid one).
Two major exhibition complexes in Moscow compete to host an international car show; 09.2005.
Ellipsis.
http://www.vmdaily.ru/article/15080.html

AP-2: *Двум лидерам не бывать* (There cannot be two leaders).
Canadian prime minister Jean Chrétien may step down ahead of time; there will be a new leader of the Liberal Party; 09.2003.
New lexical content.
http://www.izvestia.ru/world/article38568/

AP-3: *Двум... не бывать!* (There cannot be two…!)
Life insurance and life expectancy.
Ellipsis.
http://forsake.ru/14.shtml

AP-4: *Двум Park Inn в Омске не бывать* (There cannot be two Park Inns in Omsk).
Two companies want to build a Park Inn hotel in Omsk.
New lexical content.
http://sib.adme.ru/mzhkdevelopment/dvum-park-inn-v-omske-ne-byvat-7843/

AP-5: *Двум наказаниям не бывать, но одного не миновать...* (There cannot be two punishments, but you cannot avoid one…)
Individual entrepreneurs who did not reregister by 01.2005 cannot be brought to administrative responsibility, but they can be fined.
New lexical content.
http://www.klerk.ru/buh/news/23528/

AP-6: *Обама: двум великим депрессиям не бывать* (Obama: there cannot be two Great Depressions).
12.2009.
New lexical content.
HTTP://NM2000.KZ/NEWS/2009-12-06-22437

AP-7: *Двум МВД в России не бывать* (There cannot be two Ministers of the Interior).
Russian parliament passed a law banning the usage of state symbols, names of government agencies, etc.; May 2010.
New lexical content.
http://www.newizv.ru/news/2010-05-19/126460/

AP-8: *Двум национальным праздникам не бывать* (There cannot be two national holidays).
Kazakh parliament first established two national holidays; then legislators changed their opinion and voted for one only; 04.2009.
http://www.kp.kz/node/6617

Comments: The only new proverb that has a semantic connection with the traditional proverb is, not surprisingly, proverb #3, as it talks about life insurance. It is also interesting from the point of view of its linguistic mechanism, which is ellipsis (the word *death* is omitted), but the remaining construction is enough to create the necessary association. It is thanks to this association that the writer does not have to use the word *death* itself. This – elliptical – form is also better simply because most people do not like to be reminded about death and dying. All other anti-proverbs have little to do with the traditional phrase and simply discuss situations where there needs to be chosen one of two (exhibition halls – #1, leaders of the party – #2, hotels – #4, penalties – #5, national holidays – 8).

Соловья баснями не кормят (Nightingales do not live on chitchat/idle talk).
Usually said to the guests when the host invites them to the dinner table.
English equivalent: Fine words butter no parsnips.

AP-1: *Артиста баснями не кормят* (Actors do not live on idle talk).
Recipes from famous actors.
New lexical content.

http://media-kuban.ru/ki_gazeta/2010-12-31_Artista_basnyami_ne_kormyat.html

AP-2: *Бизнес баснями не кормят* (Business does not live on idle talk).
Suggestion to lower taxation on small businesses in Belorussia; 04.2009.
New lexical content.
http://www.ng.by/ru/issues?art_id=31721

AP-3: *Тимошенко опять кормит баснями о контрактной армии* (Timoshenko again gives us idle talk about professional army).
Populist promises of Yulia Timoshenko before presidential elections in Ukraine; February 2010.
Syntactic extension.
http://globalist.org.ua/novosti/society-news/novosti-ukrainy-vybory-975610152-no31665.html

AP-4: *ГФИ кормят баснями* (Inspector General is given idle talk).
Valery Lazarev, Inspector General for Ulyanovskaya oblast talks about problems in his work; the government of the region ignores his requests; 12.2008.
New lexical content.
http://simcat.ru/readnews/8732/

Comments: Only the first anti-proverb continues the idea of eating; all others lay emphasis on the idle talk, or nonsense that is being told by a presidential candidate (#3) or government officials (#4). Somewhere in between is anti-proverb #2, which talks about lowering taxation for small businesses (will it leave them more money for food?)

Утопающий хватается за соломинку (A drowning man catches at a straw).
A person who is in a desperate situation will be eager to use any means, even ones hardly helpful, to get out of trouble.

AP-1: *Адвокат Виктора Бута хватается за соломинку* (Defense attorney of Victor But catches at a straw).
But's lawyer appealed the decision of Thailand court to extradite him to the US. 10.2010.
Note: Victor But is a convicted arms smuggler (2011).
New lexical content.
http://www.voanews.com/russian/news/Victor-boot-Extradition-2010-10-08-104594094.html

AP-2: *Евро хватается за соломинку* (Euro catches at a straw).
In spite of the fact that European stock exchanges continue to show growth there is little optimism about European currency. 12.2010.
New lexical content.
http://www.finam.ru/international/imdaily0158C/

AP-3: *Лужков хватается за соломинку* (Luzhkov catches at a straw).
The mayor of Moscow, Yury Luzhkov, announced that he is not going to step down ahead of time, and will sue federal TV stations. 09.2010.
New lexical content.
http://www.spravedlivo-online.ru/content/news/SER1.php?news=11514

AP-4: *Обманутые эстонские бизнесмены хватаются за последнюю соломинку* (Deceived Estonian businessmen catch at the last straw).
"Seaside Residence Baku" company issued promissory notes for large scale real estate projects to Estonian investors who lost tens of millions; they demanded that the company be pronounced bankrupt; July 2010.
New lexical content.
http://rus.delfi.ee/daily/business/obmanutye-estonskie-biznesmeny-hvatayutsya-za-poslednyuyu-solominku.d?id=32228493

Comments: All anti-proverbs use the message of the traditional proverb: any means, no matter how unreliable, are used to try and achieve some goal, be it fighting extradition (#1), or trying to get back the money (#4), or the mayor's refusal to step down (#3).

Один с сошкой, семеро с ложкой (One with a plough, seven with a spoon).
Several people who do not work are supported by one who does all the work.

AP-1: *Четверо с сошкой и ложкой* (Four with a plough and a spoon).
Departments of Agriculture of four countries: Brazil, Russia, India and China agreed to cooperate in the food market.
Syntactic restructuring, new lexical content.
http://www.mcx.ru/news/news/show/3865.174.htm

AP-2: *Один с сошкой, четырнадцать с ложкой* (One with a plough, fourteen with a spoon).
According to this post, Russian Federation fed the other 14 republics of the Soviet Union.
New lexical content.
http://www.perunica.ru/kartinki/2895-odin-s-soshkoj-chetyrnadcat-s-lozhkoj.html

AP-3: *КАСКО с сошкой, семеро с ложкой* (Hull insurance with a plough, seven with a spoon).
The ratio of premiums and payments for obligatory motor insurance is over 70%, since basic tariffs have not changed during seven years. 10.2010.
New lexical content.
http://www.gorodfinansov.ru/news/index.php?article=11050

AP-4: *Крестьянин с сошкой, бюрократы с ложкой* (A peasant with a plough, bureaucrats with a spoon).
An individual farmer has to meet 176 norms and regulations during one year.
New lexical content.
http://www.gorod.lv/novosti/83463-krestyanin_s_soshkoy_byurokratyi_s_lozhkoy

AP-5: *Семеро с сошкой, один – с ложкой* (Seven with a plough, one with a spoon).
10% of the citizens of Russia have 1/3 of all profits; 04.2010
Antonym.
http://clubs.ya.ru/4611686018427392330/replies.xml?item_no=54795

AP-6: *В Одессе на тысячу с сошкой – шестьсот с ложкой* (In Odessa, there are six hundred with a spoon to one thousand with a plough).
There are 591 not-working people to one thousand working in the city of Odessa; 08.2010.
New lexical content.
http://www.048.ua/news/24962

AP-7: *Сколько мужиков с сошкой на одного чиновника с ложкой* (How many people with a plough to one bureaucrat with a spoon).
There is one bureaucrat per 140 citizens of Russia; 12.2010.
New lexical content.
http://www.rtkorr.com/news/2010/12/21/201533.new

AP-8: *Кто с сошкой, тот и с ложкой...* (He who is with a plough is also with a spoon…)
Hot meals for persons taking part in the harvest; 08.2009.
Syntactic restructuring.
http://www.mogved.by/ekonomika-biznes-proizvodstvo/1973

AP-9: *И с сошкой, и с ложкой!* (Both with a plough and with a spoon!)
How to choose good food to use at summer cottage (dacha).
Syntactic restructuring.
http://www.kp.ru/daily/23513.4/40097/

AP-10: *Один учитель с сошкой – десять чиновников с ложкой* (One teacher with a plough, ten bureaucrats with a spoon).
Too much paperwork and other bureaucratic requirement leave teachers less and less time for teaching; Ukraine (Donetsk).
New lexical content.

http://uznal.info/krik-2006-a12670

Comments: The majority of the new proverbs keep the message of the traditional phrase: there are fewer people who actually produce something than those who only shuffle papers. Still, there are several exceptions. Thus, #5 is about inequality in profit, not work; while #8 and 9 interpret the traditional proverb literally to state their own message: #8 is about food for those taking part in harvest work, and #9 advises how to choose food to use in summer.

И на старуху бывает проруха (Even an old woman can make mistakes).
Anyone can make mistakes, even an experienced person.

AP-1: *И на пирата бывает проруха* (Even pirates can make mistakes).
Somali pirates attacked a war ship; November 2010.
New lexical content.
http://blog.kp.ru/users/razinja/post140612025/

AP-2: *И на генетиков бывает проруха*…(Even geneticists can make mistakes…)
A critical review of a research study about the genetic pool of people living on the territory of Russia.
New lexical content.
http://via-midgard.info/news/in_russia/4668-i-na-genetikov-byvaet-proruxa.html

AP-3: *И на налоговую бывает проруха* (Even a tax agency can make mistakes).
Local branches of the tax agency in Ukraine make a lot of mistakes.
New lexical content.
http://www.ligazakon.ua/news_old/ga010288.html

AP-4: *«Ложное искушение»: и на Де Ниро бывает проруха* (“The Good Shepherd”: Even de Niro can make mistakes).

A critical review of the movie *The Good Shepherd*, producer Robert de Niro.
New lexical content.
http://www.fashiontime.ru/cinema/news/5022.html

AP-5: *И на Хакухо бывает проруха* (Even Hakuho can make mistakes).
Sumo wrestler Hakuho won 63 matches in a row, but lost in 64th; 11.2010.
Internal rhyme.
http://www.sport-express.ru/newspaper/2010-11-23/8_2/

Comments: All new proverbs preserve the original message: even an experienced person can make mistakes, be it an experienced actor and producer (#4), or experienced pirates (#1), or an experienced athlete (#5). Linguistically, the best coinage is #5, which preserves the internal rhyme of the traditional proverb (and thus creates hidden rhyme): *старуха – проруха* (old woman – mistake) in the traditional proverb, and *Хакухо – проруха* (Hakuho – mistake) in the new one, based on the fact that the name of the famous sumo wrestler rhymes with the Russian word *проруха* (archaic word for *mistake*). More than that: the name Хакухо not only rhymes with the Russian word *проруха* (mistake), but it has the same number of syllables and the same stress pattern as the original word *старуха* (old woman): both are three-syllable words with the stress on the second syllable. All these features of the anti-proverb make its association with the traditional phrase easily recognized by modern Russian speakers.

У страха глаза велики (Fear has big eyes).
Said about a person who exaggerates the danger or sees danger where there is none.
English equivalent: Fear hath a hundred eyes.

AP-1: *У страха перед КНДР глаза велики* (Fear of North Korea has big eyes).
Military conflict between North and South Korea; 11.2010.
New lexical content.

http://www.pravda.ru/world/asia/fareast/26-11-2010/1058889-kndr-0/

AP-2: *У секса глаза велики* (Sex has big eyes).
A 38-years old man is a virgin and afraid to meet women; he came to the popular Moscow newspaper and asked them to write about him, hoping it will help solve his problem.
New lexical content.
http://www.mk.ru/social/article/2010/11/19/545708-u-seksa-glaza-veliki.html

AP-3: *У соцстраха глаза велики* (Social security/fear has big eyes).
Payments for sick leaves will get smaller; 11.2010.
Hidden rhyme; homonymy.
http://www.vmdaily.ru/article/108397.html

AP-4: *У исламофобии глаза велики* (Islamophobia has big eyes).
An idea of uniting of Muslims of Russia.
New lexical content.
http://www.islam.ru/pressclub/islamofobia/isfogalut/

AP-5: *У стражи глаза велики* (Security has big eyes).
Qualities necessary for professional body-guards.
Paronymy.
http://www.hr-portal.ru/article/u-strazhi-glaza-veliki

AP-6: *У сноса глаза велики* (Demolition has big eyes).
Citizens of Sokol settlement near Moscow were afraid that all their houses would be demolished, as they were illegally built; 02.2010.
New lexical content.
http://www.kommersant.ru/doc.aspx?DocsID=1316719

AP-7: *У газа глаза велики* (Gas has big eyes).
Increase of the price for natural gas for Ukraine turned out to be lower than the Ukrainian government predicted.
Hidden rhyme.

http://www.kommersant.ua/doc.html?DocID=1507439&IssueId=7000556

Comments: There are two groups of anti-proverbs here: one (larger) preserves the original meaning, that a scared person tends to exaggerated the danger, be it danger of Islam (#4) or danger of sexual relationships (#2). The other group employs the association with this well-known traditional proverb to create a play on words and thus create their own message. Thus, #3, that talks about payments for sick leaves, uses the wordplay based on the coincidence in the form of the Russian words *страх* (fear) and *соцстрах* (social security), while #4 interprets the traditional phrase "big eyes" literally, and describes qualities necessary for body-guards (and good eye sight is obviously one of them). Linguistically, the best coinages are those that create a hidden rhyme – #3: *страха – соцстраха* (fear – social security) and #7: *газа – страха* (gas – fear); the last one is not a perfect rhyme, but it preserves the same rhythm, the same stress on the first syllable, and the new word *газа* (gas) has the same vowels, so the association with the original *страха* (fear) is clearly felt by Russian speakers, and the title makes perfect sense: the fear of increase in price for gas was exaggerated.

От сумы да от тюрьмы не зарекайся (Don't count out a prison cell or a beggar's cup).
One is never safe from misfortune or trouble; bad things can happen to anyone. Often said to a person who is very sure in his or her well-being.

AP-1: *От тюрьмы да от реформы – не зарекайся* (Don't count out a prison cell or reforms).
Reform of penitentiary system in Russia; October 2010.
New lexical content.
http://www.mk.ru/regions/tambov/article/2010/10/06/534612-ot-tyurmyi-da-ot-reformyi-ne-zarekaysya.html

AP-2: *От темницы да от больницы не зарекайся* (Don't count out a prison cell or a hospital room).
Investigation of the penitentiary medicine after the death of

Sergey Magnitsky, who died in jail because he was not given necessary medical treatment.
Note: Sergei Magnitsky was a Russian lawyer specializing in tax law who worked as a counsel for the Russian investment fund Hermitage Capital Management. He was arrested on 28 November 2008 on tax evasion charges filed as part of the investigation launched against Hermitage Capital Management. Many observers believe that the document which formed the basis of the arrest warrant had been fabricated. On 16 November 2009, Sergei Magnitsky died in a Moscow detention facility as a result of having been held in harsh conditions and denied appropriate medical care.
Internal rhyme.
http://www.novayagazeta.spb.ru/2009/95/3

AP-3: *От войны и от тюрьмы не зарекайся* (Don't count out war or prison cell).
An interview with colonel Pavel Popovskih after he spent four years in prison; he was charged with the murder of journalist Dmitry Holodov, but was acquitted.
Internal rhyme.
http://www.zavtra.ru/cgi/veil/data/zavtra/02/456/41.html

AP-4: *От ГАИ и от тюрьмы не зарекайся* (Don't count out traffic police and a prison cell).
An administrative arrest for 15 days for drivers violating traffic rules.
New lexical content.
http://www.trud.ru/article/19-01-2008/124983_ot_gai_i_ot_tjurmy_ne_zarekajsja.html

AP-5: *От сумы и кризиса не зарекайся* (Don't count out a beggars cup and crisis).
World economic crisis of 2008.
New lexical content.
www.rau.su/observer/N2_2009/029_043.pdf

Comments: An interesting feature of this group is the fact that all the new proverbs, while preserving the core message of the traditional proverb, also preserve one of the two key words from it – but use them literally, unlike how they are used in the original saying. Thus, #1-4 use the word "prison" and do talk about prison in various contexts, while #5 preserves the word *сумы* (beggar's cup; in Russian, literally, "beggar's purse" used for alms in the same way as a cup) and do mean it, as many companies and people got bankrupt as a result of the world economic crisis. Linguistically, the most interesting examples are those that retain the internal rhyme used in the traditional proverb – #2 and 3; it is made possible by using new words that rhyme with the remaining lexical content of the original proverb. Thus, we have *сумы – тюрьмы* (purse – prison) in the traditional phrase; and *войны – тюрьмы* (war – prison) in #3; *темницы – больницы* (prison – hospital) in #2.

Не было бы счастья, да несчастье помогло (There would not be luck, but for bad luck help).
Said when something good happens as a result of a problem, unpleasant event, etc.

AP-1: *Не было бы несчастья, да ЕГЭ помог* (There would be no bad luck, if it were not for Unified State Examination help).
New final exams for high school graduates in Russia, and their problems for students.
Antonym.
http://www.odintsovo.info/news/?id=21501

AP-2: *Не было бы экспорта, да кризис помог!* (There would be no export, but for crisis help!)
Economic crisis turned out to be beneficial for Ukrainian exporters of buckwheat.
New lexical content.
http://www.apk-inform.com/showart.php?id=84125

AP-3: *Не было бы счастья, да КГБ помогло* (There would be no luck but for KGB help).
Importing consumer goods from the USA to the Soviet Union with the support of KGB guaranteed the success of the transaction, for 1.5 billion dollars; 07.1991.

New lexical content.
http://www.kommersant.ru/doc.aspx?DocsID=147

AP-4: *Не было бы счастья, да ненастье помогло* (There would be no luck, but for bad weather help).
Children from Prednistrovye, where there was heavy flooding, were invited to come to Moscow by its mayor.
Paronymy; hidden rhyme.
http://www.lgz.ru/article/5799/

AP-5: *Не было бы счастья, да хадж помог* (There would be no luck, but for hadj help).
"Uralskaya nedelya" newspaper was to pay 140,000 dollars to a private company; the owner, after he had been to hudj, decided to drop his charges, and the newspaper does not have to pay anything; 12.2010.
http://respublika-kz.blogspot.com/2010/12/blog-post_8927.html

Comments: Four out of five new proverbs keep the message of the original proverb: something bad or at least unusual had good consequences, be it bad weather (#4), economic crisis (#2), or hadj (#5). The only exception is #1, whose message is exactly the opposite (it interprets the original message literally: there was no bad luck, and thanks to these exams, we now have bad luck): Unified State Exams brought only new problems to high school graduates in Russia, and thus this anti-proverb has nothing to do with the traditional one. Linguistically, the best coinage is #4, built around paronymy (and thus, hidden rhyme) between the original word *несчастье* (bad luck) and *ненастье* (bad weather). In fact, they look and sound so similar that one has to read twice to see the difference, because at first reading one can get an impression that the traditional proverb is simply used in its original form.

T

Плохому танцору и штаны мешают (Bad dancer blames his pants).
Those who cannot do something correctly often try to find the

reasons for the failure not in themselves but in some external circumstances.

AP-1: *Плохому депутату танцы мешают* (Bad deputy blames dances).
An idea to forbid members of the Lithuanian parliament to take part in entertainment shows.
November 2010.
New lexical content.
http://svpressa.ru/society/article/34249/

AP-2: *Заметки о Евангелии – Плохому пастуху овцы мешают* (Notes about Gospels: Bad shepherd blames his sheep).
New lexical content.
http://www.evangelie.ru/forum/t15548.html

AP-3: *Табачник: Плохому ректору ноги мешают* (Tabachnik: Bad rector blames his legs).
Minister of education of Ukraine Dmitry Tabacnhik about not renewing contracts with several rectors of universities.
New lexical content.
http://novostey.com/politic/news286730.html

AP-4: *Плохому танцору мешают брюки, а отечественной Госавтоинспекции – автомобили* (Bad dancer blames his pants, and Russian traffic police – automobiles).
Head of the Russian traffic police said that the increase in the number of cars in Russia during recent years is catastrophic, and that only economic crisis slowed it down.
Syntactic extension.
http://xn--80aeaiumtfabimx.xn--p1ai/news/plokhomu_tancoru_meshajut_brjuki_a_otechestvennoj_gosavtoinspekcii_avtomobili/2009-11-30-438

AP-5: *Плохому асфальту шипы мешают* (Bad asphalt blames studs).
Using studded tires in Moscow.
New lexical content.
http://autorambler.ru/journal/events/09.09.2008/560942176/

AP-6: *Плохому дипломату язык мешает* (Bad diplomat blames his tongue).
German ambassador in Ukraine said that the problem of Ukrainian youth is not that they know Russian poorly, but that they do not know English and German.
New lexical content.
http://newzz.in.ua/politic/1148851744-httpkramtpinfonews12fullid12084.html

Comments: All new proverbs preserve the original message: finding reasons for failure or problems in some external circumstances, be it blaming studded tires for the poor quality of the roads (#5), or entertainment shows for the poor work of members of the Lithuanian legislature (#1).

Без труда не вынешь и рыбку из пруда (You can't even pull a fish out of the pond without some effort).
Nothing can be achieved without effort and diligence.

AP-1: *Без труда не выловишь акта из суда* (You can't even get documents from court without some effort).
Many documents of joint-stock companies have been found void by courts.
Internal rhyme; hidden rhyme.
http://www.msn.kg/ru/news/29221/

AP-2: *Без труда не стать "Ветераном труда"* (You can't become a Veteran of Labor without effort); [literally: you can't become a veteran of work without work].
Difficulties in getting paperwork done for getting the award "Veteran Truda" (Veteran of Labor).
Internal rhyme; hidden rhyme.
http://www.rg.ru/proekt/book/68.shtm

AP-3: *Без труда не очистить дно пруда!* (You can't clean the bottom of the pond without effort!)
Volunteers cleaned the bottom of the pond in the city of Kotelniki.
Internal rhyme.

http://www.kotelniki.info/?p=462

Comments: All new proverbs preserve the key feature of the traditional proverb – internal rhyme, and thus, also create hidden rhyme by substituting a key word from the original phrase with another one, rhyming with it. Thus, we have another *труда* (labor, work, effort) instead of *пруда* (pond) in #2, and *суда* (court) in #1, while in #3 the original rhyming pair is preserved intact. Besides, the last proverb interprets the content of the phrase literally, as it does describe cleaning the bottom of the pond. The other two talk about struggling with bureaucracy (#2) and obtaining court decisions (#1), both of which require a lot of effort. Finally, there is an additional wordplay in #2, because it uses the word *труда* (work, labor, effort) twice, and thus makes a sad joke that people who worked all their lives (the title "Veteran of Labor" is given to people who worked for many years) have to fight to be awarded the title that they earned by their work.

У

Уговор дороже денег (An agreement is worth more than money).
One should carry out one's obligations, keep one's word.

AP-1: *Телефон дороже денег* (Telephone is worth more than money).
Peter Aven, president of Alfa Bank, owns 7% of the telecommunication company Altimo, and these shares cost more than his financial assets.
New lexical content.
http://www.vedomosti.ru/newspaper/article/2010/06/25/238568

AP-2: *Налог на роскошь: популизм дороже денег* (Tax on luxury: populism is worth more than money).
Suggestion to tax luxury goods looks good, even if it is never implemented; July 2010.
New lexical content.
http://www.rian.ru/analytics/20100726/258605008.html

AP-3: *Байкал дороже денег* (Baykal is worth more than money).
Demonstrations demanding to protect Lake Baykal [to stop polluting the lake with waste water] took place in Moscow, Saint-Petersburg and Ulan-Ude. 2010.
New lexical content.
http://news.babr.ru/?IDE=84836

AP-4: *Соцпакет дороже денег* (Benefits package is worth more than money).
Importance of benefits, first of all, insurance, to keep valuable employees in the company.
New lexical content.
http://www.rusconsult.ru/cms-news.php?mode=view_news&id=836

AP-5: *Репутация дороже денег* (Reputation is worth more than money).
Positive image and its importance in business.
New lexical content.
http://www.ancor.ru/company/press/in_the_press/article/articleid/1957/

AP-6: *Договор дороже денег* (Agreement is worth more than money).
Essential contractual conditions in Russian Civil Code.
Hidden rhyme; paronymy.
http://zakoni.com.ua/?q=node/41

AP-7: *Покупатель дороже денег* (Customers are worth more than money).
During crisis, retailers who offer best prices win even if they lose profit.
New lexical content.
http://www.interfax.ru/business/txt.asp?id=120746

AP-8: *Перевод дороже денег* (Transfer [of money] is worth more/more expensive than money).
Review of the ways one can transfer money in Russia today, and

their costs.
New lexical content.
http://www.aferizm.ru/bb/bb_perevodnie-sist.htm

AP-9: *Власть дороже денег* (Power is worth more than money).
Belorussia refused the offer of $3 billion from Europe on the condition that presidential elections will be open and fair; November 2010.
New lexical content.
http://dec19.org/?p=1327

AP-10: *Здоровье нации дороже денег* (The health of the nation is worth more than money).
How government will fight illegal sales of alcohol. January 2011.
New lexical content.
http://www.prime-tass.ru/news/articles/-201/%7BBFD8426B-C5C5-4D05-AE4F-73FF1ED04CFB%7D.uif

AP-11: *Ипотека 2010: оптимизм дороже денег* (Mortgage loans 2010: optimism is worth more than money).
Mortgage market in Russia was improving in 2010, as compared to 2009: more loans, lower interest rates.
New lexical content.
http://www.asvbroker.ru/2010/06/22/ipoteka-2010-optimizm-dorozhe-deneg.html

Comments: There are two groups of anti-proverbs here: the first group (larger) continues the message of the traditional proverb: there are things in life that are more important or more valuable than money, be it benefits for employees (#4), clean water of Lake Baikal (#3), or the positive image of a company (#5). The second group interprets the traditional proverb differently, and, using the polysemy of the word *дороже* (which can mean "more valuable" or "more expensive"), describes situations when to transfer money one has to pay a larger sum than the sum being transferred (#8) or when assets in communication business (*telephone*) cost more than financial assets (*money*); #1.

Ум хорошо, а два лучше (One brain is good, but two brains are better).
Two people can solve a problem that one person cannot solve alone.
English equivalent: Two heads are better than one.

AP-1: *Ум хорошо, а две пары зимних шин всегда лучше!* (One brain is good, but two pairs of winter tires are always better!)
Importance of choosing good winter tires.
New lexical content.
http://shinimport.ru/um_horosho_a_dve_pary.html

AP-2: *Ум – хорошо, а два диплома – лучше* (One brain is good, but two [college] diplomas are better).
Why people are getting a second higher education.
New lexical content.
http://topcareer.ru/db/tc/893EFA5779199B02C3256F39003FB817/education.html

Comments: These two anti-proverbs provide textbook examples of a situation when the traditional proverb has nothing (#1) or very little (#2) to do with the new coinages, and the association with it is used with the only purpose – to catch readers' attention.

Что у трезвого на уме, то у пьяного на языке (What is on the mind of a sober person, a drunken person has on his tongue).
A person who is drunk loses self-control and talks about intimate or touchy things that a sober person will never discuss.

AP-1: *Что у парикмахера на уме, то у клиента и на голове* (What a hairdresser has on the mind, the customer has on the head).
Hairdressers' contest in Mogilev oblast.
Defeated expectancy.
http://gorad.by/by/page/town/943

AP-2: *Что у правительства на уме, то у Кудрина на языке?* (What the government has on the mind, Kudrin has on the tongue?)

Minister of Finances of Russia says that the government does not have money to increase pensions; February 19, 2011.
New lexical content.
http://news.argumenti.ru/society/2011/02/94536

AP-3: *Что у власти на уме, то у Иванова на языке* (What the authorities have on the mind, Ivanov has on the tongue).
Deputy prime-minister Sergey Ivanov said that "people are our second oil."
New lexical content.
http://www.city-n.ru/view/116317.html

Comments: Two of the new proverbs keep the original message of the traditional proverb, only adjusting it to their situations (#2 and 3): what everyone (in the government) is thinking about is what one person says out loud; this is achieved by keeping the key words: *на уме – на языке* (on the mind – on the tongue). Anti-proverb #1 interprets the phrase differently, and by substituting *на языке* (on the mind) by *на голове* (on the head) creates a catchy title about hairdressers' contest; it has very little to do with the original message, but uses it very cleverly by creating a certain defeated expectancy.

Устами младенца глаголет истина (Truth speaks through the child's lips).
A child who is not burdened with conventions of the world of adults can say things which a grown-up person will never say.

AP-1: *Устами наборщика глаголет истина* (Truth speaks through typesetter's lips).
Typos sometimes reveal the true meaning of some government programs that are not affordable for most people.
New lexical content.
http://www.perunica.ru/iumor/1990-ustami-naborshhika-glagolet-istina.html

AP-2: *Устами Жириновского глаголет Кремль* (Kremlin speaks through Zhirinovsky's lips).
Liberal-Democratic Party of Russia introduced a bill to the Rus-

sian parliament, according to which national languages should be taught only to students of that nationality; Vladimir Zhirinovsky is the leader of the party.
New lexical content.
http://www.ufagub.com/index.php?option=com_content&view=article&id=33334860:2011-02-09-01-00-05&catid=34:2010-03-20-22-17-34&Itemid=7

AP-3: *Устами Данилкина глаголет Генпрокуратура?* (Prosecutor general's office speaks through the lips of Danilkin?)
Judge Danilkin, who presided over the hearing of Khodorkovsky's second trial, simply used the charges of the prosecutors in the text of his decision; 27.12.2010.
New lexical content.
http://www.newsland.ru/news/detail/id/607001/cat/94/

Comments: Only the first new proverb has a semantic connection with the traditional saying; the other two simply use the structure, but for a different message: someone uses someone else to voice their ideas: Kremlin uses the leader of a party (#2); prosecutors' office uses a judge (#3).

Ученье свет, неученье тьма (Learning is light, ignorance is darkness).
Said as advice to study, to emphasize the value of knowledge.

AP-1: *Ученье – свет, неученых – тьма* (Learning is light, the amount of ignorant people is enormous).
Problems in the Russian educational system.
Homonymy.
http://www.newtime.su/news/reforma/

AP-2: *Ученье – свет, учебников – тьма* (Learning is light, the number of textbooks is enormous).
Problems of textbooks for Russian secondary schools.
Homonymy.
http://www.kommersant.ru/doc/284365

AP-3: *Ученье – свет, а безработных – тьма* (Learning is

light, the number of unemployed is enormous).
High unemployment forces many people to go back to school in Germany; February 2010.
Homonymy.
http://www.mk-germany.de/node/100

Comments: An interesting feature of this group of anti-proverbs is that they all use the same linguistic mechanism – homonymy between the Russian words *тьма* (darkness) and *тьма* (a great many): in the traditional proverb this word is used as an antonym for light (darkness), while in all anti-proverbs it is used in another meaning – a great many.
Note: In the old Russian calculation system, *тьма* meant 10,000; in the figurative meaning it denotes an unquantifiable amount.

Ч

Человек предполагает, а бог располагает (Man proposes, but God disposes).
Said when something planned does not go as it was designed, some unforeseen events take place.
English equivalent: Man proposes, God disposes.

AP-1: *Человек предполагает, а ремонт располагает* (Man proposes, but remodeling disposes).
Cost of remodeling.
New lexical content.
http://bul-bul.com.ua/article/price.php

AP-2: *Человек предполагает, а Эйяфьятлайокудль располагает* (Man proposes, but Ejyafeljokudl [Icelandic volcano] disposes).
Eruptions of this volcano disrupted air travel in Europe in 2010.
New lexical content.
http://www.chaskor.ru/article/chelovek_predpolagaet_a_ejyafelj okudl_raspolagaet_16821

AP-3: *Эксперты предполагают, а рынок располагает* (Experts propose, but market disposes).

Analysis of stock market volatility; 14.02.11.
New lexical content.
http://www.irn.ru/articles/26784.html

AP-4: *Медведев предполагает, а Путин располагает* (Medvedev proposes, but Putin disposes).
Tensions between Russian president and prime-minister; 21.01.2011.
New lexical content.
http://www.newsland.ru/news/detail/id/619211/cat/94/

AP-5: *Госстрой предполагает, а спрос располагает* (Ministry of Construction proposes, but demand disposes).
Forecast of the Minister of Construction of Russia about housing prices.
New lexical content.
http://www.nrn.ru/article_print.shtml?id=1048

Comments: All new proverbs preserve the essence of the original message: people plan something, but some higher power interferes, be it a more powerful person (#4), or laws of free market (#3 and 5), or forces of nature (#2). Since all anti-proverbs preserve the original structure and the key words: *предполагает – располагает* (supposes – disposes), the new proverbs also preserve the internal rhyme of the traditional proverb, which makes it easier for the readers to create the association between the new version and the original phrase.

Не так страшен черт, как его малюют (Devil is not so scary as he is described). Problems or obstacles that people are afraid of in reality turn out to be much less difficult or scary.
English equivalent: The devil is not so black as he is painted.

AP-1: *Не так страшен грипп, как его малюют* (Flu is not so scary as it is described).
Swine flu.
New lexical content.
http://www.ukrrudprom.com/digest/Ne_tak_strashen_gripp_kak_ego_malyuyut.html

AP-2: *Не так страшен штраф, как его малюют?* (Fines are not so scary as they are described?)
New fines for traffic violations in Russia in 2011.
New lexical content.
http://102km.ru/news/350988.html

AP-3: *Не так страшен кризис, как его малюют* (Crisis is not so scary as it is described).
New products and surprises from Apple and Nokia; 04.2009.
New lexical content.
http://www.sotovik.ru/news/hi-techweek/ne-tak-strashen-krizis-nokia-apple.html

AP-4: *Не так страшен сладкий черт, как его малюют* (The sweet devil is not so scary as it is described).
The harm of sugar is exaggerated; a moderate amount of sugar is necessary.
New lexical content.
http://www.herpes.ru/hudo/sp/cukerman.htm

AP-5: *Не так страшен счетчик, как его малюют* (The meter is not so scary as it is described).
Introducing meters for water and gas in Russia.
New lexical content.
http://www.mk.ru/economics/article/2010/08/19/524134-ne-tak-strashen-schetchik-kak-ego-malyuyut.html

AP-6: *Немецкий язык: не так страшен Дойч, как его малюют* (German language: Deutch is not so scary as it is described).
Learning German.
New lexical content.
http://www.germania-online.ru/wissenschaft-bildung/nauka-i-obrazovanie-detal/datum/2010/07/08/nemeckii-jazyk-ne-tak-strashen-doich-kak-ego-maljujut.html

AP-7: *Так ли страшен дефолт, как его малюют?* (Is default so scary as it is described?)
The economy of Ukraine; 16.03.2011.
New lexical content.

http://finance.liga.net/economics/2011/3/16/articles/21017.htm

AP-8: *Не так страшен бакалавр, как его малюют* (Bachelor program is not so scary as it is described).
Transition to a new higher education system in Russia: bachelor and master programs instead of a five-year course for everyone.
New lexical content.
http://www.birzhaplus.ru/kariera/?61171

Comments: All new proverbs preserve the original message: some problem or difficulty turns out to be not so difficult or scary as it was initially thought, be it a new system of higher education (#8), new fines for traffic violations (#2), new research about the value of sugar (#4), or exaggerated rumors about the new type of flu (#1). Taking into account that this group is quite numerous, it is interesting to note that none of the anti-proverbs uses the association with the traditional phrase merely to attract readers' attention – they all preserve the essential meaning.

Ш

Была бы шея, а хомут найдется (If there is a neck, there will be a horse-collar).
For a person who is used to obeying and doing the work, there will always be something to do or some people willing to load him or her with work.

AP-1: *Была бы книга – читатель найдется* (If there is a book, there will be a reader).
An international book exhibition in Moscow.
New lexical content.
http://www.rest.ej.by/everything/2011/02/10/byla_by_kniga____chitatel__naydetsya.html

AP-2: *Был бы человек, а статья найдется* (If there is a person, there will be an article [of the Criminal Code]).
Arrests of political opposition leaders in Russia.
New lexical content.
http://www.grani.ru/blogs/free/entries/185462.html

AP-3: *Было бы желание, а работа в Одинцово найдётся* (If there is a will to work, there will be jobs in Odinstovo).
Job fair in Odintsovo, Moscow oblast.
New lexical content.
http://www.odinews.ru/news/Bylo-by-gelanie-a-rabota-v-Odintsovo-naydetsya/

AP-4: *Найдутся мухи – был бы мед!* (If there is honey, there will be flies!)
Changes in Russian tax code; May 2011.
New lexical content.
http://www.nalogoved.ru/art/1201

AP-5: *Круизы к Луне: были бы деньги, а «Союз» найдется* (Cruises to the moon: if there is money, there will be a "Soyuz" [Russian space rocket].
Space tourism.
New lexical content.
http://www.interfax.by/article/75698

Comments: All new proverbs keep a small fraction of the original meaning: if some condition is met, there is no doubt that there will be a necessary result, be it people who like to read (#1 – if books are available), or jobs (#3 – if there is a will to work), or spaceships (#5 – if there is money for space flights). Thus, the key part of the message of the traditional proverb is lost.

Шила в мешке не утаишь (You can't hide an awl in a sack).
It is difficult to hide something that is obvious; sooner or later it will be known.
English equivalent: Truth will out.

AP-1: *Краба в мешках не утаишь!* (You can't hide crabs in a sack!)
Customs officer in Murmansk confiscated a large shipment of illegally caught crabs.
New lexical content.
http://murman.rfn.ru/rnews.html?id=871405

AP-2: *Кроссовер в мешке не утаишь* (You can't hide a new crossover in a sack).
A new VW crossover.
New lexical content.
http://www.ma.by/?q=krossover-v-meshke-ne-utaish

AP-3: *Денег в мешке не утаишь* (You can't hide money in a sack).
Rapper 50 cent (Curtis Jackson) made 150 million dollars during 2008.
New lexical content.
http://www.kommersant.ru/doc/1014194

AP-4: *100 млн. в мешке не утаишь* (You can't hide 100 million in a sack).
Changing management of the National Reserve Bank of Russia.
New lexical content.
http://expert.ru/2010/03/22/nrb/

AP-5: *Шилина в мешке не утаишь* (You can't hide Shilin in a sack).
Investigation of the organized crime group headed by Shilin, which was abducting people.
Paronymy.
http://www.novayagazeta.ru/data/2009/134/20.html

AP-6: *Красноярск: Шиншилл в мешке не утаишь* (Krasnoyarsk: You can't hide chinchillas in a sack).
Chinchillas as pets.
Hidden rhyme.
http://www.petworld.ru/modules/news/article.php?storyid=812

Comments: All new proverbs have the same message: it is difficult to hide something, though for different reasons: it may be too big a sum of money (#4), or a large amount of illegal crab (#1), or a new crossover that everyone is talking about (#2), or the ringleader of organized crime group (#5). Linguistically, the best coinages are #5 and 6: the first one uses paronymy between the original word *шила* (awl, in the genitive case) and *Шилина* (the last name of the ringleader), while the second one uses hidden rhyme between the words *шила* (awl) in the traditional proverb and *шиншилл* (chinchillas) in the anti-proverb.

Щ

На то и щука в море, чтобы карась не дремал (A pike is in the sea, so that a crucian will be awake).
Danger or some supervisory authority exists to keep people on the alert, be attentive and careful.

AP-1: *На то и теща, чтобы зять не дремал* (A mother-in-law is here, so that the son-in-law will be awake).
Relationships between husbands and mothers-in-law.
New lexical content.
http://gazeta.aif.ru/_/online/ss/142/ss06_01

AP-2: *На то у нас и медицина,чтобы пациент не дремал* (Health care is here, so that the patient will be awake).
Quality of health care in Russia.
New lexical content.
http://www.ins-union.ru/rus/news/publications/473

AP-3: *На то и Южный, чтобы Щукин не дремал* (Yuzhny is here, so that Shchukin will be awake).
Tennis match between two athletes – Michael Yuzhniy and Yury Shchukin.
Paronymy.
http://www.time.kz/index.php?module=news&newsid=17116

AP-4: *Затем «Зенит» в лиге, чтобы «Спартак» не дремал* (Zenit is in the league, so that Spartak will be awake).
Rivalry between two Russian soccer teams: Zenit (Saint-Petersburg) and Spartak (Moscow).
New lexical content.
http://www.izvestia.ru/sport/article3745/

AP-5: *На то и общественность, чтобы чиновник с монополистом не дремали* (General public is here, so that bureaucrats

and monopolies will be awake).
Public should control the activity of government officials and monopolies.
New lexical content.
http://www.izvestia.kz/news.php?date=31-03-09&number=1

AP-6: *На то и ВТО, чтобы фермер не дремал* (WTO is here so that farmers will be awake).
When Kazakhstan joins the World Trade Organization, local farmers should increase the quality of their produce.
New lexical content.
http://www.kazpravda.kz/rus/ekonomika/na_to_i_vto_chtobi_fermer_ne_dremal.html

Comments: All new proverbs have a similar message: there is some supervising authority or a potential danger that makes people or a person be vigilant and careful, be it a rival soccer team (#4), the World Trade Organization (#6), or a mother-in-law (#1). Linguistically, the best coinage is #3, where there is a paronymy between the original word *щука* (pike) and the last name of the tennis player – *Щукин* (Shchukin) in the anti-proverb.

Ю

Что дозволено Юпитеру, то не дозволено быку (What is allowed to Jupiter is not allowed to a bull).
People with high status have more rights and possibilities than all others.
This is a calque from a *Latin proverb*: Quod licet Jovi, non licet bovi.

AP-1: *Что дозволено Израилю, то не дозволено России* (What is allowed to Israel is not allowed to Russia).
Israel sells weapons to Georgia, but objects to Russia selling even defense weapons to Syria; 4.04.2011.
New lexical content.
http://www.km.ru/news/chto-dozvoleno-izrailyu-ne-dozvoleno-rossii

AP-2: *Что дозволено Медведеву, не дозволено Белых* (What is allowed to Medvedev is not allowed to Belykh).
President of Russia reprimanded governor Belykh for tweeting during the meeting of the State Council.
Note: President Medvedev is known for his love of the Internet, in particular, his use of Twitter.
New lexical content.
http://www.trud.ru/article/31-08-2010/249448_chto_dozvoleno_medvedevu_ne_dozvoleno_belyx.html

AP-3: *Что дозволено быку, не дозволено Юпитеру* (What is allowed to a bull is not allowed to Jupiter).
Interview with a member of Russian Parliament, Natalia Narochnitskaya, who believes that Russia should choose the way of the Orthodox Church and monarchy.
Chiasmus.
http://www.religare.ru/2_31440.html

AP-4: *Что позволено Каролине, не позволено Алене* (What is allowed to Carolina is not allowed to Alyona).
World cup in figure skating in Moscow: Russian skater Alyona Leonova was the fourth; Italian skater Carolina Kostner the first.
New lexical content.
http://www.smena.ru/news/2011/05/06/18893/

Comments: Only one out of four anti-proverbs preserves the key element of the meaning of the traditional proverb: what is allowed to one person (usually higher in some status) is not allowed to another; thus, the President of Russia can tweet, but the governor cannot (#2). All others create their own message, and even though they do say that what is allowed to one person (or country) is not allowed to another, it is not because of different status, but because of some other things. Thus, the Italian skater won first place, and hence it was "allowed" to her, but not because she was of a higher status, but because she skated better (#4). The first anti-proverb in fact uses the association with the traditional proverb simply to question the alleged double standard of Israel foreign policy. Finally, the farthest from the original proverb is #3, which reverses the traditional phrase in order to claim that Russia has its own unique way of development.

Я

Яблоко от яблони недалеко падает (The apple doesn't fall far from the apple tree).
Children often are very similar to their parents. Said, as a rule, to emphasize that children have the same drawbacks, negative qualities as their parents.
English equivalent: Like father, like son.

AP-1: *«Яблоко» от власти недалеко падает* (Yabloko does not fall far from authorities).
Opposition party Yabloko [“apple” in Russian] supported the idea expressed by a Russian minister to establish criminal responsibility for denying the role of the USSR in the victory over German fascism in WWII; March 2009.
Polysemy.
http://www.ej.ru/?a=note&id=8856

AP-2: *Apple от appl'a недалеко падает...* (Apple does not fall far from another apple).
James McCartney, son of Paul, released his first album *Available Light*; September 2010.
English word with Russian morphological ending; metonymy.
http://www.liveinternet.ru/community/jam_music_journal/post134561514/

AP-3: *“Еврострой” от “Флоры” недалеко падает* (“Evrostroy” falls not far from “Flora”).
A construction firm in Saint-Petersburg changed its name, but not the quality and cost of the belt road and bridges it builds.
New lexical content.
http://www.fontanka.ru/2010/11/30/081/

AP-4: *Дырка от бублика недалеко падает* (Hole falls not far from doughnut).
Low purchasing power of the people in Kirov oblast; 2009.

New lexical content.
http://www.osobaya.net/1359

AP-5: *Брат от брата недалеко падает* (One brother falls not far from the other brother).
Negative attitude to Russia from the brother of the deceased president of Poland Kachinsky.
New lexical content.
http://cprfspb.ru/5394.html

Comments: The only anti-proverb that continues talking about the similarity between parents and kids is #2, about the son of Sir Paul McCartney releasing his first album; all other anti-proverbs describe the similarity between two entities or people, but not parents and children (though we have two brothers in #5). Linguistically, we have several interesting examples. First of all, #1, where the wordplay is based on the fact that the name of the political party is *Яблоко* (Yabloko) – which is "apple" in Russian, so the word *яблоко* acquires a new meaning. Then, #2 uses a rare device – an English word with a Russian morphological ending: to show that the second word *apple* is used in the Russian instrumental case, it is given the Russian ending *-a*; also of interest is the fact the both times the word *apple* is used in English in the Russian sentence. Finally, it is used metonimically: the Beatles' recording firm was called *Apple*.

Язык до Киева доведет (You tongue will lead you to Kiev).
By asking other people one can learn everything and find everything.
Note: Kiev was the capital of Kievan Rus, medieval state of Eastern Slavs (late 9th – middle of 13th century); thus the proverb retains the memory of the time when Kiev was "the mother of Russian cities."

AP-1: *Визит до Киева доведет* (A visit will lead you to Kiev).
Hillary Clinton's visit to Moscow, and whether Kiev will be the place of signing the Russian-American SALT treaty; 18.03.2010.
New lexical content.
http://www.kommersant.ru/doc/1338343

AP-2: *"Сапсан" до Киева доведет* ("Sapsan" will lead you to Kiev).
Speed train "Sapsan" may start going between Moscow and Kiev.
New lexical content.
http://www.ukrrudprom.com/digest/Sapsan_do_Kieva_dovedet.html

AP-3: *Какой язык до Киева доведет?* (Which tongue will lead you to Kiev?)
The status of the Russian language in Ukraine today.
Syntactic restructuring.
www.pravda.ru

AP-4: *Русский язык до Киева доведет* (The Russian tongue will lead you to Kiev).
Decision of the Ukrainian government that teaching should be only in the Ukrainian language in Ukrainian schools, starting with 2009.
New lexical content.
http://www.ntv.ru/novosti/177478/

AP-5: *Доведет ли до Киева голландский язык?* (Will the Dutch language lead you to Kiev?)
The Dutch coach of the Russian national soccer team, Dick Advocaat, promised to bring the team to the world cup-2014, which will be held in Ukraine; March 2011.
Metonymy.
http://www.kp.ru/daily/25661.3/822935/

AP-6: *Иврит до Киева доведет* (Hebrew will lead you to Kiev).
Free courses in Hebrew for new repatriates to Israel.
New lexical content.
http://bat-yam.israelinfo.ru/news/779

AP-7: *Boeing до Киева доведет* (Boeing will lead you to Kiev).
Air travel between Odessa and Kiev by Ukrainian international airlines, by Boeing 737.

New lexical content.
http://odessaglobe.com/novosti/13476/

Comments: Four of the new proverbs (#3, 4, 5, and 6) keep the idea of the "tongue leading to Kiev" and build their messages around it; three others fill the structure with something else – Boeing (#7), speed train (#2), or foreign visit (#1). At the same time, the other key word – Kiev – is used in its literal meaning (as it is used in the traditional proverb) in six out of seven anti-proverbs; the only exception is #6 – this is the case when the association with the traditional proverb is used simply to catch readers' attention. Linguistically, the most interesting case is #5, where the Dutch tongue/language is a metonymy (in this context) for the Dutch coach of the Russian soccer team, Dirk ("Dick") Advocaat, who promised to bring Russia to the World Cup -2014, which will take place in Ukraine (or metonymically, in Kiev).

Appendix

Language Mechanisms Used in Creating Anti-Proverbs[1]

The range of mechanisms by means of which modern Russian anti-proverbs are formed (and related to their prototypes) is quite wide; these mechanisms belong to all language levels, from phonetic to syntactic, though of course some of them are more common, and some of them are used only occasionally.

1. Phonetic mechanisms:
    - homonymy
    - paronymy
    - internal rhyme
    - hidden rhyme (rhyming substitution)

2. Morphological mechanisms:
    - English words with Russian morphological endings
    - neologisms

3. Lexical mechanisms:
    - polysemy

---

[1] The content of the Appendix is a shorter version of a chapter from my book *Old Wine in New Bottles: Modern Russian Anti-Proverbs* (2009), where language mechanisms were analyzed as part of the overall analysis of the anti-proverb phenomenon. I believe including a description of language mechanisms in the current dictionary will make it possible for many readers who do not have a formal linguistic training to get much more from every dictionary entry, where language mechanisms are described in brief. Thus, if one sees some vague term like *paronymy*, or *anadiplosis*, or *defeated expectancy*, one can always consult this Appendix for an explanation.

And one more thing: all the examples in the Appendix are also taken from my 2009 book (in which I used previously published collections) and are not part of this dictionary. As I have already mentioned in the introduction, I do not include such artificially coined anti-proverbs in my dictionary, but for the discussion of language mechanisms their status in actual speech is of little or no importance.

- antonymy
- synonymy
- new lexical content of the same syntactic structure

4. Syntactic mechanisms:
   - restructuring
   - extension

5. Stylistic mechanisms:
   - metaphor
   - metonymy
   - chiasmus
   - anadiplosis
   - wellerism

6. Defeated expectancy

Phonetic mechanisms

Homonymy

Homonyms are words that sound and/or look alike but have nothing in common from the point of view of their meaning. For example:

TP: *Не переходите улицу на красный свет* (Do not cross the street when the light is red). This, in fact, is not so much a proverb as a well-known saying (traffic rule), one of those basic things that kids are taught in school, hence, well-known to everyone.

AP: *Не переходите улицу на тот свет* (Do not cross the street to the other world). That is, if you cross the street when the light is red, you will get hit by the car and die.

The peculiarity and black humor of the AP is based on the play on words: the Russian words *light* and *world* are homonyms; hence, literally, (красный) *свет* (red) *light* and (тот) *свет* (the other) *world* sound and look the same.

Paronymy

Paronyms are words that sound alike, though they may have no semantic connection. There is a fine line between paronyms and homonyms, but still homonyms sound exactly the same, while the paronyms sound similar but are still different. This way of the formation of anti-proverbs is quite common:

TP: *Не отрекаются любя* ([Those who] love do not denounce [their love].

AP: *Не отвлекаются любя* ([Those who] love do not divert [their attention]).

The AP takes a line from a very popular song by the famous Russian singer Alla Pugacheva, changes one phoneme ([r] to [l] – both of them belong to the same group of so-called liquid consonants, and their articulation is very similar), and makes it a joke.

Internal rhyme

One of the typical elements of traditional Russian proverbs and sayings is internal rhyme, which, combined with a distinct rhythm, makes them easy to pronounce and remember. In this aspect, anti-proverbs are as conservative as they can be, as the vast majority of them also have a clear rhythm and internal rhyme. For example:

TP: *Кто рано встает, тому бог подает* (He who gets up early is helped by God).

AP: *Кто рано встает, с тем бог поддает* (He who gets up early, drinks with God).

The original proverb expresses a common wisdom that people who get up early manage to do more and hence, they can say that God is on their side (literally, God gives them). The AP, using similarity of the form of the verbs *подает* (give) and *поддает* (drink, in low colloquial style), makes it a wordplay.

Both the original proverb and the new version have internal rhyme: *встает – подает* (gets up – helped), *встает – поддает* (gets up – drinks), so the AP follows its prototype very closely.

Hidden rhyme (rhyming substitution)

This is by far the most interesting linguistic feature of modern Russian anti-proverbs.

By hidden rhyme I mean that many modern Russian anti-proverbs use the so-called rhyming substitution, that is, they rhyme with the traditional proverb that was used as their pattern or prototype. The rhyme is hidden, because in the resulting AP there is no rhyme per se, and in order to understand it one needs to know (and to recognize) the traditional proverb in its AP version. For example:

AP: *Из всех искусств для нас важнейшим является вино* (Of all the arts the most important for us is wine).

This language joke is based on the well-known (at least, well-known to the people who lived in the soviet era) quotation from Vladimir Lenin:

TP: *Из всех искусств для нас важнейшим является кино* (Of all the arts the most important for us is cinema).

Lenin paid much attention to this new form of mass propaganda, because he understood its possibilities, hence this famous quotation.

The AP is of course just a joke, but in order to understand the humor (otherwise, it makes little sense – why is wine a form of art?) one has to recognize the prototype sentence, and to help the reader in this the AP has the hidden rhyme, as the Russian words *cinema* and *wine* (*вино – кино*) rhyme.

Morphological mechanisms

English words with Russian morphological endings

For example:

TP: *Чем бы дитя ни тешилось, лишь бы не плакало* (Whatever the child plays with, the most important thing is that it does not cry). Thus, anything is worth allowing the child to do as long as it does not cry. Figuratively (and often ironically) said about adults who do something unusual or strange for a grown-up person, but like it anyway.

AP: *Чем бы дитя ни тешилось, лишь бы не факалось* (Whatever the child plays with, most important is that it does not fuck).

The Russian saying uses the English verb *fuck* in Russian transliteration and with Russian morphological endings of a Russian reflexive verb – as if it were a Russian verb (such a verb does not exist).

Neologisms (new words)

This is a rare mechanism; still, here is an example:

TP: *Пролетарии всех стран, объединяйтесь!* (Workers of the world, unite!)

AP: *Предприниматели всех стран, налогооблажайтесь!* (Entrepreneurs of the world, tax yourselves!)

The traditional saying is a well-known quotation from Karl Marx's "Communist Manifesto," while the new version is of course just a joke, and encourages entrepreneurs to pay taxes. The key feature of the anti-proverb is the verb *налогооблажайтесь* (tax yourselves) that does not exist in Russian, though its meaning is clear, thanks to the fact that it uses a standard word-formation mechanism. Of course, it will hardly become a regular verb, but it serves its function well enough in this new version of Marx's slogan.

Lexical mechanisms

Polysemy

Many anti-proverbs are coined by means of polysemy – two or more meanings of the same word; for example:

TP: *Сделал сам – помоги другому* (If you have finished your work, help another person).

AP: *Бросил курить сам, брось курить другому* (If you have quit smoking yourself, throw [a cigarette] to another person).

The literal translation means next to nothing: the AP uses the play on words based on two different meanings of the Russian verb *бросать* (literally, throw). In the phrase *бросить курить* it means *to quit smoking* (literally, throw smoking), but in the phrase *брось курить* (imperative of the same verb) it means *give* (literally, again, throw) *a cigarette* to another person. Since as a result the first and the second parts of this AP contradict each other, the resulting phrase is a very good example of the play on words based on polysemy.

Sometimes, the polysemantic word which is the basis of the play on words is used only once in a sentence, but both meanings are realized simultaneously, thus making the play (and the joke) even more evident:

AP: *Чтобы выжить в России, одного терпения мало. Нужно два* (In order to survive in Russia, it is not enough to have only [one] patience: you need two).

The play on words here is based on the polysemantic phrase *одного терпения* (literally, *only patience*): the Russian word *одного* can also mean *one* in the genitive case; so when you read this sentence, the first meaning that is understood is, "It is not enough to have only patience" – that is, one needs something else. But the continuation utilizes the other meaning – "one patience," and makes it a sad joke: one needs two patience(s) to survive in Russia today.

Antonymy

Antonyms are words that have the opposite meaning, and this device is used fairly often. Here is an example where *regular antonyms* are used:

TP: *Настоящий мужчина должен посадить дерево, построить дом и вырастить сына* (A true man must plant a tree, build a house, and raise a son). This saying reflects the traditional (patriarchal) view of the duties of the man.

AP: *Настоящая женщина должна спилить дерево, разрушить дом и вырастить дочь* (A true woman must cut the tree, demolish the house, and raise a daughter).

One should not look for any deep meaning or wisdom in this AP; all it does is make fun of the patriarchal mores; the joke is obviously based on preserving the same structure (a true ___ must do three things), while listing antonyms: man – woman, plant a tree – cut a tree, build a house – demolish the house, son – daughter).

At the same time, it is quite common for anti-proverbs to use pairs of words as *contextual antonyms* – that is, antonyms that have opposite meaning only in the given context, but do not have opposite vocabulary meanings. For example:

AP: *У плохого студента есть шанс стать хорошим солдатом* (A bad student has a chance to become a good soldier).

This modern proverb reflects such a fact of soviet and Russian life as military draft: all male citizens who reach the age of 18 are eligible for the draft. Students of colleges and universities get an extension, and are drafted after they graduate. Thus, many people enter colleges and universities not because they want to get a higher education, but primarily to avoid being drafted into the army. As a result, quite a few students study poorly, as they are not interested in the specialty that they have chosen. Thus, if a student is expelled he is immediately drafted, hence the moral of the proverb: if you study poorly and get expelled you will be in the army. So the phrases (*плохой) студент* (bad student) and *(хороший) солдат* (good soldier) become contextual antonyms here, though, of course, by the dictionary definitions, they are not antonymous in any way.

Synonymy

Synonyms are words that have similar meanings and can replace each other at least in some contexts. They may differ in the components of their conceptual meanings, or in their stylistic and emotional connotations.

Stylistic synonyms

TP: *По одежке встречают, по уму провожают* (One is greeted by the clothes, and seen off by the mind).

Figuratively, it is similar to the English saying *Appearances are deceptive*; *Beauty is only skin deep*, etc., thus, we first judge people by the way they look, and later on, when we learn more about them, we judge them by their inner world.

AP: *По прикиду встречают, по понятиям провожают* (One is greeted by the clothes, and seen off by the street laws).

The meaning is very much the same, but stylistically the wording is completely different. The association with the original proverb is achieved by preserving the structure and both verbs of the original proverb (*По* ______ *встречают, по* _______ *провожают*), though stylistically the AP belongs to the low colloquial register, having replaced the key nouns by their stylistic synonyms: *по одежке* (TP) – *по прикиду* (AP), and *по уму* (TP) – *по понятиям* (AP).

Contextual synonyms

TP: *Дружба дружбой, а табачок врозь* (Though we are friends, I am not going to share my tobacco with you). It means that there are limits to what friends will do for each other.

AP: *Дружба дружбой, а нефть врозь* (Though we are friends, I am not going to share my oil with you).

The AP is another reflection of modern Russian realities, where oil companies compete for oil deposits and federal government support. The association with the traditional proverb is achieved by the same syntactic pattern and common wording, except for one word: *oil* (in AP) as opposed to *tobacco* in the TP. The use of the word *табак* (tobacco) in TP is not accidental: it reflects the traditionally high value of tobacco in Russia, hence, unwillingness to share it even with friends. And since oil in modern Russia is as valuable a possession as tobacco was in the old days, this is a good example of contextual synonymy.

New lexical content of the same syntactic structure (partial or complete)

This device is used very often. Let us have a look at some examples, ranging from one new word and up to a completely new (lexically) sentence:

TP: *Молчание – знак согласия* (Silence means agreement).

AP: *Венчание – знак согласия* (Wedding means agreement).

The traditional proverb expresses an old wisdom: if a person you are talking to is silent when you have suggested something, it means that that person agrees with you.

In the new version, the word *молчание* (silence) is replaced with the word *венчание* (wedding) and of course means a completely different thing: if you have a wedding, it means that the other person agrees to marry you.

The extreme version of this mechanism is the case when nearly all the lexical content of a familiar saying is replaced, for example:

TP: *В человеке все должно быть прекрасно: и лицо, и одежда, и душа, и мысли.* (Everything must be beautiful in a man: the face, the clothes, the soul, and the thoughts).

This is a well-known quotation from the play *Uncle Vanya* by Anton Chekhov.

AP: *В бизнесмене все должно быть прекрасно: и 600-й мерс, и дача на Канарах, и контрольный выстрел в голову* (Everything must be beautiful in a businessman: his Mercedes, his vacation home in the Canary Islands, and his control bullet in the head).

The new version has a completely new wording, except the introductory phrase: *все должно быть прекрасно* (everything must be beautiful). Thus, it is the new content per se that creates a new proverb reflecting modern-day realities: no one can feel safe, no matter how rich he or she is.

Somewhere in between are examples when the new version replaces some key words of the original proverb but keeps the rest:

TP: *Редкая птица долетит до середины Днепра* (It is a rare bird that can fly till the middle of the Dnepr river). This is a well-known description of the Dnepr River from the novel *Dead Souls* by Nikolay Gogol.

AP: *Редкий премьер долетит до середины Атлантики* (It is a rare prime-minister that can fly till the middle of the Atlantic Ocean).

The original quotation is easily recognized thanks to the same syntactic structure and partly the same wording: *Редкая/ая* ____ *долетит до середины* ______ (It is a rare _____ that can fly till the middle of ____). This AP describes a well-known diplomatic incident between the US and Russia: on March 24, 1999, Russian prime-minister Evgeni Primakov was flying to the US for an official visit, and having learnt that NATO started bombing Yugoslavia made a U-turn over the Atlantic ocean and went back.

Syntactic mechanisms

Syntactic restructuring

This device is used quite rarely as compared to many others, but nevertheless it presents an interesting case: by restructuring the original syntax, an anti-proverb creates a new meaning while leaving the lexical content intact. For example:

TP: *Мусор из избы не выносить* (Do not carry your garbage out of the house). This is an interesting example of old advice which became a proverb: traditional prejudices required not to take the garbage outside, but burn it in the stove, as it was believed that an evil person could bring bad luck to the house saying some special words about the garbage.

AP: *Мусора, из избы не выносить* (Cops, do not carry [me] out of the house). This joke is based on the coincidence of the two Russian words: *мусор* (garbage) in the original proverb, and *мусор* (slang for policeman) in the anti-proverb. But more importantly, the syntactic structure is also changed in the AP, and even though both sentences are imperative constructions, in the AP *мусора* is the address, not the object of the action *carry out*. Thus, we are dealing with a situation when police officers come to somebody's home and the drunken person says to them: cops, do not carry me out of the house; leave me alone. Thus, by restructuring the original phrase an old proverb becomes a language joke by means of the different syntax:

TP: Object – adverbial of place – verb

AP: Address – adverbial of place – verb

Extension of syntactic structure

It is quite rare that extension of the syntactic structure is used as the only mechanism for creating a new proverb; much more often, it is just a vehicle for other more obvious means – lexical, phonetic, stylistic, etc. Still, there are examples where *syntax* itself is the key method used to create an anti-proverb:

TP: *В вине мудрость* (In wine there is wisdom). This is a Russian translation of the old Latin maxim, *In vino veritas*.

AP: *В вине мудрость, в пиве – сила, в воде – микробы* (In wine there is wisdom, in beer – power, in water – microbes). This joking extension, using the true fact (there are quite a few dangerous microbes in unfiltered water), twists it in such a way that it turns out that the most useful drinks are wine and beer, as they do not have any microbes!

Stylistic mechanisms

These figures of speech are used to create modern Russian anti-proverbs. Let us have a look at some examples.

Metaphor

Metaphor is the understanding of one concept in terms of another, based on their similarity; for example:

TP: *Дети – цветы жизни* (Children are flowers of life). This is a well-known quotation from Maxim Gorky (from his story "Former People," written in 1897). Often used in emphasizing the importance of children in life of any person, and of the society in general.

AP: *Дети – цветы жизни. Дарите девушкам цветы.* (Children are flowers of life. Give flowers to girls.) This is just a joke, based on the play of literal and figurative meanings.

Metonymy

Metonymy is another name for an object based on some connections between them (special, causal, part and whole, etc.). Let us have a look at an example:

TP: *Долг платежом красен* (The debt is made red by the payment). The literal meaning is that one should promptly return the money one owes to somebody. Figuratively, it can also mean that anything that you owe someone (not necessarily money) should be promptly returned.

AP: *Долг платежом зелен* (The debt is made green by the payment). The literal meaning is the same; figurative meaning is absent.

In the TP, the adjective *red* is used in its old meaning – "beautiful, good looking" (thus, for instance, Red Square in Moscow is, of course, "beautiful square," not a square red in color). Thus, *the debt is made red by the payment* means that it is good (morally correct) to pay your debts, both monetary and others.

Green is quite opposite in its etymology, and originates in the realities of modern Russian economy, where the dollar, especially in the early 90s, was considered the most reliable currency. Since dollar bills are green, the AP uses metonymy and in fact says that one should pay one's debts in dollars.

Chiasmus

Chiasmus is an inverted relationship between the syntactic elements of parallel phrases. For example:

TP: *Молитва – это разговор с Богом* (Prayer is a talk with God). This is a commonly accepted understanding of what a prayer is.

AP: *Когда ты говоришь с Богом – это молитва. Когда Бог с тобой – это шизофрения.* (When you talk to God, this is a prayer. When God talks to you, this is schizophrenia.) The extension, by changing the subject and the object in the subordinate clause, makes this unexpected (though from the point of view of a psychiatrist, probably logical) conclusion.

Anadiplosis

Anadiplosis is repetition of the last prominent word of a clause in the next one, with an adjunct idea. Here is a good example of this rare stylistic device:

TP: *Дуракам закон не писан* (Fools recognize no laws). This traditional expression is used in situations when someone does a clearly foolish thing, often even detrimental to one, and thus, someone will say, *Fools recognize no laws*, meaning, what can you do with such a person?

AP: *Дуракам закон не писан. А если писан, то не читан. А если читан, то не понят. А если понят, то не так.* (Fools recognize no laws. And if they recognize them, they have not read them. And even if they have read them, they have not understood them. And if they have understood them, they understood them in the wrong way.) This is a very interesting example of stylistic development of a traditional proverb: anadiplosis does not change the meaning much and only emphasizes that no matter what fools do, they will never understand any commonly accepted rules of human society.

Wellerism

This type of stylistic device, based on the wordplay involving a metaphorical and literal sense, got its name after Sam Weller – Mr. Pickwick's witty servant in Charles Dickens's novel *The Posthumous Papers of the Pickwick Club.* Sam was fond of following well-known sayings by his own conclusions. Soon after publication of the novel (1836-1837), such witticisms started to be called *wellerisms*. For example:

TP: *Какой же русский не любит быстрой езды!* (What Russian is not fond of driving fast!) This quotation is taken from the novel *Dead Souls* by the famous Russian writer Nikolay Gogol (1809-1852).

AP: *"Какой же новый русский не любит быстрой езды?" сказал гаишник, пересчитывая бабки* ("What new Russian is not fond of driving fast?" said the policeman counting the money.)

The new version, as was already mentioned, is one more allusion to modern Russian mores. At the same time, this AP clearly follows the structure of wellerisms, as it uses the play on words comparing a well-known quotation to a facetious sequel.

Defeated expectancy

Defeated expectancy stands aside from the rest of linguistic mechanisms. The thing is that it is not a mechanism of creating some (stylistic, ironic, emphatic) effect, but rather the result of some other device. The reason I thought it necessary to analyze it separately is the fact that defeated expectancy is a key feature of many anti-proverbs (in fact, the reason for creating many of them), so it makes sense to see how this effect is achieved.

The device itself is a very old one and is traditionally used to attract attention of the reader to some element of the text that receives prominence due to an interruption in the pattern of predictability. In other words, it is based on the fact that usually the reader, on the basis of his or her background, general knowledge, or previous context expects to see a continuation that makes sense (predictable); so when this expectation is ruined, the result is an additional emphasis on the part that is surprising. Of course, it is mostly used to create language jokes instead of some serious or traditional maxim, but is also used as a stylistic device in poetry. Just to give a classic example, it is the essence of the well-known poem "November" written by British poet Thomas Hood (1799-1845):

> No sun – no moon!
> No morn – no noon –
> No dawn – no dusk – no proper time of day.
> No warmth, no cheerfulness, no healthful ease,
> No comfortable feel in any member –
> No shade, no shine, no butterflies, no bees,
> No fruits, no flowers, no leaves, no birds! –
> November!

The last line – November! – receives prominence exactly because by the time the reader reaches it, he or she expects one more negation, and the first syllable of the word *November* seems to confirm this expectation – only to show that the reader's expectancy will be immediately defeated.

Here is an example of this popular stylistic device:

TP: *Всех денег не заработаешь* (One cannot earn all the money). This is an old expression, usually said to people who are dedicating all their time to earning more and more money. It is a common sense maxim, which says: no matter how much you can earn, there will be much more money that one has not earned, while one is spending (or as many will say, wasting) life on that, depriving oneself of many other aspects of life. Thus, the moral of this saying is not that it is bad to earn money, but rather that one should not dedicate all life to that.

AP: *Всех денег не заработаешь – часть придется украсть* (One cannot earn all the money – some money will have to be stolen). As we can see, the extension gives the proverb a new meaning, and is quite alien to the original one. The way to do this is standard for this pattern – the extension creates a completely new context, so the old, traditional, part acquires a new meaning, as well: now the beginning (*One cannot earn all the money*) is not a warning that there are other aspects of life which one can miss if dedicating all the time to money, but rather a justification of stealing; since it is impossible to earn money anyway, there is no other choice but to steal some part of it. Thus, this AP is a great example of defeated expectancy, built on the fact that the familiar maxim gets a completely new interpretation due to the extension (some money will have to be stolen).

Index

The traditional proverbs are listed in the order of the Russian alphabet, by the first notional word, shown *in italics*

А

Аппетит приходит во время еды (Appetite comes with eating)

Как *аукнется,* так и откликнется (As you sow you shall reap)

Б

Баба с возу кобыле легче (It is easier for the horse when a woman is off the cart)

Бабушка надвое сказала (Grandmother said ambiguously)

Кто про что, а вшивый все про *баню* (No matter what other people are talking about, a person who has lice will talk only about the bath-house)

Не лезь поперек *батьки* в пекло (Do not get into fire ahead of your father)

Семь *бед* – один ответ (Seven troubles – one/the same responsibility)

Лиха *беда* начало (Beginning is a difficult problem)

Бедность не порок (Poverty is not a flaw)

На *безрыбье* и рак рыба (In the absence of fish, even a lobster is fish)

За одного *битого* двух небитых дают (In exchange for a beaten one they give two unbeaten)

Первый *блин* комом (The first pancake is a flop)

Бог дал, бог и взял (God gave, God took back)

Бог любит Троицу (God loves Trinity)

Бог терпел и нам велел (God suffered and told us to suffer, too)

До *Бога* высоко, до царя далеко (God is up high, the Tsar is far away)

На *Бога* надейся, а сам не плошай (Trust in God but rely on yourself)

В

Кому *война*, а кому мать родна (What is war to some people is mother to others)

Волка ноги кормят (Legs feed the wolf)

И *волки* сыты, и овцы целы (Both the wolves have eaten and the sheep are unhurt)

Волков бояться в – лес не ходить (If you are afraid of wolves do not go to the forest)

Г

С *глаз* долой – из сердца вон (Out of sight, out of heart)

Не говори *гоп,* пока не перепрыгнешь (Do not say "gop" until you have jumped over)

Дурная *голова* ногам покою не дает (Silly head does not allow the legs to have some rest)

Повинную *голову* и меч не сечет (The sword does not chop off the head admitting guilt)

Голь на выдумки хитра (Poor people are creative)

Незваный *гость* хуже татарина (An uninvited guest is worse than a Tatar)

Пока *гром* не грянет, мужик не перекрестится (Until the thunder roars, a Russian will not cross himself)

Не было ни *гроша,* да вдруг алтын (There was not a single penny and all of a sudden there are several)

Назвался *груздем,* полезай в кузов (You say you are a mushroom, so get into the basket)

Гусь свинье не товарищ (A goose and a swine cannot be friends)

Д

Дают – бери, бьют – беги (If they offer you something, take it, if they start beating you, run)

Дело (работа) не волк, в лес не убежит (The work is not like a wolf – it will not run away into the forest)

Делу – время, потехе – час (There is time for work, and there is time for play)

Летний *день* год кормит (A summer day feeds a year)
Не в *деньгах* счастье (Happiness is not in money)
Деньги дело наживное (Money is something that can be earned)
Деньги не пахнут (Money has no smell)
Деньги счет любят (Money likes to be counted)
Маленькие *детки* – маленькие бедки (Little kids – little problems)
Чем бы *дитя* ни тешилось, лишь бы не плакало (Whatever the child plays with, the most important thing is that it does not cry)
От *добра* добра не ищут (One does not leave something good for another good thing)
Доверяй, но проверяй! (Trust but verify!)
Долг платежом красен (The debt is made red by the payment)
Мой *дом* – моя крепость (My home is my castle).
В *доме* повешенного не говорят о веревке (In the house of a person who was hanged one does not talk about a rope)
Все *дороги* ведут в Рим (All roads lead to Rome)
После *драки* кулаками не машут (One does not wave fists after the fight)
Скажи мне кто твой *друг,* и я скажу тебе кто ты (Tell me who your friend is, and I will tell you who you are)
Старый *друг* лучше новых двух (An old friend is better than two new friends)
Друзья познаются в беде (Friends are tested during bad times)
Дружба дружбой, а табачок врозь (We are friends, but we will not share tobacco)
Заставь *дурака* богу молиться – он и лоб расшибет (If you force a fool to pray to God, he will hurt his forehead)
Дуракам закон не писан (A fool observes no rules)
Чужая *душа* – потемки (Another man's soul is dark)
Дыма без огня не бывает (There is no smoke without fire)

Е

Тише *едешь* – дальше будешь (The slower you go, the farther you get)

Ж

Семеро одного не *ждут* (Seven [persons] don't wait for one)
Куй *железо*, пока горячо (Strike while the iron is hot)
Жизнь прожить – не поле перейти (Living life is not like crossing a meadow)
Не до *жиру*, быть бы живу (It is about survival, not about wealth)

З

Закон что дышло – куда повернул, туда и вышло (Law is like a shaft – you can turn it any way you like)
Слышал *звон,* да не знает где он (He's heard the ringing but doesn't know where it's coming from)
Слухами *земля* полнится (The earth gets filled with rumors)
Неча на *зеркало* пенять, коли рожа крива (Don't blame the mirror if your face is crooked)
Из двух *зол* выбирают меньшее (Out of two evils choose the least)
Мал *золотник*, да дорог (Zolotnik is small but expensive/valuable/precious)
Не все то *золото*, что блестит (All is not gold that glitters)

И

Игра не стоит свеч (The game is not worth the candle)
Не красна *изба* углами, а красна пирогами (A house is made beautiful not by its interior, but by its food)

К

Терпи *казак,* атаманом будешь (Be patient, Cossack, and you will be ataman [hetman, leader])
Под лежачий *камень* и вода не течет (Water does not flow under a stone that lies still)
Капля камень точит (A drop [of water] wears away stone)
На чужой *каравай* рот не разевай (Do not open your mouth to somebody else's pie)

Кашу маслом не испортишь (Too much butter won't spoil the porridge)

Клин клином вышибают (A wedge is removed with a wedge)

Куда ни кинь, всюду *клин* (No matter where you cast lots – everywhere there is a narrow plot)

Черного *кобеля* не отмоешь добела (A black dog cannot be washed so as to make it white)

Коготок увяз – всей птичке пропасть (If one claw is caught, the whole bird is lost)

Не плюй в *колодец* – пригодится воды напиться (Do not spit into the well—it may be useful to drink water)

Старый *конь* борозды не испортит (An old horse will not spoil the furrow)

Даренному *коню* в зубы не смотрят (Don't look a gift horse in the mouth)

Копейка рубль бережет (A kopeck saves a ruble)

Большому *кораблю* – большое плавание (A big ship needs a big sea)

Нашла *коса* на камень (The scythe struck a stone)

Ночью все *кошки* серы (All cats are grey at night)

Страшнее *кошки* зверя нет (There is no scarier animal than a cat)

Не родись *красивым*, а родись счастливым (It is better to be born happy than to be born beautiful)

Всякий *кулик* свое болото хвалит (Every sandpiper praises his own swamp)

Курица не птица, баба не человек (A hen is not a bird; a woman is not a human being).

Л

Одна *ласточка* весны не делает (One swallow does not make a spring)

Лес рубят – щепки летят (When they chop down wood, woodchips will fly)

Чем дальше в *лес*, тем больше дров (The farther into the forest, the more wood)

Лбом стену не прошибешь (You can't break a wall by beating your head against it)

На *ловца* и зверь бежит (Wild animals run into hunters)
Дорога *ложка* к обеду (A spoon is important/valuable at dinner time)
Близок *локоть*, да не укусишь (Your elbow is close, but you can't bite it)
Против *лома* нет приема (There is nothing you can do against a crowbar)
Поспешишь – *людей* насмешишь (If you do something in haste, you will only make people laugh)
Свои *люди* – сочтемся (We are close relatives, so we will pay back what we owe)

М

Мавр сделал свое дело, мавр может уходить (The Moor has done his duty; he can leave)
Два *медведя* в одной берлоге не уживутся (Two bears will not live in the same hole)
О *мертвых* – или хорошо, или ничего (About the dead – either good, or nothing)
Не *место* красит человека, а человек место (It isn't the place that graces the man, but the man the place)
Свято *место* пусто не бывает (The holy place is never empty)
Насильно *мил* не будешь (You can't win love by force)
Худой *мир* лучше доброй ссоры (Better a bad peace than a good quarrel)
Горбатого *могила* исправит (Only death will cure the hunchback)
Москва слезам не верит (Moscow does not believe in tears)
Муж и жена – одна сатана (Husband and wife are the same devil)
Русский *мужик* задним умом крепок (The Russian is wise after the event)
Кто платит, тот и заказывает *музыку* (He who pays orders the music)

Н

Благими *намерениями* вымощена дорога в ад (The road to hell is paved with good intentions)

Что русскому здорово, то *немцу* смерть (What is good for a Russian, is death for a German)

В *ногах* правды нет (There is no truth in the legs)

Своя *ноша* не тянет (A burden of one's own choice is not felt)

У семи *нянек* дитя без глазу (Seven nannies have a child without an eye).

О

Всякому *овощу* свое время (Every vegetable has its season)

С паршивой *овцы* хоть шерсти клок (Even a bad sheep can give a bit of wool)

Овчинка выделки не стоит (The sheepskin is not worth tanning)

По *одежке* встречают, по уму провожают (One is greeted according to one's clothes; one is seen off according to what one knows)

Видит *око*, да зуб неймет (Eye sees but teeth cannot reach)

В тихом *омуте* черти водятся (Devils live in a quiet water-hole)

Охота пуще неволи (Desire is more powerful than coercion)

П

Написано *пером* – не вырубишь топором (If something is written by pen, it cannot be cut out by an axe)

Из *песни* слова не выкинешь (One cannot drop a word out of a song)

Береги *платье* снову, а честь смолоду (Look after your clothes since they are new; and after your honor since you are young)

Плетью обуха не перешибешь (One can't break a head of an axe with a whip)

Один в *поле* не воин (One man in the field is no worrier)

Каков *поп,* таков и приход (Like priest, like flock)

Привычка – вторая натура (Habit is a second nature)
Дурной *пример* заразителен (A bad example is contagious)
Нет *пророка* в своем отечестве (There is no prophet in his own country)
Простота хуже воровства (Simplicity is worse than stealing)

Р

Работа дураков любит (The work likes fools)
Кто не *работает*, тот не ест (He who does not work, shall not eat)
Семь *раз* примерь – один отрежь (Measure seven times, cut once)
С милым *рай* и в шалаше (With your loved one, even a hut is heaven)
Где тонко, там и *рвется* (It will break where it is thin)
Риск – благородное дело (Risk is a noble deed)
Где *родился*, там и пригодился (Where one was born, there one was useful)
Своя *рубашка* ближе к телу (One's own shirt is closer to the body)
Не имей сто *рублей*, а имей сто друзей (Don't have a hundred rubles, rather have a hundred friends)
Своя *рука* владыка (One's own hand is the master)
Рыба тухнет с головы (Fish begins to stink at the head)
Рыба ищет, где глубже, а человек – где лучше (Fish seek where it's deeper, and people where it's better)
Рыбак рыбака видит издалека (A fisherman sees another fisherman from afar)

С

Не в свои *сани* не садись (Do not sit into somebody else's sledge)
Всяк *сверчок* знай свой шесток (Every cricket should know its place)
Свет клином не сошелся (The earth is not only limited to this small plot of land)

Седина в бороду, бес в ребро (Grey hair in the beard, devil into the rib)
В *семье* не без урода (The family is not without a freak)
Сила есть – ума не надо (If one has muscles, one does not need brains)
Лучше *синица* в руке, чем журавль в небе (It is better to have a chickadee in the hand than a crane in the sky)
Скупой платит дважды (A miser pays twice)
Слезами горю не поможешь (Tears will not alleviate the grief)
Слово не воробей, вылетит – не поймаешь (A word is not a sparrow, once it flies out, you won't catch it)
Слухом земля полнится (The earth gets filled with rumor)
Перед *смертью* не надышишься (You can't breathe enough before death)
Двум *смертям* не бывать (а одной не миновать) (There cannot be two deaths (but you cannot avoid one).
Соловья баснями не кормят (Nightingales do not live on chitchat/idle talk)
Утопающий хватается за *соломинку* (A drowning man catches at a straw)
Один с *сошкой*, семеро с ложкой (One with a plough, seven with a spoon)
И на *старуху* бывает проруха (Even an old woman can make mistakes)
У *страха* глаза велики (Fear has big eyes)
От *сумы* да от тюрьмы не зарекайся (Don’t count out a prison cell or a beggar’s cup)
Не было бы *счастья*, да несчастье помогло (There would not be luck, but for bad luck help)

Т

Плохому *танцору* и штаны мешают (Bad dancer blames his pants)
Без *труда* не вынешь и рыбку из пруда (You can’t even pull a fish out of the pond without some effort)

У

Уговор дороже денег (An agreement is worth more than money)

Ум хорошо, а два лучше (One brain is good, but two brains are better)

Что у трезвого на *уме*, то у пьяного на языке (What is on the mind of a sober person, a drunken person has on his tongue)

Устами *младенца* глаголет истина (Truth speaks through the child's lips)

Ученье свет, *неученье* тьма (Learning is light, ignorance is darkness)

Ч

Человек предполагает, а бог располагает (Man proposes, but God disposes)

Не так страшен *черт*, как его малюют (Devil is not so scary as he is described)

Ш

Была бы *шея*, а хомут найдется (If there is a neck, there will be a horse-collar)

Шила в мешке не утаишь (You can't hide an awl in a sack)

Щ

На то и *щука* в море, чтобы карась не дремал (A pike is in the sea, so that a crucian will be awake)

Ю

Что дозволено *Юпитеру*, то не дозволено быку (What is allowed to Jupiter is not allowed to a bull)

Я

Яблоко от яблони недалеко падает (The apple doesn't fall far from the apple tree)
Язык до Киева доведет (You tongue will lead you to Kiev)